# Lower Cape Cod

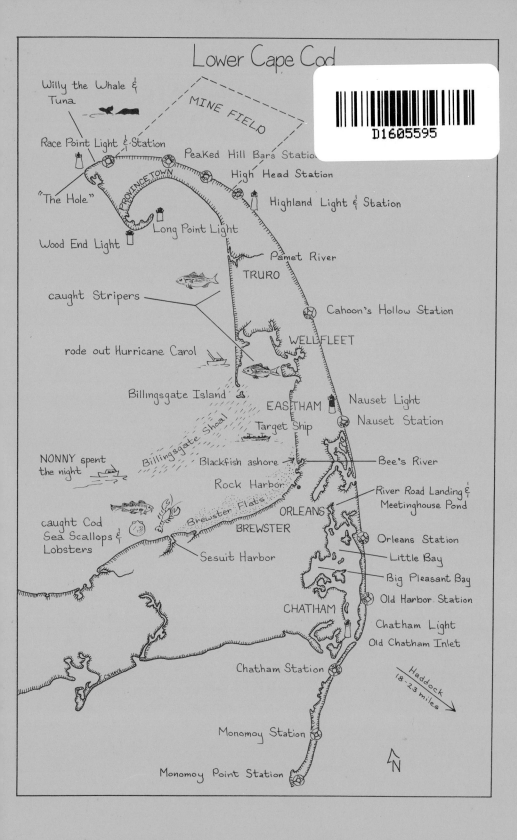

Willy the Whale & Tuna

MINE FIELD

Race Point Light & Station

Peaked Hill Bars Station

High Head Station

Highland Light & Station

"The Hole"

PROVINCE TOWN

Long Point Light

Wood End Light

Pamet River

TRURO

caught Stripers

Cahoon's Hollow Station

rode out Hurricane Carol

WELLFLEET

Billingsgate Island

EASTHAM

Nauset Light

Nauset Station

Target Ship

NONNY spent the night

Billingsgate Shoal

Blackfish ashore

Bee's River

Rock Harbor

River Road Landing & Meetinghouse Pond

Brewster Flats

ORLEANS

caught Cod Sea Scallops & Lobsters

BREWSTER

Orleans Station

Little Bay

Sesuit Harbor

Big Pleasant Bay

Old Harbor Station

CHATHAM

Chatham Light

Old Chatham Inlet

Chatham Station

Haddock 18-23 miles

N

Monomoy Station

Monomoy Point Station

# Cape Cod Fisherman

# Cape Cod Fisherman

## by Phil Schwind

International Marine Publishing Company
Camden, Maine

Printed by Maine Coast Printers
Rockland, Maine

# Dedication

She never had a boat named for her, and she would have liked it if I hadn't been so superstitious about re-naming boats. She opened scallops beside me until her hands were cut and bleeding and would never have sufficed for a hand-care advertisement. She toted fish to market, and cooked them when there were too few to sell. She held one end of a plank while I secured the other, handed me tools, ran errands while I repaired motors, and swabbed copper paint on hulls, leaving me only to cut the waterline. She answered a thousand telephone calls and arranged charter dates, monitored the radio-telephone, and ferried me home over the road when I made a strange harbor.

For those who read between the lines, this is not just a book about fishing and boats. This is a grateful acknowledgment that I couldn't have done it without the help of my wife Helen. So, I would like to dedicate this book to her, humbly and lovingly.

# Contents

# Introduction

*Whitecap* is gone, sold and trailered away. In her place there was
for a while a sense of relief. Let the wind blow as it would, let the
tide be high or low, let the fish bite or disappear, I couldn't care less.
Scallops, flounders, striped bass — they were all something to eat, not
something to catch from a boat to make a living. When the wind beat
against the side of the house in the night and rain or sleet drummed
on the windows, I could roll over in bed and think luxuriously, "No
boat to worry about, no lines to part, no rails to hang up under the
dock, no more midnight boat drill."

On the other hand, there was a wrench when they trundled *Whitecap* off over the hill, as if a tried and trusted friend were leaving, and
there was an emptiness. I thought, "I hope they treat her well and
don't abuse her." With her went the golden, glowing sunrises and the
damp, salt-smelling cleanness of early mornings on the water. There
went peaceful, tired evenings, coasting home to rest. Beside her like
a cloud swirled the bark of her bold exhaust and the chuckling of
gentle water along her side as she rested obediently at anchor. In the
wake of her blunt, scuffed stern churned the memories of eager hopes
and honey-sweet triumphs. We had made a team, *Whitecap* and I.
Boating and fishing for a living are not all trials and toil and danger.
Maybe I could get a smaller boat, one I would feel less personal
about . . .

To many men who live with them, boats are female beings and
highly intimate, the relationship depending on the man and the boat.
"She's Grandma rocking me home at night," one skipper will say, or
another about another boat, "She's a bitch and the only way to get

along with her is to drive her." Perhaps this is not true about some men, and perhaps some boats are male or, more unlikely, inanimate.

*Sunshine*, my first boat, was all female, an old-maid, inadequate little school teacher of a boat who taught me — how she taught me — and we muddled along together for eight years. My second boat, known variously as the *String Bean* and the *Eel Car*, I never got really intimate with, though goodness knows she caused me hard work and heartaches enough. An underprivileged drab she was, who should have been retired to the old folks' home long before I met her. *Nonny*, who followed, was princess, mistress, and helpmate all in one. For nine years *Nonny* and I went everywhere in the waters surrounding Cape Cod, everywhere a small boat could take me, and everyone who went with us fell in love with her. It was a wonder my wife wasn't jealous, but she didn't seem to be, in spite of the fact that I spent more time with *Nonny* than I did at home. I think my wife came to love and trust *Nonny* as much as I did. There was a real sense of loss when I parted with *Nonny*, but, like a lot of men who have prospered slightly, I foolishly sold her off and bought a bigger, showier baggage named *Whitecap*. Not that *Whitecap* ever let me down after our first year together while we were getting to know each other. For fifteen years we lived together, through loads of fish which put her scuppers under and even through a hurricane offshore. She was a capable, handsome wench, a vixen who would soak you with spray in a light breeze but bring you home little wetter through weather no thirty-five-footer should be caught out in.

And now *Whitecap* is gone. For a while I thought, "No more boats. Anyone who buys a boat is crazy or will soon be driven so." But I know where there's a pretty little nineteen-footer, with a bow like *Whitecap's* and enough bearing aft to get up and go . . . Maybe . . . No, you fool, think back over the boats you have known.

# Part One

SUNSHINE

# 1

# I Am Introduced to Fishing

It was Arthur Clark who talked me into buying *Sunshine*, he and my first winter's fishing on *Sea Pal*. I've wondered since just how much Arthur knew about boats. He was a native of Eastham and sort of a relative, since his father was my maternal grandmother's first cousin. Tall, slightly stooped, dark and brown-eyed, with an eagle's beak of a nose, he often made me suspect there was Indian blood somewhere back in the Clark line. He owned his own one-man garage and was a whiz with the Model T's and Model A's of the day, but I came to suspect his knowledge of boats came by a sort of osmosis, he being a Cape Codder and all, rather than by experience. Many years and several boats later I know I should have asked, "If there's so much money in boating why aren't you at it instead of grinding out a living as a mechanic?"

Fresh out of the city because of the Great Depression, I was willing to take any kind of work, for I was trying to raise a family. At my attempts to make a living scratching quahogs by hand on the flats of Eastham's West Shore, Arthur would say, "If you only had a boat you could long-rake a great many more quahogs." Then he'd go on to tell about Ebenezer Cummings and Benny Bangs Nickerson and the old days. "Bushels and bushels they got," he'd say, "a bucket to a bucket-and-a-half to the rake." Bushels and bushels was the kind of talk I liked, being young; sometimes my wife and I worked a whole tide for a meager bushel. Boating sounded romantic; I could visualize myself wearing a jaunty cap and being referred to as "Captain." (Actually, the title "Captain" as commonly used on Cape Cod is an honorary one with a slight tinge of irony. Just as any dignified

*3*

man over fifty and below the Mason-Dixon line who drinks bourbon may be called "Colonel," so anyone on Cape Cod with a boat bigger than a rowboat may be called "Captain" or more commonly "Cap'n.") So Arthur baited the hook with his stories.

I got my first taste of commercial fishing the first winter we spent on Cape Cod; that would be the winter of '34 and '35, when I went hand or striker on a bay scalloper. I guess the skipper should go nameless, for while the stories I have to tell about that winter are pretty wild, they are true, and I have no desire to hurt anyone's feelings. Suppose we call the skipper "Bart," because that wasn't his name, and the boat we might call *Sea Pal*.

Ashore one day for lack of a crew, Cap'n Bart was stuck to his hubs in mud by Boat Meadow, where he had been gathering thatch, dead marsh grass, to bank the foundation of his house, as was the practice in those days. Having been helped myself in the same sort of situation, and because it was the way people lived then, I stopped, threw him a rope, and pulled his car off the beach. Out of gratitude (or because he couldn't find anyone else to go with him) he offered me a job culling scallops aboard the *Sea Pal*. Thirty-five cents a bag for twenty bags a day, which amounted to seven dollars, seemed like a fortune since there wasn't much of any other way of making a dollar at that time of year. Of course the captain's lay seemed astronomical; twenty bags at three and a half dollars a bag, less only my thirty-five cents and the fifty cents the openers got. I had much to learn about boat expense.

*Sea Pal* was in those days a fine boat painted dark green with black trim. She was thirty-eight feet long with a beam of thirteen feet and drew a good four feet of water. She was powered with a four-cylinder Lathrop, rated at forty horsepower. The story was that she had been built as a swordfisherman by a couple of partners who had had a falling out and sold her cheap to Cap'n Bart.

Although I didn't fully realize it at the time, this was lesson number one: Never buy a boat on equal shares with someone else, because someone — some one person — has to be captain. Not that a captain on Cape Cod considers himself, or is considered, any better than the striker (the old phrase was "hand"). There is no caste. (To my surprise, I found it quite different in Florida, at least among charter and private boatmen, where owners seldom greeted captains socially, and mates sat at a still lower table.) Here on Cape Cod one man is thought to be as good as another — no better. But some one person has to make the decisions. A boat can't go two ways at once.

My first day scalloping I remember as though it were only last year. I had spent eleven dollars for a new suit of Black Diamond foul weather gear, Canadian black rubber, and while it was very heavy it was the very best. Cap'n Bart greeted me with ridicule and perhaps a little envy. "Boy," he said, "I don't know why you go scalloping when you can afford gear like that." Somewhere along the line I had already learned a lesson that was brought home to me again and again in later years: When it comes to boating and fishing the best is none too good. So we went dredging (or, as it is more commonly called here, "dragging") for bay scallops, and my education began.

A scallop drag in those days (and they have changed but little since except in rare cases) was a rectangular frame perhaps eighteen inches high by five or six feet wide, made of two-inch angle iron. It was towed on edge by a rigid, V-shaped bridle made of inch-and-a-half round iron, and was followed by a bag usually six feet deep, made on the bottom and sides of two-inch steel rings connected by metal links made for the purpose, and rope netting clipped together on top. This ponderous affair was towed behind the boat at three or four miles per hour, scraping up shells, rocks, and weeds as well as scallops. The sand supposedly washed out through the net bag. After about fifteen minutes, or when the deck was cleared of the last tow, the three-quarter-inch rope was thrown off the hauling post aft by the striker, and, before it came tight, was wound by the captain three or four quick turns around the winch head, which was powered by the motor. The boat was cut in a slight circle to starboard so the drag, as it was winched aboard, cleared the rail. The whole load was dumped on deck, then the drag was flipped overboard again, right side up with the bail or bridle forward, and the rope was caught on the fly by the striker and secured to the hauling post. This last business of catching the rope as it was running out one learned very quickly or lost an arm in the learning. The culling, on the other hand, was a tedious, back-breaking chore. Braced against the roll of the boat, one scratched over the load on deck, picking up scallops individually as they were uncovered and shovelling overboard all the half ton or so of trash. It was hard, wet work, but the money seemed good. Looking back on the lessons I learned, some of our experiences seem frightening and almost unbelievable.

It was winter and it was cold, and because Rock Harbor is landlocked at low tide we spent a number of nights offshore, anchored by the drag in the lee of Billingsgate Island. That meant a fire all night in the Shipmate stove in the almost airtight cabin. When we turned in the first night I complained about the smell of gasoline in the cabin. "Oh, sure," said Cap'n Bart, "the gas line leaks a little bit. But it's a good thing because it keeps you continually aware of the danger of fire."

Maybe so, but when the stuffy cabin drove me on deck in a sweat before daylight next morning, my first breath of fresh air hit me between the eyes like a hard-swung two-by-four. After that I never turned in without first wedging the companionway door slightly ajar. I felt I'd rather be cold than sick or dead from gasoline fumes.

Then there was the way Cap'n Bart started a fire in the Shipmate. After the ashes had been drawn and thrown overboard he'd dump in a half bucket of coal. Over this he'd pour a good quart of lubricating oil, then half a cup of gasoline. I tell you truly! Leaving the cover off the stove, he'd stand back, light a match, and toss it into the stove. There'd be a whoosh, the gasoline would puff flame clear to the overhead, and he'd jump to slap on the stove cover. That was bad enough, goodness knows, but when the flame had died down and gone out, still not hot enough to ignite the coal properly, he had a tin measuring cup, brought along for just this purpose. He would draw off another quarter cup of gasoline, take off the stove cover, and throw the cup, gasoline and all, into the hot stove. There would be an explosion as the gasoline caught fire and the cup would ricochet from overhead to bulkhead and half a dozen times more about the cabin while he was slapping on the stove cover. The first time he pulled that trick he caught me unaware and trapped forward. The second time I headed for the deck and comparative safety. Before he could try it a third time I saw to it the galley was well supplied with hard pine kindling, and for the rest of the time I fished on *Sea Pal*, the kindling never got low.

Cap'n Bart wasn't the only wild man in the Bay.  Let Cap'n Sim Smith, later of the *Lucky Lady*, tell it:

"We was all out draggin' in the Bay.  There was Finlay and me in Finlay's boat, and there was Ralph Hansen.  There was Zibe Crosby, and there was Foster Atwood in the *Sea Urchin*.  Old Charlie Campbell was with him.  All of us that night, we went into the lee of the Horseshoe.  Jack Bonnell and Everett was there in their boat.  They never *had* to go draggin' 'cause they had enough money.  I asked Jack that afternoon if they was goin' to stay out and Jack said yes, and they was goin' to have steak for supper.  I knew very well I wasn't goin' to have steak for supper — I was on Finlay's boat.  So that night we went into the Horseshoe.

"Ed Hunt, his boat was leakin' quite bad.  She was twenty-six foot long and fourteen foot wide.  Painted green, she was.  He went close inshore in the Horseshoe to lay, 'cause she'd ebb out dry there and he could get a good night's sleep.  'Course, Ed, he always used to sleep in the bunk with his foot hangin' over the edge, and when the water hit his foot he'd get up and pump.  It was kinda cold, of course, and he'd always wake up when the cold water hit his heel.

"So anyway, we was all layin' off the Horseshoe there, and all at once we heard this noise, somebody hollerin'.  And we couldn't make out just what it was down in the cabin there, so we went on deck and this voice says, 'I'm sunk!  I'm sunk!  I'm sunk!'  Well, old Charlie Campbell, he was on the *Sea Urchin* along with Foster Atwood — and I can see him standin' there now.  Finlay had his searchlight on, tryin' to find the feller on the Island or whoever 'twas hollerin', and there stood Old Charlie in his underwear and with his socks on.  And he says, 'Think nothin' of it, Ed, I'm drunk, too.'

"Poor Ed, he swum or walked ashore, and he had a blanket over his head and a loaf of bread under his arm, and he wasn't drunk 't all.  He was sunk, and he was prett' near froze to death standin' on the Island.  So we finally shacked him aboard, and, of course, there was plenty of bootleg liquor around in those days, and the boys, they got a couple of drinks into him.  And of course, they had to get warmed up, too, 'cause they'd heard Ed hollerin' he was sunk and they knowed how cold he was.

"Well, anyway, the next morning she was ebbed out all dry, Ed's boat was, and Ed, he got some caulkin' off the other boats, and he went ashore and caulked her. Far as I can remember, he went fishin' that day when the tide come in."

The weather was getting worse and the lost days more frequent, and the scallops weren't getting any thicker. The episode that finally turned me off was a display of temper the likes of which I had never seen before.

*Sea Pal's* heavy-duty Lathrop motor was a workhorse, practically indestructible — I mean that literally. The day came when the motor stalled. No amount of cranking and diddling would start it. Each time he cranked, each time he made an adjustment, Cap'n Bart got madder and swore longer. I knew very little about marine motors in those days, but I did know enough not to offer any suggestions. Nothing seemed to work and it looked as though we would be broken down all day, until one of the other boats came to tow us in that afternoon. And then the skipper blew up. *Sea Pal* had been ballasted with neat, fifty-pound pigs of iron and one of these came to Cap'n Bart's hand. He yelled, "Goddamn you, if I can't start you nobody ever will!" And with that he belabored that insensate piece of machinery with a pig of iron, not once, but many, many times, until his hands were bleeding and he was sobbing with frustration and exhaustion. Then he crawled to his bunk blubbering.

I was slightly frightened and completely puzzled, for I had never seen a grown man carry on so. Curious to see how much damage Cap'n Bart had done to the motor, I climbed down, expecting to see broken fragments. I found one broken sparkplug, a considerable disarrangement of wires, and a few bright places on those pie-plate size cylinder heads. I fished in the junk box. (Lesson: Every well found boat should carry a junk box of odds and ends of machinery, used sparkplugs, bits of wire, odd nuts and bolts, rusty nails and screws of various sizes — just junk that ordinarily would be thrown overboard but might someday come in handy.) I found a used sparkplug and cleaned it as best I could. I found a wrench, took out the broken plug, replaced it with the cleaned one, and connected the wires where they seemed to belong. Then I backed out of the engine hold, made sure everything was clear and barred over the flywheel. The steady chunk, chunk, chunk of that good, old, indestructible motor greeted me. I reached for the throttle, speeded it up and slowed it down again. Finally I soft-talked Cap'n Bart into dragging scallops again. In later years I realized what had happened: Overheated by the heavy work we had been doing, the magneto had quit, but once it had had enough time to cool off properly, no amount of beating with a pig of iron on the heads of that motor made any difference.

If the motor hadn't had it, I had, though I didn't come off totally free. I quit and went back to hand-scratching quahogs the rest of the winter, but from then on I dreamed of a boat of my own.

# 2

## Sunshine Launched

In the spring of 1935 Arthur Clark came up with a proper boat within my price range. *Sunshine* had been built for a Dr. Hill, so I was told, as a yacht tender. She was an open boat, twenty feet long, six feet in the beam, round-bottomed, and she drew about eighteen inches standing. She had an old Leroy tractor motor in her, but the motor had been sunk and was good for nothing but a mooring. Arthur pointed out that there was no better motor for a boat than a Model T Ford engine, which could be bought in any junk yard for a dollar. He would even help me install it. Judging by his interest, I think he was going fishing vicariously.

I paid twenty-five dollars, put *Sunshine* on a trailer and brought her home. My education in boat building had begun and was to continue for the eight years I suffered with the little witch. *Sunshine* was a well-built craft, planked from stem to stern without a single butt, and copper-riveted, but she had been terribly neglected. Some previous owner had left her bow down during the winter, and ice formed in her and sprang both garboard planks and her forefoot as well. Once I had cleaned her up and taken off the many lead patches this became painfully apparent. Even more upsetting, she had to be "fixed" before I would dare take her to sea.

Arthur dolefully shook his head and apologized for having talked me into buying such a hunk of junk. I talked with one boatman after another. They'd squat down and peer up through the three-inch gap on either side of her keel. They'd knowingly jab a knife point into her planking. (I found this to be a sure sign of a man who doesn't know much about boatbuilding — jabbing a knife point into unoffending planking is akin to kicking the tires of a car.) Then they'd say wisely and smugly, "Well, her planking seems sound enough and she used to be a pretty little thing, but she ain't worth patching up; and furthermore, there ain't nobody around here who knows that much about boatbuilding." I was considerably disillusioned; I thought that everyone on Cape Cod knew everything about boatbuilding.

There was someone who knew "that much"; there was Mac McKoy. Mac was one of a kind, a genius in his peculiar way, a small man physically but feisty. Nothing ever suited Mac the way it was, and he was never interested in just any old job that just any old wood butcher could do. Mac wasn't even satisfied with the way chickens were bred, and bred his own until the hens laid eggs too big for a standard eggbox; in fact, nine out of a dozen were sure to be double-yolked.

I went to Mac one day to buy a dozen eggs, and while he was putting them in a paper sack I said casually, "You hear about that sticking I took on that boat I bought? I've had every boat expert in town look at her, and they all say the best thing to do is to burn her up. She can't be fixed."

Mac peered at me over his heavy glasses, one bow of which was a piece of heavy copper wire. "Who says she can't be fixed?"

I named the experts.

Mac put the price of the eggs in his overalls pocket. "Got a few minutes?"

I said I had.

"Drive me over and let me take a look."

I drove Mac over and he took a look. He crawled way up in the eyes of her inside and asked for a flashlight. He came out and pried up under *Sunshine*'s bow with a four-by-four. I noticed he didn't jab her planking with the point of his knife. He looked at me over his glasses. "You want to fix her?"

I said I did.

"Take me home to get some tools, then go to Harry Snow's hardware store and get six feet of three-eighth-inch solid brass curtain rod, six three-eighth brass nuts and washers, and a seven-inch by half-inch galvanized carriage bolt (you can't buy anything as big as that in brass locally). We can counter bore and bung the galvanized bolt so we won't set up electrolysis."

I did as I was told, and that afternoon Mac "fixed" *Sunshine*. He bored straight through the three forward pairs of ribs, planks, ribs and all. He sawed off the brass curtain rod to length, threaded it, and screwed on washers and nuts. He bored up through the forefoot and projecting end of the keel, slightly off-center to get new wood. Then with a car jack putting on pressure against the forefoot we tightened first one nut and then another. The garboard planks crept beautifully into place, the ribs nestled into the slots cut for them, the forefoot and keel snugged up tight. A flat file took off the corners of the brass nuts where they hadn't pulled flush into the planking, and a light caulking and a couple of coats of paint finished the job. In later years when I got into boat repair work myself, by necessity, I often thought of Mac's dictum, "Don't ever take *nobody's* word that a boat can't be fixed."

Then we scraped and painted and puttied. We rigged tiller lines, and Arthur installed the Model T on a new bed. We rigged an exhaust line of galvanized pipe out through the stern, and put controls where they could be easily reached. After Mac's repair job there was one feature which bothered me: along both bilges there were seams which looked too wide to hold caulking; furthermore, the edges of the planks didn't line up smoothly. (I later learned the reason, and another lesson: Look to see if each plank lines up with the edges of the one above and the one below. If not, there is a loose fastening somewhere that ought to be replaced. This is particularly so where the ends of two planks in the same strake don't match each other. Either the butt block behind the joint is rotten, or some of the fastenings have let go.) However, it was some three or four years before I finally found out what was wrong with *Sunshine*'s seams. I consulted Mac and he suggested that if I was doubtful I should caulk all the seams, and then, anywhere they were wider than the thickness of a pencil, I should cover them with sheet copper. "And," he said, "don't put all your tacks in a line or you'll split the plank. Stagger the tacks, first one up and then one down."

I did as Mac suggested and spent fourteen dollars for copper flashing. I remember the price well, because it seemed somewhat out of proportion to spend fourteen dollars on copper for a twenty-five-dollar boat. The patch job held up well, for it was three years before winter ice, poundings, and rough usage finally pulled the tacks

and I had to do the repair job which should have been done in the
first place — had I known enough. But that comes later.

There is a thrill to launching a boat, a thrill that never dims in all
the years to come. The hard work is finished, all the hopes of a new
year are before you. And a boat never again looks as pretty as she
does on launching day. It was a proud day when we launched *Sunshine*, all gleaming white paint and shining copper — and I got myself
into one hell of a mess. There were no launching ramps in those days,
and no four-wheel-drive vehicles. We put *Sunshine* carefully on a
great old homemade, four-wheeled trailer. (As I remember, it was
made from a Chandler car chassis and probably weighed more than
*Sunshine*.) For hauling we had our ever-used, ever-abused Model A
Ford, with oversized tires. Carefully I drove down the road, then
out across the sand track to Bee's River — most of the way in low
gear. Years before, blackfish (the smallest species of whale, driven
ashore for their "head" oil) had been buried along this shore. Where
their natural oil seemed to have made a hardened spot, I swung
around and started to back down the river bank. And then I got
stuck, the Model A up to her axles in sand, the boat and trailer at a
fearful angle, neither in the water at low tide nor out of it at high.

Sometimes I have been accused of being over optimistic and over
trusting of strangers, but so many people have helped me when I've
been in a jam that I can't be any other way. Around the point of
the beach there came three strangers, men I had never seen before
and never saw again. Shop workers they said they were, all older,
bigger, stronger men than I. They took in the situation as they came
closer and, all without ever asking, found boards for shovels and
driftwood planks for pries. They not only got the boat and trailer
down into the river bed (it was low tide) but, what was even more
helpful, they unloaded the boat, hitched up the trailer, got the Model
A unstuck and cleared up the whole area. All for no more than a
sincere thank-you. (Sometimes when I've fished a sunken week-end
admiral with a too-small boat out of the water, or waited late at night
at the harbor for one of the boats overdue and perhaps in trouble, I
think of times like the first launching of *Sunshine*, and can do no less
than hope that I, too, can be of help.)

# 3

〰〰〰〰〰〰〰〰〰〰〰

# First Trip

One trip in *Sunshine*, with the Model T for power, stands out in my memory among the many I made that summer. It was my first trip and I was to gather lessons thick and fast. Before daylight I drove out the sand track to Bee's River where *Sunshine* was moored against the bank. I had made everything ready the night before — I thought. In the dark I cranked the Model T, which was set in such a way between the bedding timbers that I couldn't spin the crank, only pull it over a quarter turn at a time. Arthur was a good mechanic and the motor caught immediately. What I didn't know and found out the hard way was that when a Model T is installed in a boat there is, in effect, no clutch. As soon as the motor fired the propeller began to turn. It was simply good luck that I hadn't thrown off my mooring lines. Mind you, this was my first trip, it was still pitch dark, and, as I said, they had buried blackfish along this shore.

The motor fired, the propeller turned and *Sunshine* went into an unbelievable, twisting, wringing spasm which nearly threw me overboard. I jumped for the knife switch which cut the motor, and the spasm stopped. I sat on the stern deck and wiped the nervous sweat from my forehead while I thought it out. I had no flashlight; indeed, I had no life jacket, no fire extinguisher (except a bucket of dry sand) and no lights of any kind.

I felt along the motor and shaft where I could reach it. Everything seemed to be as it should. There was only one other moving part, the propeller. I shucked off my clothes and dove under *Sunshine*. It didn't strike me as unusual or peculiar that I should dive overboard in the pitch dark, alone and in a fast-running tide. It was simply something that had to be done, so I did it. I found the trouble by feel. I had picked up in the propeller a length of half-rotted drag rope, three-quarter-inch manila, which had been used to tow in those dead blackfish weighing sometimes as much as a ton, and then discarded because it would forever stink of dead blackfish.

Coming up for air two or three times and fighting the fast-ebbing tide, I hurriedly unwound the rope and threw it up on the beach. Never since have I felt right in throwing over old rope, used burlap bags, or any other substance which might foul a prop.

The tide was dropping fast. (It drops vertically about two feet an hour here.) Shivering with pre-dawn chill and nervousness, I fired up the motor again, fought off the two mooring lines, and without taking time to put my clothes back on, I felt my way, vulnerable and naked, out of the twisting channel and into the open Bay.

The sun came up shortly and it turned into a beautiful day, flat calm, warm and sunny. I headed north where the quahogs were supposed to be thickest. I wanted to stand up and throw out my chest — *Sunshine* was *my* boat, and *I* was *Captain* — but the controls were so low it was more convenient to kneel on the deck. The feeling of pride and accomplishment were almost suffocating. My troubles were over — I thought.

Listening to the old-timers had taught me that when I got to the grounds I was to slow down, bring the boat up into the wind, drop over my first anchor, and then, still heading into the wind, run out all forty fathoms of my anchor rode. At the far end I dropped over the second anchor, cut the motor, and then let myself fall back until the bow anchor took hold. Since there was no wind I ran the rode out with the tide.

A long rake, or as it is more commonly called hereabout, a bull-rake, is very much like an oversized garden rake on the end of a long pole, except that it has a bag of netting or a basket of wire behind the teeth. I had bought from Nate Clark, Arthur's brother, an old "channel" rake with twenty-eight three-inch teeth spaced an inch and a half apart. It was satisfactory, though somewhat heavy for the depth of water I was in. This rake is thrown, teeth down, off the stern or bow as far as possible, or to the length of the pole, which in this case was thirty feet. The pole is then put over one shoulder and the rake worked, or "jigged" toward the boat, with the pole, as it is worked in, climbing farther and farther over the shoulder. The teeth, of course, are always buried in the sand. As the rake comes to quahogs, the quahogs are raked out of the sand, up over the teeth and into the net bag. When so much of the pole has been pulled in that the weight of it overbalances that part of the gear still in the water, it is given a twitch to break the rake clear of the sand and rapidly turned so the teeth are up and the bag holding the quahogs down. Then it is brought in, hand over hand, until the rake is at the boat's rail. I had listened to all of this but found there was a knack which I was slow in learning.

As the day wore on I wore blisters on both hands and both wrists as well as my shoulders, but I was happy. As I worked along the rode my pile of quahogs grew. (I got six bushels that day at a dollar and a quarter a bushel.) I owned my own boat and I was making money for the first time in weeks instead of spending it. I laid back my head as bullrakers have done for untold years and in sheer exuberance I yelled, "What a da-a-y!" I should have kept my mouth shut.

There have been times in the years and boats which came after *Sunshine* when I have been accused of being timid. Well, maybe I am. I prefer to think that I weigh the profit against the cost. I fished days when much bigger boats ran for shelter. I've knowingly headed into bad weather when there was good and sufficient reason, and I've been, as the saying goes, "shellacked" for going. I got shellacked that day in *Sunshine*, but good! There is one weather sign, which I know but didn't then, that a boatman must watch for in Cape Cod Bay in the summer. If the sun comes up on a morning that is dewy wet, with flat calm or a light southerly breeze, if the tide is on the ebb and will start to flood about noon — he looks out for a "smokey sou'wester" when the tide turns ("smokey" because the air will be full of haze). Nobody had told me, so I sat peacefully munching my cheese sandwiches as the noon whistle blew in Orleans. The light southerly breeze carried the sound all the way to North Eastham. The tide turned and the southwest wind came up. In fifteen minutes all the water around me was "feather white," and the wind whistled. Inexperienced though I was, I knew this was no place for *Sunshine* and me. Before the wind got any stronger I had better streak for the south end of town and Bee's River.

I lashed down my thirty-foot quahog pole with the rake forward and the end tailing out behind me. I dropped back to pick up my stern anchor; then hauling myself by brute strength to where my bow anchor held short, I checked to see that everything was secure. With my lesson about the clutch in mind I bent over the motor. In my hurry to get fishing there were several things I had neglected to finish, thinking I could do them on blowy days. One of these unfinished projects was building an engine box or cover around the Model T.

Heading up into the rapidly building seas, I cranked the motor, and when it fired I jumped to pull the bow anchor. I needn't have hurried. *Sunshine*, with the throttle open to start, stuck her nose right through the first wave. Solid water came pouring over the bow. It soaked me all right, but I had no time to worry about that for it drowned out that Model T. I dropped anchor and enough rope to hold me. I pumped out the bilge and sat down to contemplate a soaking wet motor.

It's kind of funny now, looking back on all the equipment I didn't take, to think the one thing I did take was a quart of kerosene to dry out the wires if they got wet. (I guess hardly anyone uses kerosene or range oil nowadays, but it still works — I know because I dried out motor wiring with it no longer ago than last winter.) I wiped off the plugs and wires with my handkerchief and shirttail as best I could and doused everything with kerosene, and then I thought through my dilemma. If I started the way I had before I'd get more of the same. Well, in that case, the thing to do was to put the anchor over the stern and start downwind. If I took a wave over the stern, at least the motor wouldn't get wet. It worked. In fact I had set the anchor so short that my first surge ahead broke the anchor out of the sand and it really steadied me as it dragged behind until I could find time to bring it aboard.

It was a slow, tedious, four-mile trip back along the length of the town to Bee's River and a safe mooring. I think I learned another lesson that day: The quickest way to learn to handle a power boat, though it's neither pleasant nor safe, is to start off in a boat that is relatively small for the size of the seas. When I came to bigger boats and bigger seas, I found I had learned my lessons well. That day I learned just how much I could quarter the seas and stay dry, and since the whole trip was broadside to the wind and in the trough, I found that if the seas were long enough I could speed up and run comfortably in the trough quite a way, if I was ready to chop my throttle and swing head up into the first breaking sea that came. That little trick saved my life and my boat a good many years later. Eventually I made Bee's River and tied to the mooring stakes I had put down along the river bank.

*Sunshine*, I had already begun to suspect, was not designed for Cape Cod Bay even in the summertime. She was not high-sided enough; a foot of freeboard plus a four-inch wash rail was hardly safe in seas which commonly built up two or three feet high, even on a calm day. However, we worked the summer out, *Sunshine* and I, bullraking some, going to Billingsgate Island for steamer clams, and even trolling for mackerel occasionally just for the food and the fun of it.

# 4

## Brad Takes Me to Pleasant Bay

That winter Brad Steele and Pleasant Bay in Orleans came into my life together. Brad was a likeable rogue, as salty as they come. He bragged of having been cook in the Coast Guard and from him my wife got many of the recipes she uses today for fish and shellfish. There was never anything Brad didn't know how to fix, and if he didn't he'd bluff and usually make the bluff stick. His happy-go-lucky swagger was a part of Brad and he had an unfondness for shaving, though his father, Old Bill Steele, was still barbering in his nineties. Pleasant Bay was a much smaller body of water than Cape Cod Bay, being perhaps a mile across (distances are so hard to judge on the water) but full of shallows and trickeries as I was to learn over the years.

"Since you have a boat and no know-how," Brad said, "and since I have the know-how and no boat, why don't we pair up and go bull-raking together in Pleasant Bay this winter. They're getting rich over there."

Maybe *they* were getting rich, but we never did. However, I learned a lot about boats and bullraking and Pleasant Bay. Brad was the most unconcerned, casual partner with whom I ever fished. I could tell when he was completely contented, which was often, for he used to sing in a salt-cracked voice, "It was the *Greasy Heman* that sailed upon the sea and towed along behind her the little *Willy D*." I often wondered if there were more to the song than that couplet; anyway, after that winter *Sunshine* became *The Greasy Heman*.

We trailered her over to Pleasant Bay and bullraked for big quahogs most of the winter, though we made side excursions. Brad borrowed somebody else's skiff scallop drag, a rig somewhat like the one we used on *Sea Pal*, but light enough and small enough to be hauled by hand. He talked me into going dragging for scallops. What I didn't know was that we were illegally dragging seed scallops, immature scallops without the required "well-defined" growth ring. (I had never heard of them.) Somehow, Elmer Darling, the shellfish constable then (to whom I was to owe much in later years) never caught up with us. We were doing well, dragging most of the day, opening most of the night and peddling scallops door-to-door at fifty cents a pint in between. Until we lost the oil in the base of the Model T! That day I remarked to Brad that the motor seemed to be pounding awfully.

"No, no," said Brad, "Model T's always pound in a boat."

I looked down into the bilge. "Brad," said I, "the bilge is full of oil."

Brad went into his song about the *Greasy Heman*.

I shut off the motor and checked the oil level. In those primitive car motors there were two brass petcocks in the base. If oil flowed out of the opened top petcock the oil level was all right. If it didn't flow through the top one but did through the bottom one, the motor was still all right but needed oil. If no oil flowed out of the bottom one you were in trouble. No oil flowed out of the bottom one; we were in trouble.

As so often happened, help came along about that time in the form of the shellfish constable. Luckily for us, we had drifted a long way from the seed scallop bed. We hailed "Dar," who sold us on the spot a gallon of oil — he just happened to have a spare gallon (Dar had been around a while) — and we limped back to Quanset Pond in the nor'west corner of Pleasant Bay, where we were tying up. By the time we got that far the motor was pounding again, so after we had moored and shut off we disconnected the motor and turned it bottom up right there in the boat to examine the base for oil leaks. There was a leak, all right. Into the cast base had been brazed a bronze drain plug about an inch in diameter. It had rusted out completely. Brad rowed ashore in the skiff we were using for a tender, cut down a young cedar tree, and rowed back. He whittled out a cedar plug big enough to fill the hole where the drain plug had been and drove it in.

"There," said he, "that's better than the original because it can't rust out." We ran with it all the rest of the winter.

Brad was full of make-do's. An expansion or freeze-out plug rusted through? He took a five-cent piece, put it on the end of a piece of pipe, held against it a ball peen hammer, and hit the hammer a lick with a heavier hammer. It concaved the coin just enough so that it exactly fit where the freeze-out plug had been. "Much better and no more expensive," said Brad, "A freeze-out plug costs a nickel and will rust out. That five-cent piece is a nickel and it is good United States money, so it will never rust out."

With Brad I learned the hard way about the "window-pane" ice in Quanset Pond, that is, salt ice mixed with a good deal of fresh water and about the thickness of a window pane. It can carve a boat almost as quickly as though it were actually made of glass. We broke through window-pane ice early one morning, eager to get back to our bullraking. In an hour or so I said to Brad, "Somehow, this boat seems to be leaking."

"Not at all," said Brad, "just enough to keep her sweet."

"Then," said I, "you take a turn at pumping, I'm tired."

Brad pumped a little, then threw down the pump. "You know," said he, "I think you might be right." We picked up the anchors and headed for Quanset, where Brad drove *Sunshine*'s bow hard up on the beach. Sure enough, there where the curve of her water line had cut through the ice, the ice had cut a hole through her big enough to stick your fingers through. I suggested buying copper, and Brad was horrified. Buy copper? When there was a dump nearby? We went to the dump and found an old copper wash boiler. Brad cut out the bottom with his jackknife and a hammer, and we tacked the oval-shaped piece over the hole. "Too bad we didn't take the whole wash boiler," Brad said, "then we could have put another piece on the other side and had winter sheathing so we wouldn't have to worry about ice again this year."

Another trip that winter stands out in my mind. My lessons were already beginning to pay off. It was in February, late one afternoon; the rest of the bullrakers had gone ashore for it was bitter cold with more than a spit of snow in the air. Brad was determined to finish up his last bushel of quahogs and I couldn't very well leave without him. Finally, we topped off our measure and picked up our anchors.

The Model T ignition system had a series of four coils, one for each cylinder. They built up an unbelievably high voltage, and when the switch was turned on there was usually a quite audible buzz. That night there was no buzz. "My God!" Brad said, "The battery has gone dead. We'll be out here all night. Even if we drift over to Chatham it will be morning before we get there and we'll both be frozen dead."

I said nothing but kept on patiently cranking. I pulled up and pulled up, again and again, trying to snap the motor over. Brad said, "You're wasting your strength." But I kept on cranking. And then, for some unexplainable reason, the motor came to life, the generator took over the spark load and we headed for home. (Lesson: When things don't work, don't just sit there and moan — do something.)

Brad also initiated me into the mysteries of ranges. It is by ranges that the alongshore fisherman orients himself. He goes where he wants to go and then studies the shore. Off here, to nor'ard, for example, is a tree which lines up exactly over the center of a white house, and off to west'ard (as nearly at right angles as possible), a telephone pole ranges over the corner of a patch of white sand. As the boat moves away, the tree or pole "walks" along the shore.

Brad recited for my instruction a set of ranges. "You see that white spot on top of Dr. Hill's rock? Well, that white spot lines up with that brown rock in the middle of the field."

"Brad . . .," I said.

"Do you get it?"

"Yes," I said, "I get it, except that the white spot is a sea gull which is apt to fly away any time, and the brown rock you ranged on is a cow — and she's moved already."

# 5

≈≈≈≈≈≈≈≈≈≈≈≈≈≈≈≈≈≈≈≈≈≈≈≈≈≈≈≈≈≈≈

# Back to Cape Cod Bay

Too small or not, *Sunshine* was back in Cape Cod Bay the next summer with a new motor we could have carried in a half-bushel basket, a single cylinder, three-and-a-half horsepower Kermath. The Model T of the year before had died and Nate Clark had the little Kermath for sale. He, too, was a good mechanic. Years later it came out that the little motor had been sunk at least three times before I paid five dollars for it, but Nate had overhauled it so well that I could set the impulse on the magneto, push the flywheel over with my foot, and depend on it to run all day. The copper gas tank which came with it held three gallons and I don't remember ever having to fill it more than once a day.

Bob Whiting went with me that summer of 1936 to Billingsgate Island for soft-shelled clams. Bob had not only been a motor mechanic in the Coast Guard during the last of the rum-running days, but had worked off-Cape in a machine shop. From somewhere he came up with a tremendous marine clutch, almost as big as the motor. The trouble was, the shaft of the clutch was far too big to fit the little Kermath. In no way discouraged, we set the motor up on blocks, rigged a hose in and out of a washtub full of water for cooling, filed off by hand enough of the clutch shaft so that it would fit into the coupling of the motor, and started the rig running. Then we bore down on the shaft with a big, new flat file. The job would never have passed any machine shop inspection, but it worked. The fact was that while the Kermath was rated to turn about 800 rpm, it was so overloaded that I doubt we ever got much over 300. Thus, any vibrations due to imperfect milling were reduced to negligible proportions.

Clamming was good at Billingsgate and there were days when we came home so loaded we kept our fingers crossed to ward off a wind that would sink us. Our speed was, to use a kind word, leisurely. If the weather was calm the four-and-a-half-mile trip usually took us something over an hour. We found it was quicker than rowing, for one day the motor failed.

We had left Bee's River at daybreak and had gotten maybe a mile offshore when, for no reason we could see, the motor quit. The motor would fire once when the magneto impulse was set, but since the first explosion flipped that off, one explosion was all we could get, crank or tinker as we might. My February experience with Brad in mind, I had shipped a pair of ten-foot oars; we got them out, rigged a pair of rope rowlocks, and headed back across the tide. For an hour or more we strained at those cussed sweeps, and it became more and more evident that we weren't going to make it home on that tide.

Finally I said to Bob, "Give me your sweep and twist that animal's tail one more time. Maybe she's cooled off enough to run."

He did and it did and we cheered and just made it back to our stakes in Bee's River before the motor conked out on us again. The next day we had a new second-hand magneto. The summer went by in a haze. Between us we dug most days five barrels of clams, which is fifteen bushels or twenty-five hods. For a while we were paid a dollar a bushel, until we had fish-buyer trouble. He got snuffy and insisted on bigger measure to take care of shrinkage. We took a day off and landed a market at Bass River at three dollars and fifty cents a barrel, delivered. The rest of the summer, while Bob and I were offshore digging clams, my wife drove each day to Bass River with twenty-five hods of clams in the Model A. How much profit there was in driving thirty miles a day for a dollar and a half might be debatable, but at least we were independent of the fish buyer.

# 6

=========================================================

# Sunshine and I Go Back
# to Pleasant Bay and Scalloping Alone

That winter *Sunshine* and I went over the road again by trailer to
Pleasant Bay and went scalloping alone. Let it not be supposed that
the gear I used on *Sunshine* was such a ponderous affair as we used in
*Sea Pal*. Hand scallop dredges, or skiff drags, as they are more commonly called, were and are light rigs which have changed little in de-
sign since they were first developed some time in the late 1880's. A
two- or three-foot-wide demi-hoop of half-inch iron is followed by a
bag, the lower half of which is usually formed of two-inch rings, the
upper half of twine. The bag can be led on the bottom by a slightly
looped chain, a single bar, or a loop of lead rollers an inch or so in
diameter. The average drag will hold from one to two bushels of
trash and scallops. It is towed along the bottom of the bay, then
hauled aboard by hand and dumped. When the drag is over again
and the next tow started, while the boat, cut in a circle, pretty much
takes care of herself, the dead shells, stones and weeds are pushed or
shoveled overboard. The scallops are picked out and bagged, ready
to take home for opening that night.

It was this winter that we learned about scallop-opening, though
we continued to add to our experience and skill for the next twenty
years. Cape scallops (or "bay scallops" as they are called hereabouts)
are a relatively limited crop. Geographically they extend no further
south than northern New Jersey, and north seldom beyond Wellfleet.
They are a biennial crop, living in from one to perhaps thirty feet of
water for from twenty-six to twenty-eight months, and are harvested
only in the fall and winter, after the spawning season (in Massachusetts, not before October first nor after April first).

In the days when we started whittling, every kitchen on Cape Cod became a shucking house in a scallop year. Granted the state maximum catch of ten bushels per day, the routine went something like this. I would struggle into the kitchen at three or four o'clock with ten full bushels of scallops. Two or three of these were dumped into the kitchen sink, the rest stacked just outside the door. Side by side, sheathed in rubber aprons, our hands protected by gloves or bandages, my wife and I would start "peeling."

A scallop is a relatively agile shellfish as long as the water is warm and he is young, but as the water chills and the scallop grows older, the upper shell gathers grass and parasitic shellfish such as "quarter-decks" and barnacles. In opening, the side uppermost is the "dirty" side. Looking down on a scallop, the right side of the hinge is straight and the left side slightly hooked. A special round-pointed knife is slipped in between the shells near the hinge, held tight against the top shell until the adductor muscle is cut, then turned with a prying, twisting motion to flip away the top shell. A semi-circular cut counter-clockwise around the top of the lower shell lifts and flips away the "guts" leaving the adductor muscle clean and waiting to be sliced away from the lower shell into the waiting pan or bucket. There is a trick to it, a knack, and while a greenhorn may take all afternoon to open a bushel, a good opener will open better than a gallon of "eyes," or a bushel and a half of scallops in the shell in an hour.

Opening, we learned, was where the profit was; a poor opener left "a third for the shell, a third for the cat, and a third for the scalloper." We learned to whittle clean because the crop was limited. Together, my wife and I would open scallops as long as I could keep my eyes open; then, leaving her to clean up the kitchen, I would stumble into bed. The next morning I would pick up my ten wet bags and take off for *Sunshine* and the scallop grounds. After my wife had gotten the kids off to school, she would set to and open scallops all day. Again about three or four o'clock, just when she had finished the catch of the day before, cleaned up the kitchen, bandaged her cut hands and sat down to a cup of tea, I would come in again with another ten bushels, and away we would go.

But we had days off from opening. Poor *Sunshine* was beginning to teach me that hauling over the road is not the best thing in the world for a wooden boat. I don't know how many times that winter she sank — six maybe. There is no sicker feeling than to arrive at the shore in the morning, all ready to go offshore to make a day's pay, and find the boat sunk on her mooring. Oil all over everything — I never got all the oil off — and how to handle a sunken boat? How to get it ashore? I learned.

If friends were fishing from the same landing they stopped and helped, if not, I did it by myself. Elmer Darling, the Orleans shellfish constable, helped me again and again. Captain "Old Dave" (to distinguish him from "Young Dave," his son) Delano, who later fished with me in *String Bean* as well as *Nonny*, and all the rest of the commercial scallopers who fished from the River landing that winter were always ready to help. But there were days I had to do the whole thing myself.

I rowed out a good strong piece of rope, secured it to the bow and cast off the mooring. Then I rowed back to shore to make the other end of the rope fast to the Model A. I hauled her as far up on the beach as she would go and then, with a sad little thing like *Sunshine*, I could wade out along her rail, lifting with all my might, and jam a knee under her. (A knee in this case was simply three short lengths of plank nailed together flatways in a triangle.) Then I bailed with a bucket, or several buckets if my friends were still around. Gradually I'd gain enough so the water wasn't flowing in over the rail almost as fast as I was bailing it out. There is an amazing amount of water in a boat even as small as *Sunshine*. Once she was reasonably clear, I could open the sea cock to drain off the rest of the water as the tide dropped.

Every time *Sunshine* searched for the bottom that winter I had to take off the magneto, go to my nearest friend's house, track in mud and slush on my boots, wash out the mag with hot water and soap, and then leave it in the oven to bake. Back to the boat I'd go to take out the motor, take off the copper base, and drain all the salt water from base, gas line, gas tank, and carburetor. Everything had to be flushed with clean oil, filled with new gasoline and reconnected. Then back I'd go for the magneto, hook it up, and crank. All winter that little jewel started up every time, and chugged as peacefully as

though it had never been swimming — although by the end of the
year the magneto was beginning to falter occasionally.

With the motor taken care of, the next thing was to discover why
the boat had sunk.  Usually the cause wasn't hard to find; while
*Sunshine* was full of water, the water would pour out of the weak
place.  As often as not it was another piece of that copper sheathing
I had put on the first year.  Once the whole stern let go.

I had hunted for the leak from one end of the boat to the other.
I could find no weeping copper — as a matter of fact, by this time I
had replaced almost all of it.  As I rounded the stern I jabbed it with
my knife — yes, I did — and the water squirted out.  I went back and
pried at the copper strip I had tacked over the seam where stern and
planking met.  The whole stern dropped off in my hands!

What to do now?  True, the tide was still dropping, but it was
barely above freezing, and building a new stern is somewhat more
complicated than replacing a mere strip of copper.  However, what
else could I do?  I raced to Nickerson Lumber, gobbling my cheese
sandwiches as I went.  I'd have no other time to eat today.  I bought
a clear piece of white pine, raced the four miles home for tools, raced
back to the boat and started to work.

The new wood had to be scribed and cut, using the old stern as a
pattern, then the new wood beveled all around the edge.  Cut and try,
cut and try.  I had to hurry because the tide had turned.  Back to the
Smith Brothers Hardware I flew for copper nails I had forgotten the
first time.  (*Sunshine* was copper-fastened, remember?  I knew enough
not to use galvanized nails in a copper-fastened boat because electro-
lytic action would eat out galvanized nails in a matter of days.)  Starting at the bottom, one by one the nails were driven in.  Before I
reached the top planks I realized I wouldn't have time to caulk if . . .
I dropped the nails and went to caulking the seam between the new
stern and the planking.  By this time the water was above the knees
of my boots and rising fast.  Caulk a little, nail a little.  Before I had
finished *Sunshine*'s stern was water-borne.  The soft pine swelled as
I had hoped it would and the nails held.  That stern was still in *Sunshine* when she was deliberately destroyed by fire some years later.
Not too long ago someone asked me how I learned the boat-building
trade.  Putting on that stern was one way, though I don't recommend it.

# 7

∽∽∽∽∽∽∽∽∽∽∽∽

# New Ribs

There is a great deal more to boatbuilding than patching. Frank Ryder taught me that the next year, 1937, and *Sunshine* was our patient. We had been shellfishing together alongshore all spring and summer, clamming, razor-clamming, moon-snailing — doing whatever came along.

In this day when so many young people are going back to the shore for their living, liking the freedom and the independence, it bothers me there aren't more Frank Ryders around to steer them straight. Frank knew so many ways to scratch out a living. Round-wrinkling, or moon-snailing, was one. The moon snail is a savage predator which can clean out a clam bed or a mussel flat. It is edible, so I am told, though few local people bother with it. We made our money picking up moon snails and selling them to the codfish hand-liners out of Chatham for bait, particularly in the spring.

I don't know whether moon snails come out when the moon is up; I do know that the best time to gather them is just at daybreak, on low tide, on a muggy, foggy morning. They can be potted or trapped, but we went by rowboat, armed simply with buckets and scratchers, and picked them up by the bucketful.

Undoubtedly I owe as much to Frank Ryder as to any man I ever fished with. He was small and grey and stooped, and almost stone deaf. He was an old bachelor who lived alone except for as many as seventeen cats. He was stubborn and opinionated. He was gentle and patient. He knew more about boats and fishing and the motors of his time than any man I ever met. I saw him frightened only once, and that situation was enough to scare any man with a tinge of intelligence. I never saw him angry or jealous in all the years I fished with him.

As I say, we had been shellfishing together all summer when Frank remarked he'd like to try a little flounder dragging that winter but had no boat. I suggested *Sunshine*, but reminded him she leaked pretty badly. (She'd been on a mooring all summer and was not much trouble as long as she rested there quietly.)

We put her on the beach and looked at her bottom. I noticed Frank didn't do much jabbing with his knife blade. Instead, he studied her from the inside, and without a word he began to pull off her inside sheathing. Then, and only then, did I discover the reason for those poorly fitting planks along the curve of her bilge: almost every rib on both sides was broken — thirty-four ribs altogether. (I found out later she had been dropped off a trailer before I bought her.)

"Well," said Frank moderately, as was his way, "that's not impossible. We'll have to get some white oak, and a saw table to cut it up on. We'll have to rig a steam box. Believe I've got a piece of oak driftwood down to the shore."

He had, and we borrowed Bernard Collins' saw table. I have often wondered since, having become more familiar with power tools, what the salt and sand in that driftwood did to the saw blade, but Bernard never complained. "Thirty-four ribs," Frank said, "that'll be thirty-four pieces six foot long and an inch square — better make it forty, we might break some."

We got an armload of old cardboard posters from the movie theatre to make patterns of. With a pair of dividers Frank scribed and cut each pattern separately, numbering them as we went along.

Many years afterwards, when the Army Corps of Engineers planned to dump the spoil from Wellfleet Harbor on the best striped bass grounds in Cape Cod Bay, I went to argue with them armed with a chart, a parallel rule, and the rusty dividers I had carried aboard each boat in turn as I fished. The engineers went into polite hysterics at the dividers. Said I, "Don't laugh; if you had been brought home by any piece of equipment as many times as I have by these same dividers . . ." They listened and moved their spoil dump away.

I asked Frank if he was going to cut the curve of the ribs a little slack so the seams would pull up tight as we fastened. "No," he said, "the oak is going to relax a little after it's steamed." We went down to his fish shanty on the shore and laid out a long two-by-twelve, also driftwood. Frank laid down a pattern on the plank. "Now," he said, "when we bend the ribs around, the top end will bear here." And he drove in a spike. He laid down a pattern and drove in another spike at the sharpest bend. "The middle will bear against this spike, on the inside, and while I hold the rib bent you drive a spike right here so the bottom end will be outside. That way we've got a little sharper bend than we need."

I was curious to see the steam box — but it wasn't a box. It was a borrowed plumber's furnace, an old teakettle filled with water only half way up the spout so the steam could escape, and a long inner tube cut in the middle, one end bound tight around the kettle spout and the other end suspended open from the ceiling. Into this end we slid half a dozen pieces of oak. Once the steam started out Frank timed it. We found that twenty minutes was long enough; we could then bend that tough white oak and almost tie knots in it. We steamed the ribs, half a dozen at a time, wound them around their spikes, and secured them in position. There we left them to cool all night.

The ribs went in place as though they had been fitted, as in a way they had been. We worked without clamps, and since there was no power at the shore in those days, we drilled and counter-bored everything by hand, one of us on the outside to drill and drive the rivets, one of us inside to back the ribs and to set the bushings on the rivets. At first it was a little difficult, working with someone as deaf as Frank, but we worked out a series of taps on the hull which worked even better than words. We had cleaned out all the seams before we started and the planks pulled in as tight and smooth as they had ever been.

When we finished the ribs we put in new tie timbers, thwartship, laid a new water-tight deck, and installed a Model A motor. (Model T's were getting scarce by this time, but Model A engines were available in any junk yard for from a dollar, take what you get, to three dollars, guaranteed, meaning that if the head or block was cracked you could bring the motor back and try a new one free.) Suddenly

I had a boat, if not exactly new, at least far better than I had started with. What a difference it made to have a friend and partner to work with, a partner who knew what he was doing and spared no pains in the doing.

Not that we didn't have troubles. I think no one ever fished all winter without troubles. The gear pump for the motor's salt-water cooling system froze, so we learned to save our urine in the morning to thaw the pump with (it was easier than carrying a teakettle of hot water with us!). We hung both coil and condenser on the engine box to get them as far away from the motor heat as possible. Several times we limped home, pouring salt water over the condenser to keep it cool. Then we had a spell of losing rudders; we lost three, as I remember. We found that by coming along slowly and dragging a bucket off one side or the other we could manage to make it home to the mooring in the River leading up to Meetinghouse Pond. We learned that a rudder's counter-balance can be a very fussy thing — one of our replacement rudders had too much and very nearly capsized the boat before we trimmed it down.

Frank taught me to coil down our gear at night in the reverse order from that in which it went overboard in the morning, for some mornings it was covered with snow and frozen. First, the two drag warps were coiled down separately, then the drag doors, then the drag in neat folds, and on top of all the cod end with the puckering strings firmly tied while the rope was still unfrozen. Small lessons as they were, they became second nature and saved me endless trouble in later years.

Flounder dragging that winter, for all the hard work, was pleasant and profitable. We had not one sinking; in fact, we had hardly a leak. True enough, *Sunshine* was too small for the work to which we put her, dragging a fifty-foot net and bringing in some days as much as a thousand pounds of flounder. On some days we had to run ashore every so often to land what we had caught and then go back to work. It was asking a lot of a little boat, but she was willing and the Model A gave us power to spare.

Flounder dragging in the tidal ponds off Pleasant Bay is a highly specialized type of fishing; without Frank's guidance I would probably never have learned it. By a special act of the Massachusetts legislature, flounders may be dragged in these waters only between the first of November and the first of May. The gear is a miniature version, with some local adaptations, of the offshore otter trawlers' gear. The doors (or "boards" as they are more commonly called) are in effect paravanes, spreading a tapered net pocket out and down until it fishes, or is dragged, along the bottom, gathering everything in its way, marine grasses in abundance, fishes of all kinds, and, hopefully, flounders. The boards are hauled to the boat by hand, then the grasses and fishes have to be shaken down into the net little by little until the whole load is in the cod end, a net made of smaller mesh and heavier twine. Then the whole load has to be rolled aboard by brute strength and dumped on the deck. The grass and trash fish are thrown overboard, and the flounders are usually culled two ways, small and large. Frank's cull, I found, was somewhat larger than the average fisherman's.

"If you take all the little flounders this year," he'd grumble, "what are you going to catch next year? Besides which, the little ones ain't big enough to bother with; they don't make nothin' but slime."

Consequently, the prices the fish buyers paid for our fish were somewhat higher than average. Five cents a pound for small and seven for large was the usual price, but we were more apt to be paid seven and ten, so that actually we took home more money than we would have if we had taken smaller fish.

The next spring Frank went back to clamming, and I went back to bullraking in Pleasant Bay. That summer *Sunshine* paid a bonus. Our daughter Paula, who was in grade school at the time, was suddenly having trouble with her eyes. "No more reading," the doctor said, "no more music lessons, no more close work. Get her outdoors, make her use her eyes on distant objects." So Paula went with me every day. Fortunately, we enjoyed each other's company. On the trip to and from Pleasant Bay it became her duty to steer. I picked out ranges as far away as possible.

"Bring the Chatham Coast Guard Station right over the end of Namequoit Point," I'd say, and she'd strain to focus on the Station a good five miles away. "Now bring the Chatham radio tower right in the center of the Narrows," and she'd squint to bring the bearing in line.  It was rough on the youngster, and I don't think she's cared much for boating since, but it was, so the doctor said, a blessing for her eyesight.

And so the seasons came and went.  The next winter I went scalloping alone since Frank had other fish to catch.  Now it was my turn to help others in trouble.  Dar broke down and I returned one of his many favors by towing him through a howling snowstorm back to The River.  Old Man Chipman broke down in the miserable cross rip where the fast-running tide through the Narrows meets the sweep of the sou'west wind across Pleasant Bay, and I came along just in time to tow him out of danger.  I was learning the boating business; help a little, be helped a little.

# Part Two

STRING BEAN

# 8

## Frost Trouble

In the winter of '38-'39 I decided I had outgrown *Sunshine*. Several of us had been scalloping in Pleasant Bay — Skrag Baker, Chet Higgins, Huck Grozier, and some others. Most of the other boats had power-driven winches, and try as I would I couldn't compete with them hauling by hand. Furthermore, since Pleasant Bay isn't more than a mile across, they could go on the roughest days in their bigger boats, whereas I lost a good many days because of the weather.

One blowy day I was sitting disconsolately ashore when my eye took in a weather-beaten hull which lay half in and half out of the water. She was thirty feet long and "lean as a greyhound" I thought romantically. (Actually she was as lean as a string bean and would "roll your eyes out" and scare you half to death when she lay in a trough between seas.) She had a chicken coop house, a stubby mast and boom, an immense Hathaway winch, and a well-rusted, four-cylinder Dodge motor, a '23 or '24.

I hunted down Joe Peters, the owner, and had a talk with him, but he had been longer in the business than I. He insisted on one hundred dollars cash before I went to work on the "vessel." The only concession he would make was to guarantee the motor would run or no deal.

I asked the opinion of people who knew the boat. One of my failings was, and perhaps still is, that I'd ask everyone's opinion and then disregard all the advice I got. Captain Dave Delano (and captain he was rightfully if his word was honest — and I never had reason to doubt it — for he claimed to have an unlimited license in sail and steam) guardedly conceded she was more boat than *Sunshine*. He also offered to help me with her; in fact, since he wasn't doing anything in particular, he offered to go scalloping as a hand if I bought her.  Dar said she had been run up on the beach under her own power, but he couldn't remember when.

I bought her and she was a slut.  She should have been dragged to the boneyard and burned long before I ever bought her.  About the best I can say of her is that she gave me a lot of experience.  As usual, I had to learn the hard way.

Captain Dave and I put *Sunshine* on her mooring and went to work on *String Bean*'s bottom in the freezing cold.  She wouldn't take much caulking, although I don't expect we tried too hard, and almost all her fastenings seemed solid.  She was cedar-planked and copper-riveted.  I rather suspect she had been a seine boat, propelled by oars, until someone in the distant past built her up, cut in a shaft log, and installed power.  We did what we could for her bottom and daubed on a can of Tarr and Wonsan's copper bottom paint.  We had to heat the paint in a bucket of water with a blow torch held against it, and ourselves with an occasional dollop of Captain Dave's Hudson's Bay Rum (he always seemed to have a full bottle in his sea chest in the landward side of his little fish shanty by the river).  We launched her without too much trouble and got Dean Davenport, a sort of lesser Mac McKoy, to work on the motor.

In many ways that old Dodge was way ahead of its time.  It had a twelve-volt ignition system when everyone else was using six.  Dean said the twelve-volt coil and condenser wouldn't stand up in a boat so he put in six-volt equipment and a six-volt resistance — don't some of the modern high-speed motors have the same arrangement?  I believe the Northeast combination starter-generator was one of the finest pieces of automotive electrical equipment ever made.  (Years later, when *String Bean* had long since "gone to heaven," Freddy Harris took the starter-generator and made an electrical, push-button steering apparatus of it so he could steer Bruce Hammatt's *Ann H.* from the masthead when they went sticking swordfish as far offshore as George's Bank.)  Dean got the motor running, as I expected he would — and little enough pay he got for working there in the cold on the edge of the river.  Captain Dave and I took off for Pleasant Bay to see that everything worked.

It did, more or less. I had hooked up the tiller lines backward, so that when I steered to port we went to starboard, and vice versa, but it was a small matter to change them once we had run into the river-bank. We made our way down the river, across Little Pleasant Bay, through the Narrows and out into Big Bay. Compared to the ride in *Sunshine* it felt as though we were on a pleasure cruise in a yacht. We chucked over the scallop drag and made a slow, cautious tow. The chain-driven winch clanked most alarmingly when I threw it in gear, but the drag came flying aboard. Beautiful! Then we made a serious tow and filled the drag with rocks, shells, mud and — I guess — some scallops. I gingerly pushed the winch in gear and started to haul back. Everything worked until the full weight of the loaded drag came on the boom end. Then things parted. Mast and boom came crashing down. Stays flew in every direction. The drag disappeared below the surface again as the rope ran out. I jumped for the switch to cut the motor — the way we were rigged we had to be going ahead with the boat in gear for the winch to work.

Captain Dave and I looked at each other. He said moderately, "Something must have parted." It had. The bow stay, which took most of the load, had pulled the whole of the upper stem clear. The wood, hidden by a coat of dirty grey paint, was nothing but powder, dry rot. Captain Dave had been to sea for a good many years and parted stays were nothing new to him. While we lay there rolling I cleared the side stays and wreckage and he spliced a new piece of rope to the end of the cable bow stay. Then when we had swayed the mast upright, he spliced the rope into an immense bronze mooring eye which came through the original, lower stem. We secured the side stays, rehung the boom and stayed it, fired up the motor and carefully put the winch in gear. Everything worked. The next tow was even better and by the time the afternoon was over it began to look as though I had a profit-making boat. It looked that way.

I got to the river early the next morning to rig a new bow stay before Captain Dave got there. It was a good thing I did. Lying to Captain Dave's stakes, the *String Bean* was more than half sunk. The motor wasn't quite underwater, and we'd had sense enough to put the new battery in a box high above the deck, but I was still pumping when Captain Dave got to the shore.

We put the boat on the beach to find the leak. We found it; the whole boat leaked at almost every seam. The reason she hadn't taken any caulking was that she had been full of frost when we worked on her before launching. Mud, rotten caulking, planks and all had frozen together. Our trip down the Bay and floating overnight for the first time in years had thawed all this out and let the river run in. I really learned how to caulk a boat then. For four days I lay full length on the beach or knelt on a hatch cover, in freezing cold and surrounded by slur ice, digging out old caulking and pounding in new. I caulked that bitch from bow to stern, from keel to above the water line, every seam on both sides. By the end of the week we figured she was ready to go. We launched her on the high tide. I stayed aboard until dark — there were plenty of odds and ends of repairs to keep me busy — then set the alarm clock for midnight to check her again. She didn't leak enough to catch the bilge pump. It looked as though I might begin to get my money back — I mean, it didn't seem as though anything else could go wrong.

Any old-time scalloper will tell you scallop dragging differs from any other kind of shellfishing. When you go on working the same place for quahogs and clams, from day to day you either have to work longer or your take gradually falls off. Scallop dragging is not that way. You can go day after day, doing as well as or even better than the day before. And then, all of a sudden, "there ain't no more." They are gone.

The day after the caulking was finished, after everything was put in order, was the day the scallops ran out. Captain Dave and I went back to the spot we had worked on the last trip. Tow after tow brought in hardly enough to eat. I tried faster tows and slower; I tried more scope and less. I tried every place I had ever caught scallops and places I had never caught scallops before. It was all the same or worse. I said to Captain Dave, "We're jinxed."

Dave said, "I've been watching Chet and Skrag and the rest. They've been steaming all over the Bay. They haven't stayed long enough in the same place to make more than one tow."

We picked up and ran over to Chet. As we came alongside he threw his boat out of gear. "The boat looks nice," he said, "how does it fish?"

I said I couldn't catch enough to feed the cat.

"Me, too. And Skrag's got the same thing. It looks as though we've had it for this year. You can't catch them twice." And had it we had for that year. To this day when I talk about buying a new boat, and how I'll catch so many fish at such a price, and how the boat will be paid for in so many days, my wife will look at me sorrowfully and say, "Seems as though I've heard that song before." How right she is.

# 9

## Around the Cape

Both boats, *Sunshine* and *String Bean*, were hauled out on the shore for the winter and I went about other things. Frank taught me about eel spearing, one more of the many ways he had of making money in an off season. It is done either from a small rowboat before the freeze-up, or, if the salt ice is thick enough to be reasonably safe, through a hole chopped through the ice.

In all the salt water ponds there are fresh water seeps, known as spring holes. Here the temperature of the water remains relatively constant, slightly above that of the surrounding salt water. Into these spring holes the eels work themselves at the first frost, and there they bed down, moving little except during the winter thaws when they apparently settle themselves more comfortably. All winter the eels are semi-dormant and will hold still long enough when they are speared to let themselves be yanked into the boat or out onto the ice.

A good eel spear is a tool to be cherished. When I started the old-timers spoke with reverence of Kent spears. Then a blacksmith named Barrus apparently took over where Mr. Kent left off. Since the Barrus spears, nobody has made a decent eel spear. Peter Bruce tried, but his best spears were all made by welding together pieces of old Barrus spears.

The six or eight tines of an eel spear were made of tool steel, reputedly imported from England. The tines were about ten inches long, a quarter-inch square at the shank and tapering to a blunt point which turned back on itself, inward, toward the center of the spear, tapering within an inch or so to a needle-sharp point which looked up. These six or eight tines straddled a slightly heavier, slightly longer "knife" which took the brunt of the blow when the spear was jabbed into the bottom. The tines had to be limber enough to spring out when jammed around an eel or, as sometimes happened inadvertently, a stump or tree limb two or three inches thick, but they had to be tough enough to spring back when the eel or branch was removed. The tines, each one slightly longer than the one inside it, fanned out so that with the knife they formed pretty much of a straight line across the bottom. They were welded to a shank which in turn was secured to a slender hard-pine pole, about fourteen to sixteen feet long, or for deeper water, as long as twenty feet. The pole, not more than an inch and an eighth thick at the bottom, tapered to less than three-quarters of an inch at the top.

Whether from a boat or through a hole chopped in the ice, the spear was jabbed or "jobbed" into the bottom and snatched back, thus hooking the eels on the upturned points or barbs. I soon learned that resistance on the snatch-back meant an eel and kept the pole coming smoothly *but quickly* all the way up until the eel dropped off into the boat or onto the ice.

Thirty or forty pounds of eels was a day's pay. The eels were put into a used wooden nail keg and shipped to commission men in New York, where they commonly brought upwards of twenty cents a pound. There are wild stories of eelers running into beds of eels and getting several hundred pounds in a day. These stories are not so improbable as they sound, for I myself that first winter speared more than a hundred pounds on several different days. There were mornings after a big day when my shoulder ached, my wrist was so swollen that I couldn't button my sleeve, and my right hand was so lame I had to exercise it before I could close it around the pole. But a confirmed eeler will tell you it is a sport that beats any other kind of fishing.

The next spring, the spring of 1939, I was right back at quahoging again. In between the days I went bullraking in *Sunshine*, I spent all I made rebuilding *String Bean*. I ripped off all the old cabin and tore up the deck (both were full of dry rot) and built new. The new cabin was boxy and square, but it was solid and tight. I took out the old Dodge and bought a "new" second-hand one, same make and model, for ten dollars. Then I sold the dump truck body that came with the motor for ten dollars, so the motor cost me nothing except for Dean's work and some odds and ends. While I was learning more of boatbuilding I bethought myself of a partner. I went to Frank and asked him if he'd like to go handlining in Cape Cod Bay. He thought it might be a good idea.

At last we were all ready to make the trip out of Pleasant Bay, over Chatham Bar, around the tip of Cape Cod, past Provincetown. And don't you know it blew easterly for a solid week! The seas on the bar at Chatham were absolutely prohibitive; even the old-timers, experienced as they were at running the bar, laid up. Frank and I checked everything. We took little trial runs down into Pleasant Bay, testing this and that, making new arrangements. I borrowed an old chart and studied it nights. Frank brought aboard his old compass and we checked our courses against the chart. I even went all the way and bought a fire extinguisher, though I still carried the old standby, a bucket of dry sand. I tried to borrow a couple of life preservers from one of the old-timers. He snorted, "What the hell do you want them for? The ones that put on life preservers and leave the boat to swim ashore are the ones who get drowned. The only ones who are ever saved are the ones who stick with the boat." So eventually we went without life jackets. As a matter of fact his advice was sound except in case of fire or being washed ashore in a heavy sea. Not that I'm against life jackets, but since hearing that advice so grumpily given many years ago, I've noticed that most survivors of most boating accidents are not those who put on life jackets and try to swim ashore.

The day finally came when the surf on the bar moderated so we could cross. From the time we left Pleasant Bay everything was new and exciting. We went down the channel from Orleans to Chatham, dodging the shoal water as best we could — there were no channel markers in those days. When we got just inside the bar I motioned to Frank to take the wheel. The breaking surf on each side of the narrow channel frightened me a little. "Not me," said Frank, "you're the captain." So we slid out, the motor purring sweetly, the ground swell which ran a little up the channel lifting us and sliding us down the other side exhilaratingly.

Once we were outside the breaking seas I headed north. I left the wheel and went back to the stern to yell in Frank's ear. "How far offshore shall I go?"

Frank shrugged his shoulders. "You're the captain. Go where you want."

I found out later, the hard way as usual, there is more to it than that. If the tide is running north and the boat is going north she should get offshore to take advantage of the tide. If, however, the tide is running the other way, as it usually was when I made the trip, the boat should get in as close to the breakers as the captain dares, right in the suds, to get out of the tide.

We were making good time that day. The motor was running smoothly, the temperature stayed down, the generator was putting out. (That was as far as our instruments went.) The ground swell was long and slow so we ran easily up over one wave, ten or twelve feet high, and coasted down the other side in an endless rise and fall, as easy on that windless day as breathing. The water under us was green as bottle-glass. Since *String Bean* was a double-ender she left hardly any wake at all, just a string of slightly soiled bubbles over the ever-changing swirl caused by the propeller thrust. Offshore there was nothing but the horizon, slightly hilly because of the ground swell; inshore the beaches sparkled with the white lace of the surf and the sand which seemed whiter than life in the distance. The brown of the dunes rising sharply gave way to narrow strips of light green and dark, and the houses way inshore looked like little cubes, white or dark. The Coast Guard stations as we passed them looked like children's blocks, all white with red tops: Chatham, Orleans, Nauset. Then Nauset Light looking even more miniature, though we could see the flashing light even in the bright sunlight. I asked Frank what the next Coast Guard station was.

"Cahoon's Hollow," he said. "Want me to spell you?"

I nodded and turned the wheel over to him. I went into the cabin where the motor sounded suddenly loud. I looked proudly at the work I had done, took out a sandwich and poured a cup of coffee from a thermos bottle safely wedged where it couldn't roll off and get broken. I went aft to sit and admire my boat, the lovely day, and the unfamiliar shore as it floated by, for it seemed the shore was moving, not we. Strangely, I began to be uneasy. I watched Frank's steering critically. While I had turned just a little to meet the crest of each wave, Frank held her steady, disregarding the waves as though they weren't there. I stood it as long as I could; then I went and took over the wheel again. It wasn't that Frank was doing anything wrong (Lord knows, he'd had a great deal more experience than I); it was just that *I* wasn't doing it. I noticed several years later when we fished Frank's boat, *Nauset*, the position was reversed. He was the one who took us over the bar, coming and going, and he was the one who took us through all the rough water. I got to steer only when he wanted a few minutes relief, and I'm sure my steering never really satisfied him, if only because *he* wasn't doing it.

We came to the high, somehow unfriendly cliffs at the Highland. Frank motioned me a little inshore so we took Peaked Hill Bars on our starboard. Not that there was more than an infrequent sea breaking there that day, but I had gotten into the habit of going the way I would if it were rough, even when it was calm — just as later I made a habit of constantly checking my compass course even though I knew what the course was and how I should be heading. Didn't *that* little habit pay off when I was running at night or in a fog, or worst of all, in both?

Our only trouble that day came when we were going through the tide rip at Race Point. So far as I can verify, it is always rough there, even on a flat calm day. We tossed about a bit and then suddenly the motor stopped. The quiet was disconcerting after the steady drumming of the motor. Fortunately we were through the race and the tide was with us. "Now," Frank said calmly, "what do you suppose is the matter?" We threw off the engine cover to check. Spark? Yes. Gas to the carburetor? Yes. Then why did she stall? I hit the starter button, the motor picked up, and we were off again. We found later that the float in the Dodge carburetor had a way of hanging up in rough water. Diddling a little brass rod that was hung on gimbals cleared her immediately. The strange part of it was that she wouldn't do it if it was very rough, only if it was a little bit rough.

We were around the Cape and into the Bay, with only the long, straightaway run to Rock Harbor ahead of us. This was familiar water and the trip was relaxing to the point of boredom, except for cutting across Billingsgate Shoal as we skirted the Island. We figured the distance from Orleans to Orleans was somewhere between eighty and ninety miles and we were home in eight hours and five minutes — not bad for a skinny old boat and an ancient four-cylinder motor. I never made much better time in any of the many trips I made around the Cape.

The next morning in Rock Harbor the *String Bean* was half sunk. I began to understand why she was sometimes called the *Eel Car*: the water flowed in and out of her the way it does in and out of an eel car. I put her on the beach and found half the caulking out of one garboard seam. From then on, after every rough or long trip, the story was the same. I found out years later when we stripped and burned her that her shaft was bent. We'd pound in the caulking and she'd lie at the dock for three weeks without making enough water to prime the bilge pump, but if I took her out and worked her hard I had to do midnight boat drill or she would be half sunk the next morning. That bent shaft apparently wagged the shaftlog so badly that it worked out all the caulking, even though the vibration was hardly noticeable on deck.

Frank and I fished together off and on in Cape Cod Bay for two summers. I learned to handline codfish and flounders on Dennis Ledge, and tautog on Stony Bar off the Eastham shore. I caught my first striped bass one day when I was alone and had to carry it to Frank for identification. We scratched quahogs by hand on the flats at Eastham on the high course tides.

To those who do not live by the tides, the term "high course tide" may have no meaning. Because of the gravitational pull of the sun and the moon, and a whole lot of other esoteric factors I was never quite clear about, the vertical rise of the tide in Cape Cod Bay varies from something under eight feet to something over eleven feet. Since the tidal flats slope only slightly, the distance from shore to low-water mark varies greatly depending on the vertical drop of the tide. That part of the beach where the horizontal distance from beach grass to low water is roughly one thousand paces on an eight-foot tide will be perhaps fourteen hundred paces on an eleven-foot tide. The sand flats in between, which are covered by up to three feet of water on an eight-foot tide, are bare or nearly so on an eleven-foot tide, and of course the flats beyond, which are quite unwadeable on a poor tide, are most productive (because they are less frequently fished) on a good tide.

Frank and I, and frequently my wife, headed toward these off-shore flats on the high course tides. We'd wade out with a falling, ebbing tide, whether it came at noon or at midnight, each clad to suit his fancy. My wife usually dragged along in hip boots, I usually wore sneakers and a very skimpy pair of bathing trunks she had knitted for me of raw wool, and Frank wore sneakers and pants chopped off at the knees. I don't suppose the man ever had on a pair of bathing trunks, since his generation thought them effeminate and slightly indecent on a male. We hand-scratched quahogs three or four hours until the coming or flood tide drove us ashore, leaving our take bagged up and marked with wooden floats on the end of ropes long enough to let the floats show at high tide. When we had ac-cumulated twenty bushels or so we would run down from Rock Harbor in *String Bean* over the high tide, haul the quahogs aboard and carry them back to the harbor.

We drove the quahog draggers crazy by going to Billingsgate Island and bullraking in a bight (called "Back of Lou Gann") where they couldn't drag at low tide. One day we came in with seventeen bushels, which was more than the draggers themselves had caught. They fixed us, though. They went out over the high water and dragged where we had been raking and cleaned out that honey hole.

Frank often said we weren't making much money, but we were having a lot of fun, and my lessons were progressing steadily. *String Bean* rolled so badly when she lay nearly in a trough that we finally put up a steadying sail. To the stub mast which stood some four feet above the cabin overhead we attached a narrow triangle of can-vas (an old, cut-up tent fly, really) and ran it clear back to the haul-ing post aft. It didn't stop her from laying her scuppers under, but it did slow down that deadly snap-back.

I learned not to come cowboying in to a landing because reverse won't take hold if the motor stalls — and I re-learned that one again and again in later years and later boats.

I learned a lazy way to steer a straight course in a fog: I could throw a length of rope over the stern, correct the course by compass, and simply watch to see that the rope trailed straight behind. I bought a compass and life preservers, just in case, and was pretty mad at the compass manufacturer afterward. It was a lovely, chrome-plated compass, built for an automobile. The trouble was — and I didn't recognize it until a very confusing foggy day — one read the back of the compass, not the front. In any decent boat compass the desired course is lined up with the lubber line. If the boat is headed north and strays off to no'theast, the compass strays off to no'theast and the helmsman knows to turn back to port. With this compass read from the back, when the boat strayed off to no'theast the compass said she had gone to port. (That compass was one of the very few things ever stolen from me in thirty-five years with never a cabin door locked. And the thief did me a favor.) We got that matter straightened out when I bought a new compass.

# 10

‱‱‱‱‱‱‱

# Blackfish

The one type of fishing I did in *String Bean* that was both exciting and profitable was chasing blackfish. The blackfish is the smallest member of the whale family, seldom more than thirty feet long. They came frequently into Cape Cod Bay in the summer to have their young. Schools of blackfish occasionally numbered as many as a hundred, and were so commonplace as to cause little excitement except when they stranded themselves ashore or when they were driven by what might be called, I suppose, the last of the drift whalers on Cape Cod.

The Nye Oil Company in New Bedford had a virtual monopoly in this business; at least they were the only ones paying for the head oil when the fish came or were driven ashore. The Baker brothers, particularly Cal and Warren, had the contract, and it was through them that I got into the blackfish-driving business.

Blackfish have a failing which made our method of operating possible; they are very much a schooling fish (perhaps "herding animal" would be more precise). They could be herded or driven by a couple of power boats, by one in a pinch, as easily as a flock of sheep can be driven by a trained dog. Let one blackfish get stranded and the entire pod would stay with it until they, too, were stranded. Knowing this, Warren, who was dragging quahogs in an old catboat, *Trade Winds*, would seize any opportunity to drive blackfish onto the beach. There were times, however, when the job needed two boats, and thus Cal enlisted my help. The blackfish would be herded or milled gently, patiently, until the tide had reached tip-top high water, then they would be frightened ashore and driven until they were stranded and had no chance to get off. One school we drove in by

Bee's River consisted of one hundred and thirty of these great beasts.

Warren had picked them up on the flood tide out by Billingsgate Island and herded them slowly toward the Eastham shore. In the shallow water they balked, and it was here that *String Bean*, Cal, and I came into play. Back and forth we went outside the school, back and forth, ever closer, wheeling away only to turn back stragglers. The water was so shallow the fish couldn't have sounded if they had wanted to. Finally in exasperation, Cal yelled, "Let me take this boat!" He hooked the throttle wide open and drove us right through the middle of the school. Water flew and so did those great flukes, coming completely out of the water right alongside our rails. If one had hit us we would have been swimming with the blackfish. (As a matter of fact, when we finally got ashore we found we had cut three of them with our propeller, we were that close.) It worked. We made so much commotion cutting back and forth in figure eights, into and out of the school, that they spooked and in trying to escape toward the beach were stranded.

We had waited so long on the falling tide that few of the boats in Rock Harbor would have had enough water to get in, but we put *String Bean*'s keel on the bottom and literally churned a channel through the clear, white sand.

Then the murder started. I know of no other word that would fit. Those great beasts, their thin external skin as black and shiny as patent leather, beat the sand with their tails; they sighed and cried like monstrous babies. Their gasping was pathetic to hear as the tide ran out and left them helplessly high and dry, but what fisherman stops to listen when there is money to be made? Armed with a razor-sharp lance on the end of a ten-foot hickory pole, Cal came up behind the flipper of the nearest blackfish and beat the creature three or four times over the head. When I protested Cal explained, "You have to warn them you're here. I've lanced fish I didn't warn first and had them jump clear off the sand. Somebody could get hurt that way."

Cal drove the lance into the side of the creature, again and again, trying to make a bigger and bigger hole. Blood poured out in torrents; "gushed" is a more exact word. It splattered us and dyed the beach a bright red. One and then another he killed, working down the beach through the whole school.

It was dark before we finished lancing; my job was to hold a flashlight so Cal could see.  Sometimes the fish were so close together we had to climb on one while it was still alive to lance another.  Behind us blackfish in their death throes were heaving and moaning with blood-choked sighs.  Their great tails lashed the sand making a sound like a whole herd of horses galloping across hard ground.

Once they were all lanced we went back to the first Cal had killed and the flensing began.  Cal made a tentative cut just back of the "melon," a watermelon-sized hump where the forehead would be. I grabbed the flesh thus loosened with a baggage hook and pulled while Cal cut deeper and deeper until the whole melon came loose. Strangely, there was no blood in this part of the blackfish, but the melon was so full of natural oil that if I squeezed it between my hands while picking it up the oil ran out as out of a sponge.  Cal explained that he didn't want to cut too deep because the "horse" under the melon was tough and without much oil.  One by one the melons were cut off and dragged to a waiting truck.  It was in no way pleasant work — the panting, crying, sucking, still-dying blackfish everywhere in the dark; blood and guts and grease soaking us from head to foot; and gnats by the millions filling the calm, muggy night air.  It was no wonder that by the time we were through the whiskey bought "on the company" had disappeared and we were all slightly drunk.  Clothes worn in this work never lost the blackfish smell, and for days afterwards everything we touched smelled of blackfish; doorknobs, furniture, bathroom fixtures — everything. We got so we were no longer aware of it, but our poor wives . . .

We drove to New Bedford before daylight the next morning to cut up the melons.  It seemed a terrible waste that no more of the blackfish was used than that little forty- or fifty-pound chunk.  Tons of oil from the blackfish's thin coat of blubber, more tons of perfectly good red meat were wasted, buried on the spot above the tide line by bulldozer before they could rot and foul the air any more.  "Not economically practical to try to save it," Cal said.  A few hardy souls would carve off steaks after we were through and they unanimously declared it as good as beef, (I don't remember anyone's coming back for more) and occasionally a dog owner would carry home chunks to be frozen for his dogs.  All the rest was wasted.

In New Bedford we had a crew of seven men; Rusty Knowles and

I, the two Bakers, and three men from the Nye Oil Company.  I have forgotten old Cap Brown who lived in Orleans.  Cap was an ex-whaler and apparently the only one besides the company officials, who knew the whole refining process.  A small man, white-haired and twisted with age, he was always pleasant and garrulous except when asked questions about refining the oil.  "If I told you," he'd say, "that would be two of us who would know."

Six of us would go to carving up the melons; the seventh man was kept busy sharpening knives; great, heavy butcher knives which had to be deadly sharp.  Warren sliced the more or less round melons into two-inch slices.  Cal cut the slices into two-inch square strips.  With the black, or skin, side down, the rest of us cut the strips into wafers, not much more than a quarter of an inch thick, cutting not all the way through but as far as we could without breaking the strips into tiny pieces too hard to handle.  These sliced-up strips were thrown into vats or try kettles where Cap Brown took over, ladling and stirring them as they cooked until he felt all the oil was cooked out.  This was as far as the company would let us follow the process.  Rumor had it that when the oil was drained off it was refrigerated for a long period and then refined further.  How much refined oil they got from each blackfish we never knew.  Each one yielded about a gallon of raw oil.  Even in those days, a jeweler friend told me, the refined oil sold for as much as sixteen dollars an ounce, for it was the very best watch-makers' oil.  During the Second World War the government halted the sale of blackfish oil because it was being used in aeronautical instruments since it did not congeal at cold temperatures.  (Nowadays nobody wants it because the synthetics are better and cheaper, which is a blessing as far as the blackfish are concerned.)

Blackfishing was only a sometime thing, and I'm sure my wife, at least, was relieved when it was over.  I didn't regret the experience but it was hard, disagreeable work.  Even though the money was good, I wasn't sorry when my fishing took me another way.  I think Frank and I might have gone along in *String Bean* indefinitely, working together when it paid, working each at his own fishing when that seemed better, but two events interrupted.  I came down with sciatica and was laid up for months, and Frank bought a boat himself, a Provincetown "single dory."

# 11

≈≈≈≈≈≈≈≈≈≈≈≈≈≈≈≈≈≈≈≈≈≈≈≈≈≈≈≈≈

# I Start the Long Years
# of Striper Fishing

It was the winter of '42 and '43 when I went to bed with sciatica. It was that next spring when the doctor came up with the notion that I must stop making a living scallop-dragging, long-raking and shellfishing generally, lest I become a chronic sciatic case because of the back strain and general exposure involved. It was pretty depressing. For eight years I had struggled along, learning the trade the hard way, and now I had to turn my hand to something else. I twisted and turned and fretted in my mind. As soon as it was warm enough I put in a big kitchen garden to help out a little with the finances. (I never did like farming but I could work bent over without any severe pain, so long as I didn't straighten up.)

Frank had bought a boat, I knew, about a thirty-three-footer, heavily built, a so-called "single dory." (The type of small craft we usually referred to as a "dory" was called in Provincetown a "double dory," either because it takes two oars or because it takes two men to move it — I was never sure which.) She was powered with a massive antique, a two-cylinder Lathrop, rated at twenty-five horsepower at 800 revolutions. The boat was designed low in the bow for line-trawling, with a box of a house some fourteen feet long aft. Forward she had a tarpaulin stretched over a heavy, slanting pole, a rig commonly called hereabouts a "Portland cover." No more seaworthy boat for her size has ever been designed for these waters. I had seen them coming through the race at Race Point when all that was visible at times was the top of the house. Frank was doing quite well hand-lining codfish at Dennis Ledge, I heard.

It hadn't entered my mind that Frank would take me on, crippled

as I was, until he showed up one afternoon.  As I have indicated, conversation was difficult with Frank because he was so deaf.  He brought
us a big striped bass, cleaned and ready for the pan.  I mouthed the
words, "Thank you," and reached for a pencil and paper.  "Where
did you catch it?" I scribbled.  "Did you catch any more?"

He read and nodded.  "That's why I'm here," he said.

It seems he had been peacefully handlining at Dennis when in the
distance he had seen what he took to be pollock breaking the surface.  While pollock are not usually a "money" fish, Frank was fond
of pollock fresh out of the water.  For that matter he liked all kinds
of queer fish nobody else bothered with.  Mud hake or sculpin tails
were his idea of fine chowder material.  He taught me to skin and fry
little brown skates, sold (when they were sold) as "rajahfish."  So,
since codfishing was slow, he picked up his anchor, got out old-
fashioned block-tin pollock jigs and went to trolling for pollock.

They weren't pollock at all; they were striped bass, and with two
lines over he hung two twenty-pounders at once.  Back then, striped
bass were not the popular fish they are today.  There were a few
hard-core old-timers who fished for them for the table, and a few of
an advance guard of sports fishermen who fished in the surf for them.
In fact, striped bass were so seldom caught commercially, except in
seines, that the Federal government had never put a ceiling price on
them as it had on almost every other kind of fish.  Flounders were
five cents, market cod six, haddock seven, halibut twenty-three —
but there was no ceiling price on stripers; consequently, the rare reports on striped bass landings in the Fulton Fish Market in New York
often went as high as thirty or forty cents a pound, occasionally as
high as fifty cents.  Frank said, "The more money you can get per
pound for fish the more money you can make."  His point was that
it cost as much to handle and ship codfish at six cents a pound as it
did stripers at forty.

To return to the day of his striper fishing:  The one failing Frank
had, if in fact it was a failing, was that he had to do things the traditional way, the way, as he said, his father taught him.  In fact, it was
this trait that eventually split our partnership.  Prove to him that
some new way produced better, and he would insist on doing it the
old way.  It could be very exasperating, particularly since we were

sharing, share and share alike.  On this occasion, since he had caught
stripers, he switched to traditional striper lures — eel skin rigs.  Never
mind that he had just caught two stripers on pollock jigs; pollock jigs
were for pollock and eel skins were for stripers.  Whether it was the
change of lures, or whether the stripers had sounded and stopped
feeding, he lost them.  He felt that while he was rigging the eel skins
(which is a slow, particular job) he had drifted off the fish.  His reason for coming, other than to bring us a neighborly meal, was to ask
if I felt able to come with him, simply to steer the boat — I could sit
down while steering — for half.

Did I?  I would have gone even if my wife had had to wheel me to
Rock Harbor in a wheel chair.  Sitting down all day in the sun with
my mind at rest did wonders for my back.  It was years before I
finally shook the last traces of sciatica, but before that summer was
over I was able to stand and haul my share.

*Nauset*, as Frank's boat was predictably named, was a wonderful
boat in a seaway and she was sea-kindly, for even in the roughest
weather she never threw you about — but lordy, she was unhandy to
troll from.  With that big house aft, the most gear we could fish was
two lines, one *around* each side.  (In later years, fishing alone, I
usually fished four lines and sometimes even five over the stern.)

We fished hard.  We slept more nights in the boat than we did
ashore in order to get the sunrise fishing, and all the while I was
learning Cape Cod Bay.  We ran before a nor'wester one night and
slept in the bight behind the lighthouse in Barnstable Harbor.  The
harbormaster gave us a hard time the next morning, thinking we were
German spies or saboteurs, or something.  Many nights we anchored
up after dark in Brewster Channel, and more nights in the lee of
Billingsgate Island.  Provincetown knew us, as did the basin in Sandwich at the entrance to Cape Cod Canal.  Sometimes we even ran
aground deliberately on a sandy beach when we were tired from too
long a stretch of fishing.

This was during World War II, of course, and every Monday we
had to go to the nearest Coast Guard station to get our clearance
papers renewed.  We had papers from Rock Harbor to Provincetown,
Sandwich, and Barnstable; we had papers from Sandwich to Rock
Harbor, Provincetown and so on and so on, from every harbor in the

Bay to every other harbor. We had a whole suitcase full of papers. Later that year when we fished out of Chatham we included papers to and from Chatham and all the Bay ports. The number one man at Nauset used to groan every Monday morning when we showed up at the station, for he had to sign each paper individually. Then, of course, the Bay shore was crawling with Coast Guardsmen, all youngsters from Iowa and Kansas, so far as we could tell, nice kids who knew nothing at all about salt water and whom we considerably upset more than once.

One evening we had fished until dark on Stony Bar, off the Eastham shore. We anchored up by Billingsgate and had supper, but before we turned in, the wind came in easterly. Where we lay just off the channel the flood tide runs northerly and northeasterly, so when the tide turned we would have the wind against it, always an unpleasant berth. Frank suggested we up-anchor and make for the Camp Ground shore at Eastham to ground out overnight. *Nauset* was full enough on the bilges so she lay down but very little. I hauled anchor and we ran across the couple of miles to ground out gently. I dropped the anchor in about three feet of water and payed out enough rope so we would have scope on high tide. Frank had already turned in by the time I had secured everything so I followed.

Voices woke me shortly after daybreak. Voices? What were voices doing alongside? I struggled up and slid open the after hatch. The cant of the boat informed me that we had grounded out as planned. The morning was warm and reasonably calm, but foggy; the no'theaster had died out during the night. Suddenly I was aware of two young Coast Guardsmen standing just off the stern, fully armed. In fact, my throwing open the hatch had startled them and one of them was pointing at my head what looked like the biggest revolver in the world. I felt ridiculously like a turtle, sticking its head out of its shell.

I said, "Hey! Point that thing some other way, will you? It might go off."

He did. He asked, "Are you shipwrecked?"

I said no, and explained, or tried to, that we had purposely run aground. It didn't make any sense to him. We went through the whole thing again. It still didn't make any sense to him — boats were to be at sea in, not to be slept in ashore.  I could see he was beginning to be irritated; the revolver looked uneasy.  Finally, I asked him if he wanted to see our clearance papers; maybe Coast Guard paper work would quiet him.  He did.

Climbing down into the cabin I picked up the satchel with all our papers and climbed back out again.  They went through all the papers, one by one.  Their only comment was, "You get around a lot, don't you."  I admitted we did.

A bright thought struck the other youngster, the one who wasn't carrying the revolver, "You got all the standard, required equipment?"

We had, I said.

"Fire extinguisher?"

I folded up the papers and ducked below to fetch up the fire extinguisher.

"Horn, whistle, and bell?"

I fetched them up.

"Life preservers?"

There they were.

The first one, the one with the revolver in his hand said, "You all alone?"

I said, no, my partner was asleep.

"How can he sleep through all this racket?"

I explained he was deaf and you could see incredulity deepen on their faces.  Finally, I said, "Look, would you like to come aboard and look the boat over?"

They conferred, then the itchy-fingered one stepped back three paces — he wasn't taking any chances — and the other one climbed over the stern to peer down into the cabin.  Frank used to say he got a shave once a week whether he needed it or not, and at this time he'd been almost his full week; his whiskers were long and very grey.  He lay there, flat on his back, both arms draped over the sides of the folding canvas cot he was sleeping on, his mouth wide open, his face a cloud of grey whiskers, and his upper body bare where he had thrown off his blanket — a dead, fish-belly white in contrast to the mahogany of his neck and forearms.

The youngster took a minute to accustom his eyes to the relative dark of the cabin. Then he saw Frank. "My God!" he said, "He's dead!"

I don't know that I could have convinced him otherwise without waking Frank up if Frank hadn't snored about then and thrashed over on his side, still sound asleep. I finally sold the kids the three small stripers we had caught the night before for five dollars, and I'm not sure Frank believed me entirely when the tide came in and I woke him to head for the harbor. I heard him muttering something to the effect that he couldn't possibly have slept through having his boat boarded by the Coast Guard.

We caught a few fish, not many, but the price was high so we kept on trying; we worked harder and fished longer hours. The summer was easing by, and it had been a helpful time; my sciatica pained me less all the time and *Nauset* was a joy to fish. No leaks. Actually the bilge was so dry we had to bail in salt water occasionally and pump it out again to keep the bilge smelling sweet. The monstrous old two-cylinder was a bitch to crank. It had an immense flywheel with square holes at intervals on the rim. The crank was a tapered bar which fitted these holes. You set the magneto and barred the wheel over. Theoretically, the holes and bar were designed to kick free when the motor fired, but every so often they wouldn't and Frank would get thrown clear across the cabin when the motor kicked back. I don't know why he wasn't killed. Once started, the motor ran sweetly all day, every day, and gasoline consumption was minimal.

Until one day. We had fished all the day before and well into the night. We'd anchored by Billingsgate for a few hours and then started along the south edge of Billingsgate Shoal before daybreak. The sun came up warm; the day was calm. With our lines out behind us the boat pretty much took care of herself. We didn't have to watch out for boats because days would go by in the waters we fished and we would never see another boat. I think Frank was sound asleep with his line wound around his hand; I'm sure I drowsed a little. I woke quickly enough, for from the cabin where the motor was there came the most godawful clatter, as though all the machinery in the world was being smashed. The motor stopped, and so did the boat.

Frank roused himself when the motor vibrations stopped. Said he, peacefully enough, "I wonder what's the matter now?"

I yelled in his ear, "Couldn't you hear *that*?"

"I didn't hear anything," he said, "but I guess the motor quit."

I guess it did. On examination we found the old brute had thrown a connecting rod. The cylinders had examination plates on the side, and having taken them off we found that the bearing of one of the rods — a full three-quarters-of-an-inch by two-inch babbited bearing — had let go. The connecting rod, as big around as my wrist, had jammed between the wall and the camshaft, bending the latter. If it had merely broken and torn things up a bit we could have disconnected it and limped home on one cylinder because the old thing would run about as smoothly on one as on two. That bent camshaft and the fact that the rod was jammed in so tight we couldn't stir it, even with a hammer, made the whole deal hopeless.

"Well," Frank said, resigned, "I guess we're here to stay. Won't nobody come looking for us for two or three days, maybe a week."

I shook my head. I had no liking for the idea of drifting around hopelessly for "two or three days, maybe a week." The wind had come in light northerly, the tide was due to start flooding any minute and would run toward the southeast where Rock Harbor lay. I began to strip the canvas which was only partly rolled back from the bow.

Frank asked, "What you plannin' to do?"

I motioned for him to help with the canvas. The pole which supported it over the deck in rough weather was a heavy, four-inch hard pine affair, some sixteen or eighteen feet long. We had miles of heavy handline aboard and a good quantity of anchor warp. I started to measure this off to make stays, not to cut it, but so it could be looped in the middle. Frank caught on. "Won't stand much heavy weather."

I wet my finger and held it up in the light breeze.

"Yes," he said, "I guess it will stand that much."

We lashed one edge of the canvas to the pole, then between us we juggled the pole to stand on end, braced against a kind of thwart forward. While I held this rigging upright, Frank went about securing the stays. It made a clumsy sort of rig and my back was killing me when we finished, but the breeze was just strong enough to give us steerageway. It wasn't going to be the quickest passage we had ever made, but we were gaining, helped by the fact that the tide was now with us. Away off in the distance we could see several quahog draggers out of Rock Harbor. Surely one of them would look up and see us before it was too late to get into the harbor. If not? Then we'd be two days getting home instead of one. We had some food and plenty of water for we had learned long ago not to put all our water in one container; in fact, we had several gallon jugs of fresh water stored in secure places in the cabin. The thought made me thirsty and I made as though I were holding a glass to my mouth and drinking from it.

Frank said, "Good idea. So'm I." He slipped down into the cabin while I steered with one hand and held the sheet of what I referred to with a grin as our "loose footed mains'l" with the other. Since we were running ("crawling" would be a more precise term) almost straight before the wind, I studied our piece of canvas with the idea of spreading the other half to port, so we could sail wing and wing, so to speak.

Out of the corner of my eye a movement caught my attention. I thumped the deck to get Frank, and when he came up to relieve me I climbed on top of the house to get a better look. Sure enough, some kind of boat was going to pass across our bow a mile or more away. Surely our peculiar rig would get the skipper's attention, but just to make sure I went below and got my yellow foul weather jacket and carried it atop the house.

I guess he'd have stopped even if I hadn't wildly waved that yellow distress signal, for it was Wilton Hopkins out of Wellfleet in the *Kitty W.*, with a party headed for Dennis.

He swung alongside. "What seems to be the trouble?"

I said we had thrown a connecting rod, would he give us a tow until one of the Rock Harbor draggers saw us?

Wilton said, "Well, you seem to be making out all right as long as this wind holds. I'm going on over to Dennis to try for stripers. I'll check up on you later. Don't worry, I'll see you get in on this tide." And with that he hooked up and went on about his business.

With him went the wind. It died out completely. We swung to and drifted sideways, but I was sure our troubles were over. Wilton did pick us up (he hadn't caught any stripers which made us feel better) and towed us nearly to Rock Harbor before Cal Baker in *Sea Flower* saw us and came to tow us the rest of the way in.

Did I say our troubles were over? Now came the job of installing a new motor. Shopping without me, Frank picked up a second-hand, six-cylinder Pontiac, a neat little job with divided cylinder heads, three in each. With a borrowed chain falls and some help from idling bystanders we lifted the old engine out and swayed in the new. Then began the tedious job of installing new bed timbers, and after that the alignment of the motor. I remember well how I sweated over that. The customary method was to bolt the motor down, then to insert a feeler gauge on the divided flange coupling between motor and shaft. The motor was mounted on four hangers and one or two would have to be cut deeper, the others perhaps shimmed higher. Then bolt down again. Frank wouldn't be satisfied. Finally there was no more than three one-thousandths difference. Still it wouldn't do. My back was keeping me awake nights. After two more days of cutting and shimming, bolting and unbolting, prying up and letting down, Frank still wasn't satisfied. Now, I always wondered how much Frank couldn't hear, and how much he pretended he couldn't. With my aching back to him I threw down my tools. I growled, "All right, you damned fart, if you don't like it that way, fix it yourself."

Frank said moderately, "Oh, I think it's fine. I was satisfied yesterday morning."

"Oh-h-h-h!" Words failed me. We picked up our tools and went fishing the next day. With a few minor adjustments the controls worked fine, and as far as vibrations went, we hardly knew there was a motor in the boat. We had picked up at least four knots in speed.

But the new motor seemed to have jinxed us. We couldn't catch enough stripers for the table. Apparently we were in the midst of what we later came to call the "August doldrums." The weather was hot and fair and dry. The fish had sounded and were feeding on the bottom and stayed there day after day. We weren't catching enough to pay our gasoline bill and I had a family to feed.

Frank had talked earlier about the fact that the Chatham hand-liners were doing awfully well on haddock, so well, in fact, that the line trawlers had knocked off and gone to handlining. Six and seven boxes a day, with one hundred and twenty-five pounds to the box —

at seven cents a pound plus a two-cent black market bonus! The thought made me drool. I had never fished for haddock and I had never more than the one time run Chatham Inlet. My written conversation with Frank dwelt more and more on haddock; but, after all, he had to make the decision: it was his boat, he was captain.

Finally, I said to my wife one morning as we were leaving, "Don't be surprised if we don't come in tonight. Frank has promised that if we don't catch fish today we'll give the haddock a try. We'll probably lay in P'town tonight and fish our way around to come in to Chatham tomorrow night. I'll give you a call when we do, so you can come with the car to get us." We fished all day and caught only three small stripers, "cat bass" Frank called them, only big enough to feed the cats. However, along toward evening when the tide was up, he headed for Rock Harbor again. I hastily scribbled, "Thought we were going to Chatham if we didn't catch any stripers today!"

Frank read, then said, "Well, we caught three."

I was furious. I wrote, "Not enough to feed your cats." (He had seventeen at the time.)

For once Frank lost his temper, though he never said a word. He whirled *Nauset* around, jammed the throttle wide open, and poured us out through The Slew, the gut between Billingsgate Island and Jeremy's Point. He drove us so hard he threw water clear over the house, and *Nauset* jumped so far off a wave she lost the water in her salt-water intake. Then he had to slow down.

# 12

## Chatham and Haddock

Frank was as sweet-tempered as ever when we took off from Provincetown for Chatham the next morning before daylight, having gotten our clearance papers in Provincetown the night before. He steered while I cooked breakfast and ate contentedly out in the open as I steered. I laid out new handlines and rigged the sinkers, two-pounders we had made one windy day weeks before. Frank watched me rig my hooks. "You got your hooks on backwards," he said.

Not too long before that, when we went to Chatham to pack and ship fish, I discussed gear with old Rufe Nickerson, the father of Archie, who was drowned on the bar later, and Willard, who was drowned still later down to south'ard.

I think this is as good a place as any to say how I was treated by the Chatham fishermen, and commercial fishermen generally, whether here on Cape Cod or later in Florida. Once in awhile you'll hear someone say, "Oh, commercial fishermen! They won't give you the time of day!" I never found it so. Politely and intelligently asked, they will tell everything they know — not specifics about their favorite grounds perhaps (that would be asking too much), but how to rig tackle, how to fish it, where and when to go. I can't remember a single time when commercial fishermen weren't more than willing to help out a greenhorn. And so Captain Nickerson showed me how to rig haddock gear, and he stressed the fact that hooks should be put on "front to back," that is, the loop of the line should run through the eye from the side of the hook the point is on, then the whole hook is slipped through the loop and pulled snug. If you try it, you'll see pressure on the point tends to cock the hook forward, whereas if the loop is put through the other way it tends to swing the hook back away from the fish.

I yelled in Frank's ear, "This is the way old Captain Rufe showed me."

Frank said sulkily, "He's wrong. My father told me . . ."

I screamed, "Don't give me that. When your father went fishing there wasn't any such thing as eyed hooks, they were swedged flat and you had to mouse your hooks on." Then I wrote, "You do it your way and I'll do it mine and I bet I catch more fish than you do." But he wore out two complete sets of handlines before he'd change.

We did very well for a couple of greenhorns. We were never high-line, certainly, but there were fifty-two boats out of Chatham that summer and we were frequently highline among the low boats, so to speak. There were some beauties there that summer. Old Captain Howard Eldredge had a way of tacking names on them. One he named the *Turkey Farm*; she was some sort of old navy barge, big enough for a turkey farm, as he said, and she fished four men instead of the customary two. They never mixed with the regulars, or tried to. Then there was a houseboat on pontoons with a Model A Ford for power, all the way from Fort Lauderdale — so help me. Can you imagine running Chatham Inlet in a craft like that? The poor guy! He was so high out of water that the haddock dropped off before he could get them to boat. We swung alongside one day offshore to ask how he had done.

"I've got seven," he said cheerfully.

I couldn't believe it. "Seven boxes!" I asked incredulously.

"Oh, no," he said, "seven haddock."

This craft Old Howard called the *Pigeon Loft*, and it worried him, it was so unseaworthy.

A word here about navigation as practiced in those days before radio, sounding machines, radar and loran: It was forever a wonder to me because a good many days those fishermen never saw land from the time they left shore until they picked up the bell buoy at the Inlet on their way home in the afternoon. The chart of these waters shows four-, six-, and even eight-knot tides in some places. Yet they would run out across the tide an hour and a half, two hours, or as long as four or five, they would drift and run back, drift and run back all day, and then in the afternoon they would wind up their gear, head for home, put their heads down to gut fish, and look up only occasionally to check course and time. And nine times out of ten they had to turn out to keep from running down the bell buoy. I asked Allie Griffin how he did it, after I'd chased his tail all day in a pea soup fog.

"Oh," he said carelessly, "after forty years you learn to smell your way home."

Maybe so. Maybe so. The trick is to live through those forty years while you're learning. We almost didn't.

We'd been fishing what was called "The Great Hill Ground" (Great Hill in Chatham was supposed to be visible on a clear day. The weather was seldom that clear.) It was twenty-some miles offshore, which was a far piece in our journal. Clear though the weather was when we crossed the bar, it came on thicker and thicker. That's the fog factory out there. I think Frank was as nervous as I, though he wouldn't quit while the fish were biting. I finally nudged his shoulder and pointed where I thought shore ought to be. He nodded and began to roll up his lines. I think he wanted to go home as much as I but wouldn't be the first to suggest it. He fired up the Pontiac, swung around on course and I went to gutting fish.

On a foggy day the fisherman is bound wet in a sort of cocoon. The boat is all the world, visibility limited to the perimeter of the boat. Sound is dampened, perspective is distorted, nothing beyond his touch seems real or moving. With the motor running and the compass steady on course, he may lift and fall on the swell; nothing else changes. I wouldn't even take a peek at the course Frank had picked lest I show my nervousness, but resolutely sharpened my throating knife, threw back the tarpaulin over the fish and went to gutting. Grab a haddock by the head with the left hand, thumb probing under his gill casing, the fish upside down. With the point of the knife rip his belly open, lay down the knife and twist his guts out and overboard. A cross cut at the gills and a twisting motion rips them out; they follow the guts overboard. One after another, hooking them out of one bin and when they are gutted tossing them into another. Never look up. The fog streaming by seems at times to be reeling and I have the eerie feeling that the boat is spinning round and round. Pay no attention to it, reach, rip, toss, cut, twist and toss. I stop only for a moment to ease my back and sharpen my knife. My casual glance around stops the spinning sensation but it gives rise to the feeling that we are climbing steadily uphill.

With the fish all gutted, the bin splashed out with buckets of cold salt water, I pumped out the bilge, rearranged the fish, covered them and stowed the handlines. I scrubbed down the mess where we had cut mackerel for bait, checked the gauges and went down into the cabin to get a sandwich and the one bottle of beer we allowed ourselves for lunch. Only then would I let myself check time and course.

The difficult part of this sort of navigation, at least for the greenies, was that all distances were measured time-wise at full cruising speed. The novice feels as though he is rushing through space and that if he could only slow down he would be safer. He feels so *lonely*. But reduced speed means a longer running time and then he has no idea how far he has come. Frank's eyes alternately flicked to the compass and then peered blindly against the wall of fog. The baffling part of the whole deal was that, knowing how much to allow for tide run, we knew what our time should be and we knew what our course should be, if — and that's the big word — if we started from where we thought we started.

Frank startled me by reaching up to the throttle to slow down. I made my face as much a question mark as possible. "Ten minutes to go," he said. I made my way aft to climb up through the after hatch, closing it behind me to shut out the engine noise. Just possibly, as we got closer to shore, I would be able to hear surf breaking on the bar, or possibly even the bell on the buoy which marked the harbor entrance. I wiped the wetness of the fog off my eyelashes and strained to hear, see, smell — anything. Frank shut down even more and now we crept along, searching, searching for some clue to our whereabouts.

From my elevated perch on the cabin roof I was suddenly aware that the color of the water under us had lightened. I pounded hard with my fist on the cabin roof, three times so Frank would surely sense it. I scrambled forward, pointed down and held my hands only inches apart, horizontally. Frank nodded and threw the boat out of gear. In the trough of the sea the clear sand bottom looked pale green, maybe six or seven feet down.

Miraculously, off our port counter, I heard one clear bong of the bell buoy. That's the trouble with bell buoys: in foggy weather the sea is pretty apt to be calm, and the bell doesn't ring. It was our left-over wake running by us that had unsettled the bell just enough to ring it once. We eased south slowly, and there, almost in the boat — so the distortion made it seem — was that ugly, beautiful, impersonal aid to navigation. Frank squared away on the course which would bring us through deep water into the harbor. On both sides we could barely see the breakers topping off, unreal teeth chewing by us, and then, suddenly, we ran out of the fog and were inside the land and could relax.

It wasn't just one day like this, it was an accumulation. Foggy days, rough days when *Nauset* stuck her nose through ten- and twelve-foot high seas on her way out and ran clear green water off her stout tarpaulin forward, or rode them dizzily on her way in while I held my breath and hoped she wouldn't broach side to and drown us. It was Frank's responsibility; he was captain and it was his boat. If we both got drowned it was his fault. I deliberately closed my mind and let Frank make the decisions. It has to be that way.

So it was that with fall well on, with more days lost because of the weather, with rougher water and fewer fish, I was perfectly willing to call it a season and go back to scalloping in *Sunshine* back in Pleasant Bay.

Our various experiences that summer and fall convinced Frank that *Nauset* wasn't designed for the kind of fishing he wanted to do. While the little Pontiac had performed faithfully, it was an old motor and really not quite big enough for the boat. The house aft was a complete nuisance while trolling, a detriment. *Nauset*'s bow and rails were very low, built that way certainly for the type of work for which she was designed, but not satisfactory for the kind of work Frank wanted to do. Her open cockpit was dangerous if Frank intended to run rough water: several times with the tarpaulin rolled back out of the way we had taken barrels of water over the rail and I'd had to pump desperately to clear our bilge. A higher, water-tight standing room was the answer.

Frank decided to rebuild. He quietly and kindly refused all my offers to help. "No," he said, "you've got a family to feed. I haven't, except the cats." Then he pulled out a line he used as long as I knew him, a line which guaranteed he'd get his own way, "I'm getting older all the time, and I don't feel so very well. I don't feel able to fish as hard as we did last summer." (He used the same line eight years later when I dropped him off in New Smyrna in Florida, the first time he'd ever been more than fifty miles from Cape Cod, and he made more money fishing that winter than I did. Ten years after that he complained he couldn't really do a day's work any more while he could and did run men half his age into the ground.) It was his gentle way of saying he'd rather fish alone.

# Part Three

NONNY

# 13

## Whit and Nonny

Unless I wanted to go alone in *String Bean* — and even though she was afloat and still operative that didn't especially appeal to me — I had to find a new boat. I fished for awhile with this one and that one, but Frank had spoiled me. If I was going fishing I wanted to go fishing, not sit around on the shore saying, "It's gonna blow," nursing a bottle of whiskey.

It was along about the middle of July of 1944 when Whit Scott propositioned me to go with him in the little darling later known as *Nonny*. All the time I fished with Whit, a year and a half, the boat papers said on the line headed "Name" . . . "No Name." It was only after I bought her that I thought she needed a proper name, a pert sort of pet name. *Nonny* was the closest I could come to "no name" and still show how I felt about her. She was only twenty-four-and-a-half feet long by eight feet wide, and she drew thirty inches standing. She had a little trunk cabin forward and a wonderful fourteen-foot cockpit, perfectly clear, except for a low engine box, all the way aft to the stern. She was a Shiverick boat, built in 1917 in Kingston, Massachusetts. The legends which arose around Mr. Shiverick were many. It was said he was a racing sailboat builder — certainly *Nonny* was as easy in a seaway as any sailboat ever was. He was so crabby, they said — perhaps meticulous is a kinder word — that he couldn't abide anyone else's work and so worked alone and built one boat a year. (There were at the time four Shiverick boats fishing locally.) One thing I know to be fact and not legend: No one who ever owned a Shiverick boat was ever satisfied with anything else afterwards.

When I first went with Whit, *Nonny* was powered with a little 20-40

hp Redwing. (As was later explained for me, that meant she developed twenty horsepower when she turned 800 revolutions and forty
horsepower when she turned 2300, which was tops.) Be that as it
may, the motor was old and not completely dependable, so Whit replaced it at the end of the year with a newer model Redwing rated at
25-45 hp.

We made a couple of abortive trips over Chatham Bar. On one
trip I made alone I very nearly got clobbered for good, taking so
much water over the bow I tore loose the bow light and lost the
boathook overboard. I pounded so hard coming off a sea that I
brought the fire extinguisher out of its bracket and generally scared
myself half to death. On another trip we made together down off
Stonehorse a no'theaster building against a north tide caught us in
Pollock Rip and almost drowned both of us. *Nonny* was just too
small and too slow and we were too green for that kind of fishing.

Whit suggested we quit that nonsense and make for Cape Cod
Bay to go bass fishing, and that was all right by me. To understand
our relationship, imagine yourself in a parking lot with a flat tire
when a stranger comes up and offers to help. The next time you
meet your new friend he offers to share his car with you every day.
So little did we know about each other, and yet for the next year
and a half we shared the same mattress in *Nonny*'s cabin (though
seldom at the same time), drank from the same bottle, and took the
bitter with the better, share and share alike. A small boat is an extremely intimate place. No one can slam the door and go into the
next room, or go take a walk. Each man has to put up with the
other when he snores, and each has to pick up after his partner as
his partner probably will have to pick up after him.

Whit struck the keynote of our partnership that first afternoon
on our way around the Cape. He took *Nonny* over the bar and headed north, as was proper for the captain to do. When we got abreast
the Nauset Coast Guard Station he surprised me by saying, "Want
to take over? I'm going to turn in for some shut-eye." It was flatter-
ing trust for someone he'd met "twice in a parking lot," so to speak.
I woke him in an hour as he requested.

At that time (the country was still at war) there was reputed to be
a mine field north of Race Point. All the information we could

gather was that it was closely marked with yellow can buoys and patrolled by a Coast Guard cutter, and that small boats were to turn offshore at the yellow cans and follow them around the perimeter of the mine field. I turned in at Whit's suggestion, reminding him of the mine field.

I dropped off to sleep the instant my head hit the bunk. The first I knew anything was amiss was when Whit kicked my feet to wake me. "Phil," he said, "I guess you better come on deck."

Rubbing my eyes I came on deck to find us in fog just thick enough to hide the shore. I asked where we were.

"Somewhere off Provincetown," Whit answered.

I asked if we had come to the yellow cans yet.

"Oh, sure, we passed them a half hour ago."

"Passed them? You mean you didn't turn out?"

Whit grinned and shook his head. "What do we do now?"

I said, "My God, Whit, we're liable to blow up any minute." (We found later that this was not so, that the mines were not on the surface but deep and that they were fired electrically — but we didn't know that then.) I thought furiously. "If we've been in the mine field for half an hour, figuring we're doing about eight knots, we must be right in the middle. It would be as silly to turn back as to go ahead. I've seen people swimming in the surf at Race Point, and they certainly wouldn't set the mines in shallow water." I headed for the beach. I took us right into the breakers on the shore and we came the rest of the way, not in the broken part of the water, but riding the backs of the seas as they built up to break. We never did see the Coast Guard cutter on patrol.

The trip gave me one piece of information which was to come in handy in later years: Just abreast the roughest part of the race, where tide meets wind and there is always a chop, just there and right in on the beach so close a man can all but jump from a moving boat to shore, there is deep water and no breakers. I've sneaked through that hole in heavy weather a good many times since that first trip in *Nonny*.

Once we were clear of Race Point the fog lifted and between Provincetown and Rock Harbor we caught, the record shows, four hundred pounds of striped bass. That presaged the next six weeks.

Wherever we went, wherever we fished, sooner or later the fish would surface and we'd be in business.  No big catches as later catches were rated, but three or four hundred pounds every day, seven days a week.  In the next three weeks we shipped a ton of stripers a week to New York, and during the next three weeks we shipped two tons for the three weeks.  And, believe me, we fished seven days a week.  Whit lugged an immense innerspring mattress aboard.  We had to fight to get it into the cabin.  After we had settled it, it took up so much space we had to take off our boots on deck.  I never saw my own bed at home for that first three weeks, sleeping always on *Nonny*.  We worked out a system, two hours on and two hours off, unless the fish surfaced.  Then we both came on deck, Whit to handle the boat and I to handle the lines.

Perhaps a few words are necessary to explain what we were doing.  We were evolving an entirely new concept of fishing hereabouts.  True enough, sportsmen and a few commercial fishermen had always fished for striped bass since the Pilgrims landed at Provincetown.  Stripers were frequently netted in the surf.  Wilton Hopkins out of Wellfleet, and a few others for all I knew, had been taking charter parties, very often no more than one man to a boat, and never more than one line to a man.  But nobody had ever made a business here of trolling with handlines.

Here we were with no fishpoles, only handlines, two men with usually three or four lines out.  Of course, if we hooked more than one fish at a time, or more than two, it meant going straight ahead, towing the hooked fish until the first fish was in.  This meant heavy gear.  We fished the same six-pound handlines we had fished for cod-fish.  (Not six-pound test, but six pounds to the bundle of six, fifty-fathom lines.)  We trolled almost exclusively three-ounce Japanese-feather jigs.  In order to give greater spread to our lines we rigged and stayed a fourteen-foot two-by-four thwartships, at the break of the cabin.  No give there.  (This, of course, we could take in at night and stow in the cockpit.)  Stripers being what they are, we soon learned not to wander aimlessly around, but fished just where we caught our last fish.  This meant markers of some sort, and since there were few boats, we used semi-permanent markers, usually a flag tied to the top of a long cane pole, the pole ballasted at the bottom with a couple of window weights so it would stay upright, and kept floating with a lashed-on life preserver or pieces of cork. This rig was anchored near the grounds with a rope and a small anchor. Later on, when thick weather or poor light led us astray we added another flag buoy on the other end of the grounds. If we were to fish at night, as we were soon doing, we tied a lighted kerosene lantern to each flagpole, as high above the water as we could. Our rig was clumsy, but it worked, and we found ourselves trolling twenty out of twenty-four hours. We had to come ashore sometimes, to ship our fish to New York via the fish trucks which ran regularly, and to get dry clothes and more food. We had no galley stove in *Nonny* at that time, having no room for it in the cabin with the mattress, but we did carry a canned heat outfit to make an occasional cup of hot coffee.

As I said, we tried fishing at night for about three weeks, but we both got pretty ragged, never being able to relax completely; furthermore, our night catches were not all that good. So after three weeks we gave it up, though we did still plan to fish the sunrise and sundown tides. Since Rock Harbor, whence we were fishing, is a landlocked harbor at low tide, that meant some pretty long days.

Fall came and with it rugged weather, wind and rain, and then a couple of trips without any fish. We decided to put *Nonny* on a mooring and run a line of eel pots in Pleasant Bay. We made the trip around the Cape, stopping long enough to fish off Nauset Inlet and get thrashed around some in heavy weather. We had had enough, so we quit and finished our trip to Pleasant Bay.

# 14

〜〜〜〜

# Eels

An eel pot or trap is a cylindrical container made of cellar window wire or hardware cloth, about thirty inches long and eight to ten inches in diameter. It has a twine head, called variously a "funnel" or "nozzle," at the front end, tied back inside and as wide open as possible. About a third of the way back is another. This one is tied so that the narrow mouth or throat can be pushed open from the front and yet leave no opening apparent when the eel has gone through into the back end or parlor. The head at the far end is tied tight with a pucker string. A chopped-up horseshoe crab or any other clean fish bait is placed in the parlor, the pot is buoyed with rope and a small float. The string of pots should be tended every morning, the eels caught during the night taken out, the old bait carried off to be thrown away, and fresh bait put in. We soon found that a skiff with an outboard motor was more practical than *Sunshine* in the excessively shallow water, so we fished that way until almost November.

The market in those days (and to a certain extent today) was at Christmas time; apparently eels are an Italian Christmas dish. Prices for everything but the very largest eels were low while we were fishing, so we went about building immense cars, eel-proof containers which held up to a thousand pounds of eels each. These were put in the fresh-water Widow Harding's Pond, just under our bedroom windows, and the eels were kept there until the week before Christmas when the fish buyers showed up. It was a tedious and time-consuming process, but in the end it paid reasonably good money.

We were still potting eels when the 1944 hurricane struck. *Sun-*

*shine* was safely beached and I had put out six lines, three to anchors offshore, and three spread out to posts ashore. The day after the hurricane, when I finally got to the shore, there the faithful little biddy was, partially filled with water, with five other, bigger boats hung up on her lines. If it hadn't been for *Sunshine*'s lines, all five boats would have piled up on the beach. *Nonny* had been put on a mooring, an old Model A motor and about six fathoms of chain. Tied to *Nonny*'s stern was an eel car holding about three hundred pounds of small eels.

The morning after the storm, I dodged downed trees and electric wires and finally fought my way to the river, to find *Nonny* high and dry on the far shore, sitting up as pretty and square as you please, as though we had planned it that way. Apparently she'd ridden out the first of the hurricane, but the backlash had caught her and, dragging her mooring, had put her up on the beach. Still tied to her stern was that eel car with the eels shedding slime but still alive.

Whit and I got rollers and skids and bulled the car into the river before we worked on *Nonny*. Then we rolled *Nonny* down the beach and back into the water, just the two of us, with planks, rollers and pries. The boat had suffered no damage, but the eels were obviously the worse for their drying out. Whit was for turning them loose.

I said, "T'hell with it, let's ship them to New York."

"They'll only bring a penny or so a pound," Whit objected.

"So? That's better than a dead loss."

We went to the Smith Bros. Hardware and scrounged a big, second-hand barrel. Into it we put a fifty-pound chunk of ice and two hundred and ninety pounds of small eels, running maybe three to the pound. I saw the truck driver who took the eels to New York a few days later.

"Did you ship a barrel of eels to New York?" he asked.

I said we had.

"You sonofabitch, the next time you do that to me I'll kill you."

I asked him what the matter was.

"We transshipped that goddamned barrel in New Bedford and the bottom came out. Can you imagine a thousand or more small eels squirming around on a truck depot floor?"

Since it was a second-hand barrel, I never thought to check to see if the bottom had been nailed in.  Apparently it hadn't been; but he must have gathered up most of the eels for we got paid for the full two hundred and ninety pounds — five cents a pound net.

We had to spend a week chasing eel pots which had rolled along the bottom, sometimes an unbelievable distance, during the hurricane.

# 15

# Some Other Fishermen

That winter Whit put the new 25-45 hp Redwing in *Nonny*, and I built a windshield/sprayshield. It wasn't very pretty, but it was so securely fastened that it would have torn loose the whole cabin overhead before parting company. Previously the little trunk cabin was all the protection we had from spray and the occasional driving rainstorm we fished in.

We didn't get to the Bay striper fishing that year until sometime in June, for we found we could do well picking up moon snails (locally known as "round wrinkles") for bait for the Chatham handliners — another of the many practical lessons Frank had taught me. We filled in the days with flyfishing for striped bass in Nauset Marsh and Pleasant Bay, and did very well, catching sixty-five fish averaging five pounds apiece on one day.

When we did get offshore we found the picture had changed. The year before most of the stripers had been in deep water where handlines not only were adequate but were by far the quickest, surest way to handle fish. But 1945 was a different year. There were more boats (even the quahog draggers knocked off and went to striper fishing when the fish surfaced), and there were more fish in shallow water where trolling was neither easy nor satisfactory. And Freddy Harris came into the picture with rod and reel. While the previous year we had been consistently highline, this year Freddy trimmed us more days than we enjoyed.

*Nonny* was still the most able and sea-kindly boat in the fleet. She could, even at slow speeds, turn on her heel (that ability was to save my life later). She was easy both head into and broadside to the windchop so commonplace in Cape Cod Bay, and the fact that she was relatively slow made little difference, for our runs were seldom more than four or five miles long and almost never more than eight or ten. (We had given up roaming the way Frank and I had done two years earlier, for that wasted time; furthermore, there were more fish near home, Rock Harbor, than we could find elsewhere.)

This year Freddy Harris sold off the *Geranium*. I was not the only one in those days to go to sea in a wreck. The *Geranium* was not only a wreck, she was a disaster. She got her name the day Fred bought her.

"Gosh," Freddy is reported to have said, "she's not exactly a new boat, is she."

"Well," her former owner admitted, "She ain't no geranium." The name stuck.

She leaked almost as badly as *String Bean*. She had been rigged for quahog dragging and her deck was so far out of water as to be most unhandy. She was powered with a Model A, which might not have been as old as the boat, but which should long since have been sent to the junk yard. The one weakness in Model A's, so far as using them in boats went, was the rear main bearing, which was poured right in the block and was not replaceable. Necessarily put on a slant to line up with the propeller shaft, the motor's rear main bearing invariably wore out, and when it did it leaked oil into the bilge, lots of oil. The *Geranium* leaked water and her motor leaked oil, and both got pumped out onto the deck with a hand pump.

The second year Freddy had her he either sold her or farmed her out on shares to Kid Baker, the youngest of the famous Baker brothers of Orleans. In those days none of us took parties for hire except Cap'n Eddie Horton in *The Owl*. (Cap'n Eddie predated all of us, having started "headboating" or chartering at one dollar per head in 1928.) But tourists were forever coming to the dock, watching us unload hundreds of pounds of game fish, begging us to take them fishing. It wasn't worth it; the fish were worth much more than the people. One day a party came begging us to take them fishing, and I pushed them off onto Kid and the *Geranium*. He was quite flustered. "What shall I charge them?" he whispered.

"Charge 'em five dollars apiece," I suggested. "There's five of them."

So the bargain was struck. The party was to be at the dock at four a.m., that being the proper sailing time. They were to furnish lunch and the Kid was to furnish lines, lures, boat and know-how. After they'd gone Kid came over to *Nonny* where I was repairing gear or doing one of the multitudinous chores that are always waiting to be done on a boat. He asked me what to do about all the grease and oil on the deck.

I suggested he get some dry beach sand and spread it thick. Hopefully it would soak up a good deal of oil. I didn't mean he should leave the sand on deck, for goodness sakes. But he did. He went out before daybreak the next morning with those poor, unsuspecting people with the loose sand still covering the oily deck. That deck must have been like a skating rink. I really don't know why somebody didn't slide overboard. That they did fall down, not once but many times, was attested to by their clothes that afternoon. The men had gone aboard in white flannels, and the women, too, had worn white. The seat of nobody's pants was white that afternoon and I expect the cleaning bill, if indeed the clothes could be cleaned, was considerably more than the price of the trip. Though the day had been somewhat rough the fish had "bitten good," and they were so happy and excited that they not only tipped Kid but came over to *Nonny* when we came in to especially thank me for sending them with such a nice skipper. How could I help liking people as forgiving as that?

Kid was never too hungry a fisherman. I well remember one day trolling by Stony Bar. The fish weren't hitting at all well, and Kid had gone below with his lines still out to lie in a bunk and read *True Romances* or some such pulp magazine while *Geranium* tended to herself. The rest of us realized what was going on so we dodged or changed course to keep out of the way of Kid's erratic fishing. For some reason his motor stalled, so Kid came up on deck, threw off the engine hatch, climbed down below decks to start the motor (still in gear). Of course, when the boat lost way his lines sank to the bottom, and when he started up again he had to open his throttle to the point where the motor raced and the boat surged ahead until he

could throttle back to trolling speed. Three times he went through
this routine. In the meantime he had somehow hooked a striper on
his middle line. Each time he'd stop the fish would sink; each time
he speeded up the fish would come to the surface and skitter along
the top of water. Watching, we were well aware of this, but Kid was
so intent on getting back to his *True Romances* that he never spared
his lines a thought. We got to laughing at that poor fish, alternately
being dropped to the bottom and skidded along the surface. Where
our course and Kid's passed each other, we told him what had happened and he refused to believe it until we finally talked him into
hauling in his lines to check.

*Geranium* later changed hands once or twice more and finally sank
off Dennis Ledge while sea-scalloping, though she gave enough notice
so both men could be taken off safely.

To get back to Freddy, he bought the "Needle Boat," named
*Hazel Marie*. She was much faster and abler and a great deal closer
to the water than *Geranium*, but she leaked nearly as much. Thirty-
three feet long, six-and-a-half feet wide, it was obvious why she was
always called "Needle Boat." She was low, painted light grey, and
very fast for those days, even though she had only what Freddy referred to as a "five-cylinder" Gray motor. Actually it was a six, but
one cylinder was cracked so Freddy took out the spark plug and let
that cylinder simply blow by. I had a scarifying trip in her later,
which I'll come back to at the proper time.

Freddy had only his right hand, having himself accidentally shot
off his left hand with a shotgun while he was still in high school. It
is perhaps trite to say that such an accident, while it can completely
break the spirit of some people, can be the making of the right sort.
Freddy had an oft-repeated maxim: "Anything you can do with two
hands I can do better with one." And he usually could. He was better with a rod and reel than I ever got to be. He was a better mechanic and especially a more patient one than most men who make their
living at repairing motors. He had a ham radio license, and when he
was over fifty he decided he wanted to learn to fly so he bought himself
a Piper Cub and got his pilot's license. His other maxim, by the way,
was: "If you carry an empty basket around long enough somebody
is sure to put something in it." People gave Freddy all sorts of things,

some good but most junk.  He saved it all, and seldom did anyone need a new anything but Freddy had a second-hand one.  I remember one spell when the "Needle Boat" carried six gift batteries, none of which would hold a charge overnight.  Freddy had to invest in a gasoline generator to charge them up.  Many a morning I towed him offshore so he wouldn't miss the tide, with "Little Joe" barking merrily away, charging the batteries so Freddy could finally get that five-cylinder motor running.

Rod and reel were Freddy's best tools, and how he loved to fish. He loved to fish so well that *Nonny*, day after day, had to travel in his wake.  And Whit didn't like that.  In fact, he didn't like it so much he decided one of us, he or I, should fish and the other tend eel pots in Pleasant Bay.  It just didn't work out; you simply can't do two kinds of fishing at once.  One or the other, and usually both, will suffer.  Although Whit was a remarkably successful flyfisherman he never would go to rod-and-reel fishing for stripers and eventually worked himself out of the business.

Though it was not like the year before, we had a good summer and again in the fall potted eels, so nobody went hungry.  I no longer had *Sunshine* to work Pleasant Bay.  She had ridden out the 1944 hurricane, but after that she kind of went to pieces, she needed so much repair work.  Dar, who was harbormaster as well as shellfish constable, had my permission to burn her to clear up the beach.  *String Bean*, too, went up in smoke about that time, and for the same reason.  The fact was and is, boats are like dogs; as the saying has it, a poor man owns one dog and a very poor man owns a whole lot of dogs.  The same is true of boats; they can keep a man awfully poor.

# 16

## Flounder Dragging

With *Sunshine* and *String Bean* gone and Whit talking BIG boats, I found myself on the beach for the first time in quite a spell. I made a deal with him to fish *Nonny* alone for flounders that winter, on a share. Whit was always most embarrassingly generous — he lent me rig mast, boom, and a light, V-belt-driven, winch-head hauling rig.

The rigging involved was somewhat complicated, but I was gradually coming to a philosophy almost essential in fishing alone: Fish light, fish fast, fish smart. Don't be so hungry as to want every fish in the ocean, and, as Whit had put it, "Get in while the band is playing and get out when the music slows down."

The mast was cut to a minimum fourteen feet and made from a roughly rounded four-by-four. It had to be mounted somewhat off-center because *Nonny*'s companionway was amidships. I stepped it on a twelve-inch piece of two-by-twelve and keyed the foot in. Times being hard, I put a new, shiny penny under the step for luck. The stays were five-sixteenths galvanized steel cables and led to the stern and to short chain plates lagged through to timbers.

Peter Bruce, our local blacksmith, made a gooseneck for the boom which was mounted just at the break in the cabin overhead. Knowing I would be getting loads of trash far heavier than I could handle alone, I rigged all boom stays so that I could lead them to the winch head, both topping lift and back stays.

The bearings for the winch were home made. We took a couple of old, beat-up bearing housings, ran the shaft through somewhere near the middle, heated with a plumber's furnace some reclaimed Babbitt metal and poured.  It was amazing how well they worked; in fact, looking back on it, I wonder they worked at all.  The drive for this winch was a refrigerator v-belt, a little bitty thing never made for such heavy work, but the only belt long enough that was available locally.

When I fished for flounders with Frank in *Sunshine* we used Frank's old fifty foot net, hauling over *Sunshine*'s low side by hand. It was much too big and cumbersome, so while rigging *Nonny* I went to Frank and sweet-talked him into building me a new twenty-five-foot net.  The doors, or "boards," I made from redwood, the widest wood I could find.  By dowelling two boards together I got doors two feet high and three feet long.  I went again to Peter Bruce and had him strap the edges with half-inch, half-oval-round iron.

Peter was new in town in those days.  He was a most amazing character.  He knew more about metal than any man I ever met.  He was short, very stocky, a bundle of muscle, and very, very Scottish. He was a blacksmith of the old school, an ageless sort of man who might have been thirty or fifty.  His favorite saying, overlaid with a Scottish burr so thick it was furry, was, "I dinna dr-r-r-rink, and I dinna shmo-o-oke, but I like to pr-r-r-reach a bit."  Indeed, he was a lay preacher and spent his Sundays preaching in prisons and reform schools.  Those who were smart and wanted Peter to do a job for them neither smoked nor swore while in his shop.  If a man didn't care when his job was done he wandered into Peter's shop with a can of beer in his hand, and somehow his work never got done.  Peter could weld a cast-iron stove grate, which most blacksmiths say can't be done, or silver-solder something as delicate as my wife's antique cast-iron candle snuffer shears.  He taught my son, Pete, to silver-solder stainless steel while the boy was still in grammar school, and for years after my Pete picked up spare change silver-soldering stainless steel rod guides for the Rock Harbor fishermen.

The story is told of an out-of-town fisherman who brought in a six-foot sea-scallop drag to be mended or rebuilt.  Coming back a week later, slightly under the weather from a day-off bender, he swore at Peter for not having his work done.  Peter laid his hammer on the anvil and said, "There'll be no shwear-r-ring in my shop!"

The fisherman, a much larger man, somewhat drunk and very cocky, said, "I'll swear any blank, blank, blank place I blank, blank please."

At that point Peter reached up and grabbed the fisherman by the scruff of his neck and the seat of his pants and literally threw him the length of the shop and out into the driveway. Then he turned and picked up the drag which probably weighed a good two hundred pounds and threw it after the fisherman. Said he, "And take your-r-r for-r-r-reign dr-r-r-ag and your-r-r wor-r-rk some heathen place else."

Fishermen who were there and saw the whole thing said afterwards that it was a good thing for all concerned that the shop door was open or Peter would have thrown the fisherman right through it.

So Peter did the ironwork for me, the chain plates, the gooseneck, the stay collars for masthead and boom end, wrapped the doors in half-oval round, and welded rings in the ends of the bridles or leading chains.

An explanation of the process of flounder dragging (or otter trawling) is in order. First, in the salt ponds off Pleasant Bay and Town Cove, as well as in the Bay and the Cove themselves, dragging is prohibited by law from May first to November first. (This is an old law lobbied through by the lobster fishermen to keep their pots from being smashed within the three-mile limit by the offshore fish draggers.) Contrary to the objections by the casual sportsfishermen, flounder dragging in these waters improves the fishing by "cultivating" the bottom. Frank used to say, "If you don't cultivate a garden you can't grow any vegetables, and the same holds true for shellfish and fin fish." Those ponds closed by law to flounder dragging, Ryder's Cove, Little Round Pond and Quanset Pond, no longer produce flounders. The ponds still dragged, Meetinghouse, Lonnie's, Joe Arey's and Mill Pond, still produce — if not as many as formerly, the fault may be laid to excessive offshore fishing by foreign fleets rather than to the relatively miniscule catches of the little boats inside in the winter.

A drag is a kind of open end pocket made of netting, tapering, in the case of the little drag Frank made me, from a special width of twenty-five feet and a height of three feet some thirty feet deep to a rectangle about fifteen feet wide and two feet high. At the end was a "cod end," a bag made of much heavier twine perhaps twelve feet around and six feet long. This was closed with a pucker string rove through two-inch rings. The bottom edge of the net was weighted with light chain and the top leading edge buoyed with cork floats. The whole net was led and spread by the doors which were actually paravanes or underwater kites, so rigged that when they were pulled forward they spread out and down, searching the bottom.

As the drag was towed along the bottom at the end of two ropes, in most cases about fifteen fathoms long in this water, it picked up flounders which were hiding or feeding on the bottom, but it also picked up all the grasses and marine growths. (On occasion it also picked up such embarrassing items as old Christmas trees and oil drums half full of mud. As a matter of fact, when Frank and I were dragging in *Sunshine* we picked up a whole locust tree, roots, trunk, branches and all. We had barely enough power to drag the whole thing to shore where I laboriously cut mesh after mesh to get the tree out and Frank followed, netting up the hole through which we pulled the tree.) This whole rig (the drag, not the tree) was thrown overboard starting with the puckered end of the cod end, followed by the net, fold on fold, and then the doors and together the drag warps for each side. The ropes were secured to the hauling post or twin cleats, one to each side aft, and the tow began.

The ropes in turn led from the hauling post up to the outboard end of the boom to a heavy double block, thence to a snatch block or open-faced pulley bolted to the deck, and thence to the winch head. When it came time to haul back (take the net aboard) to take out trash and fish, I threw the turns off the hauling post and wrapped both ropes around the winch head quickly. The ropes had to lead just so from the snatch block and the turns had to be put on just so or the two ropes would jump each other and then I had trouble. This was a cut-and-try thing which eventually worked out very well.

The winch head, driven by a pulley bolted to the flywheel of the Redwing, pulled the drag to the boat (in practice, with the eggbeater propeller the Redwing swung, it pulled the boat back to the drag.) I soon learned to be downwind of the net when I hauled back, so that the net would not get under the boat. The doors came out of the water and swung toward the boat. At the right instant I threw the boat out of gear and slacked off on the drag warps so the doors came to rest gently on the deck.  Then, pulling evenly, top and bottom, I pulled the net over the rail.  Once the foot rope was aboard, of course, there was no way for the flounders to get out.  The major difference between offshore dragging and dragging in the tidal ponds off Pleasant Bay and Town Cove, other than the size of the gear, was that in the ponds I was badly hampered by marine grasses.  Sea lettuce was deadly because it trapped so much mud and water; the fine green grass we call "mermaid's hair" was so fine it clung to each mesh and had to be picked off almost mesh by mesh; but the major headache was a red, brittle grass which grew in great profusion.  Each foot of net, as it was manhandled over the rail, had to be shaken vigorously to shake the weeds down into the cod end along with the fish.

When the cod end of heavy twine was reached a strap, or double piece of rope, was squeezed down on it and the lifting rope was hooked on.  I found my little refrigerator belt was hardly strong enough to lift the whole weight by itself, so I rigged two sets of double blocks for a lifting rope near the outer end of the boom.  The rope was led through them, then down through the snatch block and so to the winch head.  Then I hoisted the cod end full of fish and weeds as nearly clear of the water as possible.  When I had two-blocked my gear, I secured the lift rope to a convenient cleat, undid my topping lift and led it through the snatch block and to the winch head.  By pulling on the topping lift I managed to get the full cod end clear of the rail, but now all that weight had laid the boat down so the boom swung out too far for me to reach.  I had to secure the topping lift and repeat the whole performance with the back stay to swing the load inboard.  Finally, the pucker string was loosened and the catch dumped out onto the deck.

If it sounds like a slow, cumbersome process, it was.  Most loads were not so heavy that the topping lift-backstay process was necessary, but occasionally I got a load aboard so big and so heavy as to put *Nonny*'s plugged scuppers deep underwater.  Then, of course, all that salt grass had to be pitched overboard.  When the deck was reasonably clear the pucker string was tied again, the boat thrown in gear and cut in a circle away from the drag or starboard side, the drag payed out and the whole process repeated while the flounders of the previous tow were sorted and sacked up. A tow and the ensuing wrassle with the drag usually took about a half hour, and "paying" fishing brought aboard seventy pounds or more of flounders per tow. It was seldom big money (only twice in all the years I dragged flounders in the winter did I ever hit the jackpot, but more of that later.) It was boating and fishing and it kept the kettle boiling.

The occasional frustrations came to be accepted as part of the business. Once in a while I'd get to the shore in the morning and half the pond would be frozen over with window pane ice. It meant running alongside the ice edge, creating as much wake as possible, until the waves had broken up the ice and I could go dragging without cutting the boat to shreds. Once in a while the net would hang up on an old mooring. Then I had to throw out of gear, haul back, put a strap around the lowest part of the drag I could reach, put on all the strain I could with lifting rope and winch, and then, with the boat rail laid down, cut round and round until the net tore loose. Then I would anchor up on the nearest lee shore and go to mending the net — four knots to the mesh, and four strands from each knot, except on the gussets which were three-sided.

All in all, it was a happy time and there were bonuses. To row out to *Nonny* with the temperature in the upper twenties, make the skiff fast to the mooring, find the bilge dry and have the motor catch the third or fourth time over — that was like a Christmas present. To have the net which I had carefully faked down the night before run out smoothly and the ropes spread in their neat geometric pattern, and at the end of the tow to have the cod end sway out of water just white with flounder bellies against the twine — that was fishing. The freckles of mud from the net shaken down as the boat drifted away from it, the wet, chafed wrists and the cold feet, even these small discomforts were a part of it. The price was up and down, usually about five cents a pound for one-pound flounders and seven for large. Frank had taught me to take nothing less than a foot long.

The second or third time I went in to pay Whit his weekly share he announced that he was going to buy a fifty-footer and go to offshore sea-scalloping, he and a couple of "sooners." (They'd sooner stay ashore and talk about fishing than go.) For a number of reasons he hadn't asked me in. One, I hadn't the capital necessary. Two, by

this time I'd learned to judge how much money there was in any
kind of fishing by what the men already in it had to spend.  Three, I
didn't much admire his new partners.

"But," he said, "*Nonny* is up for sale and I'd like to give you first
refusal."  He named a price.

I shook my head.  "I don't think she's worth that much, Whit," I
said, "and furthermore I don't have that kind of money.  I'd like to
buy her well enough, but . . ."

Whit said, "You got a dollar bill with you?"

I had.

"Gimme."  I gave him the dollar and found myself *Nonny*'s new
owner.  "Pay me what you can, when you can," he said.  Do you
wonder I loved the guy like a brother?  We had a drink to the bargain
and he was paid off at his own price before the next summer was
over.  (He never did much sea-scalloping and within two years he sold
out, bought a new small boat which later became the *Flying Mist II*
and was back in the Bay striper fishing.  I offered to take him on as a
partner again, share and share alike, but he would have none of it.
"You're too goddamn stubborn," he said.  Actually we were pretty
much alike there.)

For a wonder I didn't tear *Nonny* all apart and try to improve her.
As a matter of fact, in the seven years I owned *Nonny* I changed very
little other than to put in a new Redwing and replace the deck.  She'd
been built with a concave deck and a single scupper amidships, a lead
pipe which leads out underwater.  It kind of scared me because I had
visions of that pipe letting go when I was offshore with no way to
get at that two-inch hole in the bottom.  It was good that I did get
around to changing it, for when I freed the pipe at the deck and
pushed on it, it fell out of the boat.

# 17

# Preparations for Sea Scalloping

It occurred to me early the next spring that I could go sea-scalloping on Dennis Ledge with *Nonny* — and that was pretty wild. The boats commonly engaged in that business were small if they were in the thirty-eight-to-forty-five-foot range. Except under unusual circumstances, most dragging there was done with a cable winch with gear much too heavy for *Nonny*. I proposed to fish light and fast with light gear and rope instead of cable, in a boat not much more than half the size of the regulars. However, I had one thing going for me the bigger boats didn't have.

During my first year with Whit he had had installed a sounding machine. (The machine was just being developed, and couldn't be bought, only leased or rented.) A friend of his, who just happened to be president of the developing company, installed a "Baby Bunting" fathometer (or, as they were more commonly called, a "fad-o-meter," with the accent on the first syllable) "for experimental purposes" on *Nonny*. The machines hadn't yet reached the efficiency of the later depth recorders, but in many ways our little fathometer was a tremendous help. If we knew what depth we were looking for, we could cruise along in reasonably smooth water at a reasonable speed and read the depth. In fact, with more experience, I found I could pretty well read the type of bottom. The machine sent out an electric impulse which hit the bottom and bounced back, lighting a neon bulb on a scale calibrated to indicate the depth; a sharp flash indicated hard bottom, sand or gravel, a soft, fuzzy flash indicated muddy or soft bottom, and jagged or irregular flashes meant boulders and ledge.

Of course, I had to get a drag built by Peter Bruce, and I had to get *Nonny* around the Cape from Pleasant Bay where she had worked the winter.

I talked a friend, Howard Anderson, into going with me, for it is a long, tedious trip alone. The day was lowery, with a long, greasy swell coming in from the no'theast. We cleared the bar and made our way north with no trouble. As we churned our eight-knot way past the Highland Light Howard picked up my binoculars and inspected the high, clay bank. He focused on the flag by the light. Then he asked casually, "What does that red flag mean?"

Not much interested I said, "I don't know, the Coast Guard is always playing with some kind of damn nonsense." And that was that. We swung up into P'town Harbor to pick up a mutual friend to ride with us from P'town to Rock Harbor. He met us at the dock in a perfect dither. "Don't you fools know the Coast Guard is flying small craft warnings?"

"Oh, is that what that red pennant means?"

"Yes," he said, "it is, and I'm not leaving this dock. If you take my advice you'll tie up here and take the boat home after the storm is over."

"Well," I said. "I'm not taking your advice, I'm going to Rock Harbor. Do you want to come or not? In the first place, the wind is easterly so we'll have a lee shore all the way home, and in the second place, I can't believe any no'theast storm can build up in the two hours and a half it will take us to get to Rock Harbor."

Our friend refused to take a chance so Howard and I went alone. What we hadn't realized, however, was how long that run around Land's End into P'town Harbor and back out again would take. (We found out later that the run from Race Point to Rock Harbor took only twenty minutes longer than the run from Race Point to the P'town Dock.) We churned merrily along, up by Pamet River, Billingsgate Island and into the upper Bay. We knew the tide was dropping, but with no delay we still had plenty of time to make it before the water got too thin.

We had a delay. The long run into P'town had used just enough extra gas so that halfway across from Billingsgate Shoal to Rock Harbor the tank ran dry. With that extra touch of caution I was learning the hard way, I had brought along a G.I. can of gasoline, and five gallons was far more than we needed to finish our trip. However, the tank filler pipe, which projected up through the after deck, was only one inch in diameter — and I had neglected to bring any funnel or pouring spout. So there I stood on the stern, in the pitch dark, with the boat rolling heavily in the trough, trying to pour gasoline from a G.I. can into a one-inch pipe. Most of it spilled overboard, but I did get enough in to get us home — and I had wits enough to slosh bucket after bucket of salt water over the stern before I tried to start the motor so no bit of gasoline vapor could cause us more trouble. All these years I have had to refuel only once under more trying conditions (a later story).

Before the trip around the Cape I had ordered something new from Peter Bruce; a two-box shenanigan or Nova Scotia sea-scallop drag. The first sea scallop drags used by the Rock Harbor fleet were simply adapted snow-plow drags like those used for bay-scalloping. They were changed only in that the chain-net bag was made of three-inch rings instead of the two-inch bay-scallop rings, sea scallops being so much bigger than bay scallops. Dennis Ledge is just what the name implies, a place full of ledge, rocks big as pianos and boulders, and the snow-plow drags were forever getting jammed in the rocks and causing all kinds of trouble; occasionally they were permanently rocked down and lost. The shenanigan drag, however, was designed to fish in just that kind of bottom. Instead of having heavy iron bows, the drag consisted of an iron pipe tow bar from which were suspended by swivels and chains usually three iron boxes about three feet wide and half as high, made of two-inch angle iron and backed by chain-net bags. These bags had the advantage of being so small in the mouth that they could only swallow rocks which could be handled by hand; furthermore, swiveled as they were, they could fish as well upside down as right side up and spilled nothing of their load when they were tipped over. The big shenanigans, those with three boxes, were a fright to handle. Though each box individually was too heavy to be handled by hand, when the three of them hung up in the air suspended on swivels and chains from the boom end, they cut all kinds of shenanigans (and I expect that is where they got their name).

I had ordered a two-box drag from Peter, and as was always the case, I knew I would get it only if I sat around and spurred him on. "Peter," I pleaded, "I've got the boat around the Cape, I'm all rigged to go except the drag. You promised it to me last week. When will it be done?"

"Come ar-r-round after-r-r supper-r-r," said he, "It'll be done by midnight." So after supper that spring night my wife and I drove to Peter's shop and sat by while he finished the work. Not being used to blacksmiths' shops my wife had worn her new Harris tweed coat. The fact was, I think, she planned to wait in the car, but it was cold and the wait was long. She came in, spread an old coat of mine to sit on and was warming herself by the forge, when a spark from Peter's welding flew over and landed on that new Harris tweed and burned a small hole. My wife, being a wee bit McGregor herself, has never forgiven Peter. The drag was finished around midnight, however, and the next day I set out to make my fortune sea-scalloping.

# 18

## Apprenticeship

I had put in my apprenticeship at sea-scalloping during odd springs in the years past. My first trips with John Bernard Crosby in the old Navy motor-sailer named *Marguerite* I don't remember much about; in fact, I can't place exactly which spring it was. I do remember that one spring John Bernard poured wet cement into *Marguerite*'s bilge, thinking to ballast her and seal off the leaks at the same time, only to find that cement and wood will not bond. He had to cut out all the cement by hand. I remember on those trips John Bernard had an old Chrysler Royal, a straight eight, for power. Those old Royals were always dogs for starting, and the *Marguerite*'s particularly so. John Bernard rigged up forward of the Chrysler — so help me, as I tell it, it is true — a Model A Ford, and connected it to the forward end of the Chrysler. The Ford was famously easy to start and was always dry, being in the cabin. It would be fired up, and, with the clutch let out, it would turn the Chrysler, which would eventually start. It worked, though it was pulling ourselves up by our own boot-straps, and many a morning that poor Model A pushed us out of the harbor, turning the Chrysler all the while. Once the big motor started, the Ford was shut off, thrown out of gear, and allowed to rest until the next morning. It was my introduction to tandem motors.

One trip I remember well of that spring. A crew of those "wild Wellfleeters" (as they were known then by the relatively staid Rock Harbor fishermen) had been sea-scalloping beside us at Dennis. Apparently they'd carried too much of a deckload of booze, for when their motor stalled and they'd churned their battery dead they decided that what the battery needed was more water, so they filled it with salt water. For some reason they also filled the base of their motor with more salt water. We in *Marguerite* towed them into Rock Harbor, just making the tide, tied them to the dock, and, when they awoke the next morning to find themselves in a strange harbor, got roundly cussed for not taking them to Wellfleet. Sometimes I think all the color has gone out of the local fishermen.

After that spring with John Bernard I put in several springs with Skrag Baker, another of the famous Baker brothers. Skrag was a little man in stature but a giant in his pugnacity. Though it happened before my time, it was said that he fought in the amateur fights at the old Mill Hill Pavilion in Hyannis, and while he seemed hardly heavy enough to knock anyone down, his sheer aggressiveness overwhelmed everyone who came along. I never saw that side of his character. From the time I first met him he had a most horrible cough; surely he was not long for this world; he must be consumptive. But he coughed his way through the years long afterwards, standing up to any man, and fishing alongside the best.

He had at that time a thirty-footer, a graceful, sea-kindly little thing; I don't remember that she ever had a name. The story had it that Skrag bought her for a song at the Vineyard as a double-ender, brought her home, had her stern spread and made a square-ender out of her. (Be that as it may, years later Freddy (Boo) Turner split her again, spread the two halves a foot apart, put in a new keel and lengthened her four feet. For this kind of job Freddy was a legend while he was still alive.)

In those first days when I fished with Skrag he powered his little boat with a Model A motor, and it was here that I learned about the weak rear main bearings. That Ford leaked oil so badly there were eight inches of clear lubricating oil in the bilge. Before we left Rock Harbor in the morning Skrag would take a bucket, kept especially for that purpose, bail up two gallons of oil from the bilge, pour it into the motor and run for Dennis. Once an hour he would shut off, bail up another bucket of oil, pour it into the motor — more or less — and go on fishing. It sounds impossible in this day and age of Coast Guard regulations and safety precautions, but I don't remember it ever bothered me greatly — probably because I was too green to realize the danger we were in.

One spring in the middle thirties scallops went to the unheard-of price (at that time, of course) of forty cents a pound, or three dollars and sixty cents a gallon. While we didn't get exactly rich, I thought we were doing extremely well, even on the poor lay — a third for me, a third for Skrag, and a third for the boat, after expenses. But the strike in Boston that had caused the unnaturally high price was called off and sea scallops began to slide.

Skrag had had it; furthermore, he was offered a job ashore (he had a heavy machinery operator's license). I begged him to let me keep on scalloping, and it was proof of his confidence in me that he did. I enlisted Bob Whiting as helper. Bob had served a hitch in the Coast Guard as motor mechanic, and he and I had dug clams together commercially, but if there was ever a greener couple set sail from Rock Harbor it would be hard to find. We made one trip.

On account of the tide, we left Rock Harbor in the middle of the day, planning to spend the night offshore and fish in the morning. At Dennis things went smoothly for a while and we caught a reasonable amount of scallops. Somewhere along the line Bob or I had picked up the information that sea-scallop guts were good bait for codfish, so instead of heaving the guts overboard with the empty shells as is customary, Bob shucked them into a five-gallon tin. And then the motor died. It just stopped.

I eventually found the trouble in a sort of jury-rigged electric fuel pump Skrag had installed, but while I was finding the trouble Bob had baited a handline with sea-scallop guts and was hauling in codfish after codfish. I couldn't stand it and I went to codfishing, too. Between us and before it got too dark or the bait ran out, I forget which came first, we managed to land nearly a half-ton of codfish. Now, a half-ton of codfish in a thirty-foot boat with no provision for them can pose a problem. With the motor limping, too, I felt it best to make for Rock Harbor that night. We did, and there on the dock, to our surprise, was Skrag. It was nearly midnight, so I said, "What are you doing here this time of night?"

He said, "I kind of thought you fellows wouldn't get anything and would come in."

"Well," I said, very modestly, "I don't know what we're going to do with all these codfish."

Lester Young was running a fish cart in those days, peddling fish from door to door, and as it happened he too was on the dock with Skrag. We offered the codfish to Lester at his own price. "What would I do with them?" he asked, "I got a fish cart full of haddock."

We covered them with wet burlap bags and the next morning Bob and I went from restaurant to chain store to Howard Johnson's selling codfish at five cents a pound. We got rid of them all but it was a chore. Lester said later, "Damn you! Every place I went to sell haddock you had already loaded up with codfish. I guess the next time you offer me fish I'd better buy them even if I have to throw them overboard."

We all went codfishing the next day, but the fish didn't bite, and when we got our catch to the wholesalers at Chatham the price had dropped to a cent and a half. That ended that flurry of codfishing. For that matter, it also ended our sea-scalloping; the price dropped to eighty cents a gallon, nine cents a pound. Even as sanguine as Bob and I were, we knew we couldn't make money at that price.

# 19

≋≋≋≋≋≋≋≋≋≋≋≋≋≋≋≋≋

# Sea Scalloping

Sea scallops are a deep water shellfish — so far as my experience goes, the deepest water shellfish. Usually dragged by vessels eighty feet or more long, they are found from south of Block Island to Nova Scotia, in water from eleven to twenty-three fathoms deep, and they grow to an immense size (compared to bay scallops) of perhaps ten inches or more across. The biggest sea scallops I ever dragged ran forty-four to the bushel and opened nine to the quart. I ran into them in a thick fog one Sunday and could never find the spot again. Usually the so-called "red-back" sea scallops, opening the very best, might run a hundred and twenty-five to the bushel, and they are good scallops if they cut a gallon to the bushel. They are opened on the grounds as they are caught, with a knife the size and shape of an old-fashioned case knife. The hinge side is held away, the upper shell is cut loose and flipped overboard, and the scallop eye or adductor muscle is freed either before or after the viscera, depending on the opener. The viscera and lower shell are then thrown overboard. The scallops are bagged in cotton bags holding about forty pounds, or three and a half gallons, made especially for this purpose. In the deep-water boats they are then refrigerated. Fishermen operating as I did, making port every night, were more apt to cut the scallops into new five-gallon tins furnished by the fish buyer.

I had several more things going for me in *Nonny* than on my earlier trips as an apprentice. First, the shenanigan drags were a vast improvement over the snow-plow drags we had used earlier. Second, I had the fathometer. Third, while I hadn't been sea-scalloping since my days with Skrag, I was vastly more knowledgeable at sea, thanks to my fishing and flounder dragging with Frank. It was as though I had left nursery school and had made my way part way through grammar school. I knew more than I did to start with but, as I found out, I had an awful lot more to learn.

The weather was good, *Nonny* was a dream, and the new drag worked very well. I did, as I look back on it, far better than I had any right to hope. The big boats (big only by comparison to *Nonny*, for even they were small for offshore sea-scalloping) working two men and cable winches and nine-foot drags were averaging about forty gallons of scallops a day. *Nonny* and I, with our little four-foot drag, and hauling with rope, managed many days as much or more than twenty gallons. I found I couldn't drag with the fleet; they towed much faster than I and knew no nonsense about giving a little feller a break. In fact, one of the more hardnosed characters informed me that if I didn't keep out of his way, he'd cut off my gear with his heavier drag.

I discouraged that. I had taken the precaution, in case I should hang up and not have power to pull clear or should for whatever reason lose my drag, of towing a twenty-fathom tail buoy which streamed out behind me. This consisted of a large lobster-pot buoy and twenty fathom of new three-quarter inch manila rope. So I said, "Cut me off you may, but if while you are doing it you happen to wind that twenty-fathom rope in your prop, don't expect me to tow you home. *Nonny* is only a little boat and her eggbeater of a prop wouldn't have the power to tow your great big vessel after you'd cut off my drag."

He didn't threaten me again; in fact, he spread the word and the other boats gave me a little more clearance, at least off my stern. That kind of attitude kind of took the fun out of fishing with the fleet, though. I was never one to make it hard for the other fellow deliberately, so I picked up my drag after a day or two and turned on the fathometer to go looking.

I found a spot — oh, brother, did I ever find a spot! Watching the steady seven-fathom reading on the fathometer, I suddenly came across a two-fathom drop to nine fathoms. I was prepared and dumped over a flag buoy, then I worked back to find the change in depth. It was a little slot; three and a half minutes' towing time, turn *Nonny* on her heel, and tow back three and a half minutes. Throw the rope on the winch head and haul back — two bushels of clear scallops, no trash, no rocks, nothing but clear scallops. It was a dragger's dream.

Two facts bothered me. One, if I tried to open the scallops as usual while I made the next tow, I'd get out of the hole and either sand down on the sharp rise in the bottom or drag up mostly rocks and trash. Two, if anybody found out what I was doing I'd be run down by big boats and that would be the end of that. Lately I had been getting almost twenty bushels, cutting twenty gallons, almost every day, but at the rate I was now catching scallops, I could get that many in two hours and a half. I dragged twenty bushels, which was all *Nonny* could carry comfortably in the shell anyway, then moved my flag due east exactly five minutes at full cruising speed so that no one else who saw it and made a trial tow would discover my "honey hole." Then I steamed half-way home, threw over the drag for an anchor, and went to whittling.

It worked well and nobody bothered me for several days, but of course I got hungry. The big boats had found another bed, further offshore; nobody was dragging near me. I figured if I took on another man, maybe I could get forty gallons. I hunted up Whit.

His new boat hadn't been delivered so he was more than glad to get offshore. Being Whit, he asked me how the codfish were biting.

I said, "Gosh, Whit, I don't know. I haven't had time to wet a line."

He suggested we take along a tub of trawl, bait it with sea-scallop guts, set it while we were dragging, and pick it up on the way home. It sounded like a good idea: if the scallops came the way they had been coming, it wouldn't take all day to get our forty gallons.

We started early the next morning, carrying with us a tub of trawl, standard codfish gear: five-ought Limerick hooks, three-foot gangions six feet apart, fifty hooks to the line and only six lines to the tub — three hundred hooks. By the time the other boats caught up with us we had put fifteen gallons of scallops in tins, baited and set the trawl down-tide of the hole and gone back to dragging. Don't you know, the first boat out of Rock Harbor saw us dragging, came steaming toward us, and plunked her drag right over by our flag (which was set five minutes east of us). Whit and I quickly dragged to the up-tide end of the hole, shut off and worked the drag warp over the bow for an anchor, then dropped back as far as we could toward the center of the hole and went to handlining codfish. It worked. The dragger swung down-tide of us to clear all our gear, picked up his drag and, finding only rocks and trash, headed off to where he had fished the day before.

While he was passing, the codfish started to bite. It was line-to-line fishing: as fast as we could haul one in there would be another one on. I really believe if all the fish we started that day had stayed on we couldn't have carried them, but a lot were hanging on until we got them almost up to where we could see them and then spitting the hook out. Eventually we wound up with eleven hundred pounds after they were gutted, but that took all day.

It got along toward evening and the other draggers had all steamed t'east'ard on their way home. I said, "Whit, we better head for the barn. The tide has turned and we've got to be in before seven o'clock."

"Just let's catch six more fish," he said. So we caught six more. "I meant six more apiece," he said, so we caught six more apiece.

Finally, I said, "Whit we've got to go or stay out all night."

And then, for the first and only time in nine years, *Nonny* would-n't go. That Redwing was so dependable that in the harbor on an ebb tide I used to cast off my dock lines, open the companionway door, put away my lunch, and then turn to the motor. Now I couldn't get a kick out of it. I am not much of a mechanic, finding it less expensive to hire a man who knows what he is doing and has the tools to do the work than to mess with it myself, but there comes a time when a boatman has to be a mechanic even if he is not one. This was before the days of radio telephones, and we knew all the other boats had gone home. It was in March and it was going to be cold before the night was out. Thinking that perhaps I had flooded the motor and that letting it sit a few minutes might clear the extra gas, I suggested that we rearrange the fish. *Nonny* was so loaded with codfish that her scuppers were plugged and under water. Whit started to gut fish while I rummaged for fuel for the little Shipmate stove I had installed before I started sea-scalloping. There wasn't much that we could spare that would burn, but I did rip off some of the sheathing

I had put along the rail to keep it from being banged up too much by the drag.

Whit looked up from gutting codfish and said, "Try her again."

I did. No use. Then I began checking. I had already learned one lesson that too many of my experienced friends have yet to learn: Just because a motor won't start is not necessarily an indication that the distributor points have closed up. Since that spring night in *Nonny* I've towed home many and many a boat whose skipper had buggered up the distributor points when his motor wouldn't start. I simply took off the distributor cap, made sure everything was dry inside, snapped the points with the switch on to make sure not only that the points were opening, but that the spark was hot. I won't describe all the checking I did: the Redwing was a simple little motor with four cylinders and without all the fancy gadgets which came later. Both gas and spark seemed right but the motor just wouldn't run.

I tried until after dark, until after it was too late to get into Rock Harbor, until after both the regular battery and the spare which had been fully charged were pretty well run down. And then we settled in for the night.

We built a fire in the Shipmate, fried scallops and codfish tongues and sorted ourselves out as comfortably as possible. The chimney that ran up through the cabin overhead was not high enough to carry off the smoke (it was fortunately a calm night) so we had to keep the fire hot. I said, "Whit, you turn in first and I'll keep the fire going. I'll wake you in two hours."

He started to snore almost immediately — we'd been right straight out since before daylight and this sleeping in *Nonny* was old stuff to both of us. I poked a new piece of wood in from time to time, enough to keep the fire burning merrily. At the end of nearly three hours I couldn't keep my eyes open any longer so I woke him.

I said, "I don't know what you're going to use for fuel; the sheathing wood is almost all gone."

He said, "I'll use the trawl keg." And I went off to sleep to the sound of his breaking up barrel staves. I don't know for sure when I roused myself, but I woke to the awful stench of rotten fish and a cabin full of smoke. Whit was sound asleep in the other bunk. He'd broken up the trawl keg, all right, but when he'd let the fire die down all the rotten bait that had ever soaked into that wood turned to smoke and stench. I woke him and started up the fire again. We discussed when we could begin to expect help. I stepped out onto the deck to get a breath of fresh air. "Whit," I said, "we could get into Rock Harbor by the time we got there if we took it along slow. I believe I'll try the motor again."

We had disconnected both batteries and warmed them by the stove to bring them back as much as we could. He passed one to me and I hooked it up there in the dark. More to pass the time than with any hope of starting the motor, I turned on the key and hit the starter button. The first time over the Redwing fired, and it kept on firing. To this day I have never found out what was wrong. In the middle of the Bay, in the middle of the night I was not about to experiment — in fact, I was not about to slow down and stall the motor.

I sent Whit up on the bow to cast off the drag warp. When he came back on deck I said, "You get down in the cabin because I'm not about to touch that throttle and the drag is going to come in flying. I don't want to hit you with it." He did as he was told without argument, and the drag did come in flying. It thumped on the deck and I headed for Rock Harbor without slacking off on the throttle. Not a soul was stirring when we tied up at the dock and shut off the motor. We decided that before we handled the fish we would head for Whit's house, breakfast, and some dry clothes.

Whit's wife greeted us with, "Well, where have you been? You've given me a fine night." Her hair was mussed, which was unusual for Aletta, her eyes were rimmed with red and her hands shook. I have never understood why women show relief by scolding.

We had no idea our wives would be upset since Whit and I had often spent the night in *Nonny*. Nor would they have been if it hadn't been for a busybody at the harbor, who called Aletta at nine o'clock and announced, "Your husband is in trouble or he'd have been in before seven o'clock." At nine o'clock at night, for goodness sakes! If he had to call at all, why didn't he call at seven when the tide had already dropped too far for us to get in?

Al paced the floor from nine until ten. She tried to drop off to sleep on the sofa in the living room. Finally, at ten o'clock she called my wife, woke her from a sound sleep, and told her the story.

My wife, who has had more than her share of this sort of thing, counseled wisely. "The boat is sound, the motor is new, and the boys know what they are doing. If there is anything wrong there is nothing we can do about it at ten o'clock at night, so go on and go back to bed. If they haven't come in by daylight I'll call the Coast Guard."

Al didn't take her advice, but then, neither did my wife. She couldn't get back to sleep, so around midnight she went to the phone. One of our neighbors and friends was Captain Yngve Rongner, U.S.C.G., Retired. His son Georgie was number one man at the Nauset station at that time. Captain Yngve's advice was the same, "There's nothing we can do now. Go back to bed. If they don't show up by daylight I'll call Georgie." He didn't take his own advice either. Rather than disturb his wife he put on his clothes and walked the mile or so to the Coast Guard station to arouse son George.

George set the ponderous machinery of the Coast Guard in motion. He sent out a crew in the DUKW, he alerted the Sandwich station, which sent out an air-sea rescue plane from Quonset, Rhode Island, and Coast Guard Boston, who sent out a ninety-three-footer. The trouble was nobody knew what they were looking for or where to look. If they had thought for a minute they would have called one of the dragger captains, all of whom knew what the boat looked like and where we had been fishing. As it was, nobody came within five miles of us, lying peacefully asleep just where we had been fishing (but with no lights burning to save our run-down batteries) — and it was one of the blackest nights I've ever been on the water, not foggy but heavily overcast. The Coast Guard searchers were very indignant the next morning when they caught up with us ashore, first because we hadn't shown our masthead or anchor light, and second because we hadn't anchored near the buoy where they looked for us. My wife had said she thought we were fishing "near the can buoy," so the Coast Guard searched the can buoy near Billingsgate Island, which is in shallow water where there never were any sea scallops or codfish. Our can buoy, the one referred to by the whole fishing fleet as "the" can buoy, was five miles away, at the west end of Billingsgate Shoal and on the edge of deep water, where we had always fished for sea scallops and codfish. Any one of the Rock Harbor skippers could have told them that; every one of them had seen us lying at anchor that day. But nobody thought to get one of the skippers out of bed to ask him. Finally, after running around half the night, the DUKW ran out of fresh water in her cooling system and had to go ashore for more, and we managed to "sneak" into Rock Harbor unobserved. We gave Georgie and his boys half a dozen codfish for their trouble and thanked them politely.

Poor Aletta got a double dose of busybody trouble. Some years later Whit and their son were striper fishing in Pleasant Bay in an outboard boat when the drowned body of a fisherman was brought in to the dock at Chatham. Somebody, who should have been put in jail, "positively identified" the body as Whit's and called Al to tell her her husband was drowned. She was waiting for the undertaker to pick her up to go and claim Whit's body when Whit and young Whit came walking up the road, alive and well pleased with themselves for their morning's catch.

# 20

# Night Trip to Wellfleet

After that one famous trip when Whit and I were lost at sea (incidentally, we hit the market on codfish for twenty-five and twenty-eight cents a pound and stocked over two hundred dollars, which was to that time the biggest stock *Nonny* had made), Whit's new boat was delivered and I signed on as helper Captain Dave Delano, who had helped me with *String Bean*. He, or something, jinxed us for weather. Day after day it blew so hard we couldn't get at that little honey hole of sea scallops. We did all the boat drill and preparation we could think of. We even put six-volt deck lights on the boom and rigged an elaborate lighted buoy so we could work after dark. Then came a day, windy as usual, but with a moderating trend. It looked as though the wind would go down with the sun. I broke a rule I had found expedient: Never believe the Boston weather forecast (Cape Cod being just far enough out to sea that the Boston weather is never the same as ours). That afternoon I listened to a forecast: Northwest wind, moderating toward evening. That was the way it looked and the tide was just right — we could slip out an hour before sundown, which would give us daylight to locate our spot and set the lighted buoy, and all night to fish.

We were all ready to go, so, although the wind was fairly fresh from the nor'west, we set out and made our hour's run to Dennis. With the sounding machine we found the spot, set our lighted buoy, and went to dragging. Where we were fishing the ebb tide ran toward the north. The nor'west wind against the tide, in combination with the cross rip set up by the nearby Shoal Ground, made our work not only difficult but unsafe after dark. *Nonny* was, after all, a little boat. We anchored exactly where Whit and I lay that other night and went to codfishing.

Captain Dave was a big man, red-faced and hearty. He had on that night a pair of knee-high rubber boots and he was lustily singing and pulling in codfish when a queer wave broke over *Nonny*'s stern and filled both his boots. He turned to me and "tugged his forelock" or a reasonable facsimile. "Captain," he said, "it is my firm belief, based on uncounted years of experience, that we better get the hell out of here."

I agreed with him. We fired up (not the slightest hesitation of the motor this time), cranked in the drag, and headed back to east'ard. Goodness knows where we would make a lee, but lee we must make for the wind, instead of moderating, was pricking on. It's a long churn from Dennis Can to Billingsgate Island in the pitch dark with a sea broad on your beam. Every once in a while we'd catch a breaking sea just right and it would flood the cockpit several inches deep in ice-cold salt water. Dave sheltered himself as best he could in the companionway, but *Nonny*, rigged with mast and boom, winch and all the rigging that went with it, plus Dave's two hundred and some odd pounds, and my weight to boot, was exceedingly nose-heavy, so that all the water ran forward, instead of aft and out through the scuppers. In fact, so much ran forward that I thought it best for Dave to man the hand pump; moreover, it sloshed over the motor coaming and wet the distributor so I had to keep the Redwing at full throttle lest it stall.

Dave grumbled as he pumped, "Captain, I've made an east'ard passage through the North Atlantic under sail in the winter, and I've been through a typhoon in the South Pacific, but relative to the size of the vessel and the smallness of the water, this is a nasty little hole, ain't it."

It was another of those very black nights, not foggy, but no stars, no visible lights ashore. We kept ranging east to pick up Billingsgate Light (it wasn't until the next day we learned the light was out) until I was afraid I'd run us aground on the Eastham shore. All the time the Redwing ran smoothly enough if I left it wide open, but bucked and missed if I slowed the least bit.

Dave asked me, "Captain, ain't there supposed to be a harbor at Wellfleet?"

I admitted there was.

"Ever been there?"

"Once, on tip-top high water, on a calm day in August, with a skipper who was so drunk we could have been running over dry land for all he knew."

"Well," Dave said, "that makes it easier. We've got dead low water, on a pitch black night in March, with a skipper who is soaking wet. It's only nine o'clock, and I'd sleep a lot more comfortably in bed than I would in this five-by-two-foot bunk. Let us head for Wellfleet."

I was doubtful. I knew there were rocks scattered around Wellfleet Bay, but all the time we were debating we were heading for Wellfleet, and before we reached any decision we found ourselves in the middle of the Wellfleet draggers. In those days there was no landing dock at low water. It was the practice to moor out in the harbor and row ashore in a dory. We didn't have to worry about that just yet. Startled at being so close to so many boats, I slowed down without thinking, and the motor promptly died. Before we could drift over onto the mud flat to south'ard, I got Dave up forward to chuck over the anchor. It held, and there we were one hundred yards from shore, with a motor that wouldn't start, no dory, and no one on the beach at that time of night to take us off.

By this time I had added an extension to the Charlie Noble, as Dave persisted in calling the stove pipe, so we went below, lit a fire, and had fried chunks of Canadian bacon and sea scallops. I carefully covered the distributor itself, but I took the cap and laid it alongside the stove to warm and dry. When we had finished supper I put the cap back on and the Redwing kicked off the first thing. I ran us ashore and put Dave on the beach to scrounge a dory, then dropped back to bridle two anchors to hold us no matter which way the wind or tide shifted. Even in the lee of Wellfleet Harbor the wind whistled, and we found out the next morning that it had been blowing fifty-five miles an hour, gusting to sixty. So much for weather reports.

"What do we do now?" Dave asked.

"We walk up town till we find a telephone, call my wife and get her to drive down here to pick us up." So we two fishermen, grateful to be ashore but wet and cold, walked up through Wellfleet in

the middle of the night, looking for someone who would let us telephone for help.  In the first house with lights we came to was an
elderly gentleman sitting alone, reading in the living room.  We
knocked on his door and finally tapped on his window.

He came to the window.  "Go away!" he said clearly.

I shouted, "Can we use your phone please?  We got blown into
the . . ."

"No," he said, "ain't got no phone.  Go away."

And that was the reception we got all the way up town until we
came to the telephone exchange.  I rapped on the exchange door.
"Can we please put through a call to Eastham to get my wife to
come and pick us up?" I asked.

"Company rules won't let anyone in this building after five," the
girl said, "but I'll put through a call for you, if you want."  Bless her.

I gave her the number, she called, and after a delay long enough
for my wife to wake up, get out of bed, fumble to the phone and
answer, the operator said, "She wants to know where you'll be waiting."

I said the middle of Wellfleet Square.

The operator relayed the message and my wife hung up.  We sin-
cerely thanked the girl and wandered off to Wellfleet Square.  We
waited.  Dave said, "There's hardly any wind here, but I'm frozen."
We were both of us soaked to the skin.

I said, "Don't suggest it, Dave.  My wife is a very literal person.
I said we'd be in the middle of Wellfleet Square, and that is the only
place we'll be as far as she is concerned."

We waited and got colder.  We started to walk toward Eastham to
get warm.

My wife said afterward, very indignantly, "I had to get up, get
dressed, get both the children up and bundle them up.  Then I had to
get that old Ford running, which you know isn't always easy.  And
then I had to drive all the way to Wellfleet."

That's what she did.  She drove all the way to Wellfleet in spite of
the fact that as she went by I blinked a flashlight at her and Dave
yelled at the top of his lungs.  We had walked two or three miles toward home and she drove right by us.  Far from being upset, we
thought it was funny, and the two of us sat down by the side of the

road and laughed like a couple of nuts. She did just what I thought she would, she drove directly to Wellfleet Square and not finding us there, bethought herself of the two wild men who had tried to flag her down. She came back and picked us up.

"If you think I'm going to stop in the middle of the night and pick up a couple of bums . . ." she said. But she did.

The next morning we stopped at the hardware store long enough to pick up a new bucket (we'd lost the old one overboard during the night), and a new V-belt for the winch. On the way out of Wellfleet Harbor Dave spliced a new lanyard to the bucket. He was wonderful with rope and much of the splicing I know he taught me. Macramé and crewel work he did as a pastime, the way my wife knits. I was busy trying to find my way out the channel, wondering how we managed to stumble through the night before without hitting a rock or running aground, when Dave came to me with a mock military salute.

"Captain, sir," he said, "I wish to report the bucket is half a mile astern."

"What?"

"I . . er . . had it overside to fetch a bucket of water, sir, and the rushing billows snatched it from my grasp."

I said, "You nut! All the boating experience you've had and you don't even know how to get a bucket of water from a moving boat?"

"Begging your pardon, Captain," he protested, "I've had a flunkey to do that for me so many years I've forgotten how — if I ever learned."

It was like that all day. We found our spot and went to dragging. The very first tow the V-belt we had been using parted. Refrigerator belts were simply not made for that kind of work. We put on the new one. Long before the day was finished the second one parted and we had to horse the drag off the bottom and over the rail by hand. That finished our fishing and we headed home early. The next day I went to Boston to get V-belts and pulleys designed for the job, and hang the expense.

# 21

## I Go to East Dennis and Catch Stripers

I got twin pulleys and much heavier belts, a new shaft, and bearings designed for the job. We spent the next couple of days installing them. But we had delayed too long: someone dragging in the fog came on our flag buoy and, not knowing what it marked, tried a tow. Without us there to block them off the hole, they dragged right through it. The next day Dave and I fought off the big boats and finished with twenty-eight bushels aboard (Dave was never much at whittling sea scallops), and we nearly sank ourselves with the load. The big boats cleaned out the spot and filled the hole full of rocks and junk so that it never did produce again, and we had to hunt for another bed of scallops.

I went back to fishing alone. Actually, Dave had just gone along for the ride anyway, and the best we could find after that wasn't enough for the two of us. Rock Harbor at that time was filled with forty-foot (more or less) draggers and there was little place for a cockle-shell like *Nonny*. There were reports in the paper that East Dennis Harbor, commonly called Sesuit (pronounced 'Suet) had been dredged recently. Since we were dragging right off the Dennis shore the thought struck me that it was easier to drive a car than a boat and, if the dredging was all it was supposed to be, I could go fishing any time I wanted instead of fighting the tide and going in the middle of the night. (The dredging was not completed and the tide was still a factor, though the harbor was less than ten minutes from the grounds.)

I found my way to East Dennis and inquired where Mr. Sears lived.

"Which Mr. Sears?" was the reply. "There's only one house on this whole street which doesn't have at least one Mr. Sears living in it."

"Mr. Howie Sears?"

"Which Mr. Howie Sears? There are four of them."

"The Mr. Howie Sears who was recently appointed harbormaster."

"Oh, *that* Howie Sears. That's Old Howard Sears. He lives . . ."

So I hunted up that Howie Sears and eventually wound up with a berth on the west side of the harbor. (The east side was sacrosanct because the wife of one of the selectmen liked to swim there in the summer.)

The season was wearing on and it was getting to be striper time. *Nonny* was now encumbered not only with mast, boom, winch, and a four-by-eight-foot culling board, but also with outriggers and hand-lines neatly coiled, ready for the first fish to show up. I cruised around the Ledge with varying success. I finally found a spot about three miles straight off Corporation Beach where I could be sure of ten gallons of sea scallops a day. The big boats couldn't bother me there because I was protected on the east by a sand bar which came straight up out of ten fathoms to five. On the west was a long, barren flat in about eight fathoms. North and south of me were straight ledge, and the hole itself was full of rocks apparently as big as pianos.

Oh, they tried. I hadn't any more than worked the hole out than here came Al Harding (who was later drowned sea-scalloping off Stellwagen in *Ann H.*). Al was running Tony Peters' old *Triton* that year, and pulling two seven-foot drags. When I saw him coming I ran down and told him the situation. Whether or not he thought I was lying to keep him off the spot I don't know, but he dragged right into that steep sandbank and buried both drags so deep it took him the rest of the day to get clear. Then Warren Goff tried it in *Flavia*, a monstrosity of a converted ex-Coast Guard eighty-three-footer. If I remember rightly, he lost one of his drags in the rocks and had to part one of his cables to get clear. After that the big fellows left me alone.

It was almost nine-to-five fishing. The winch worked perfectly. If I hung up on a rock I simply turned *Nonny* on her heel, cut back the other way, turned the shenanigan drag over, and went on fishing. I could leave Sesuit on the ebb tide, drag my ten full bushels, anchor up just outside the mouth of the harbor in deep water and shuck out ten gallons, then pick up and come ashore. It was too regular; I might as well have been working ashore — almost.

On the way home nights I used to stop in at the Players' Pharmacy for a cup of hot coffee. Lennie Dubin, one of the brother-proprietors, kidded me every night. "You the great striper fisherman! No stripers tonight?"

I'd say, "Not yet, Lennie, it's still too early." Then came the day when the mackerel gulls showed up, dipping and wheeling as they do only when they come back in the spring, greeting me once again with the "Fe-e-esh, fe-e-esh, fe-e-esh" call that gives them the name of "liar birds." That night I said in answer to Lennie's kidding, "Two weeks from today, Lennie. Today's Wednesday. A week from next Wednesday when I come ashore I'll show you some stripers."

He laughed and kidded and had a wonderful time. For my part, I had no idea the old-timers were so right. Frank, I think it was, had told me that stripers show up two weeks to the day after the common terns. And they did.

I had dragged nine bushels of scallops and was working on my last one. Now, I've said *Nonny* was a little boat, and all the gear, plus forty fathoms of three-quarter-inch manila rope jumbled on the deck, plus nine full bags of sea scallops in the shell, didn't leave an awful lot of clear deck room. I had just hauled back on what was scheduled to be my last tow of the day when I looked up — and all the birds in the world were going crazy a mile or so offshore: mackerel gulls, herring gulls, gannets, and even an occasional loon.

I dumped the drag, rocks and all, with the scallops on the culling board, slipped off the belts from the winch, and headed for my kind of fishing. I flopped down the outriggers and secured them. For all my care in coiling down the handlines, they had somehow got tangled, so I was nearly into breaking stripers before I could get the first lure over. I cut the motor to trolling speed and jumped for the other handline, which was in an even worse mess than the first one. Before I could get that lure free I had a fish on the first line. Not a big fish, only fourteen to sixteen pounds, but the first striper nevertheless. I hauled him in, welcomed him aboard with a clout between the eyes, chucked over the rig and went for that snarled handline. I needn't

have hurried. I picked up one more fish the same size and that was
all. They sounded. I had no idea how long they had been up and
feeding, but, as always, they can disappear in an awful hurry.

I went round and round, trolling two lines. Finally I went to cutting my scallops, not shucking the guts overboard as usual, but throwing them onto the culling board. When I had finished my ten gallons
I kept on trolling and watching; then I began to strike my scallop
gear. I'd had enough sea-scalloping for that year. First the boom
came down, and all the blocks supporting it, then the mast and guys,
then the winch, and I even unbolted the culling board. I could tell
*Nonny* was feeling fancier and freer all the time.

Finally I gave up for the day, dumped the culling board and went
ashore. I began to grin — two weeks to the day! Would I ever rub
it into Lennie tonight! I carried home all the gear that poor Model
A could stagger under, leaving the rest on the shore for the next day.
I stopped in for my usual cup of coffee — and don't you know that
Lennie never said a word about what day it was, and when would the
stripers be here?

Not one minute longer could I stand it. "Lennie," I asked innocently, "what day is it anyway?"

"The fourteenth of May," said he.

"Yes, the fourteenth, but what day of the week?"

"Wednesday . . . Oh, yeah, Wednesday. This is the day the stripers
were due. Well, where are they?"

I said as casually as I could, though I was squirming with glee, "Oh,
they're in the back of my car, under all the gear."

"Oh, sure," he said, "oh, yeah. 'Two weeks from the day the
mackerel gulls get here,' he said, now he wants to sucker me into going out to look in the back of his car."

"Suit yourself. I don't care if you want to look at them." (I'd
never have forgiven him if he hadn't.) "Why else do you suppose I've
got the mast and boom lashed alongside the car?"

That convinced him. He went out to look and admire. He told it
all over town for the next summer that I could tell when the fish
were going to get here two weeks before they actually did.

Back to Rock Harbor I was bound, but not the next day — I had
made all plans to, but the fish bit heavy in the morning, and for per-

haps the only time in my life I guessed the weather right. It looked as though it would rain all afternoon and blow half a gale, so I quit at the last minute with the fish still hanging on, and sneaked into Sesuit. The boats from Rock Harbor were too far from home to get back in as I did. They had gotten there late anyway, because of the long run (yes, I had stopped on the way home to brag), and about the time the fish sounded it did come on to rain and blow and most of them took a pasting before they could get into Rock Harbor that night, with no fish to speak of. I was slowly learning the trade.

# 22

## Harris and I Learn the Striper Business

It was that year I paired up with Freddy Harris, and no man, even including old Frank, had so much influence on the way I was to live for the next twenty years. Freddy, as I have said, had accidentally shot off his left arm just below the elbow when he was in high school. He went off to Cornell University to study engineering and got interested in the mechanics of light, but his family's finances took a downward turn in his third year and he never finished. He was about my height, and his five-foot-ten frame was a little heavier than the one hundred and fifty pounds I carried then. His hair turned an early grey, and in a way he was rather handsome, or perhaps dignified is a more descriptive phrase, which is strange, for he was not one of the most dignified people I have ever met. He had that dry, hardly smiling sense of humor that some of the older Cape Codders wore. He had a way of turning a phrase to suit the situation.

"How long a line do you need, Fred," someone would ask.

"Just as long as from you to the fish and half an inch longer so the fish can get hooked," he'd solemnly answer. Looking at the traffic building up on the Cape even in those years, he'd say, "There's an awful lot of it, ain't there, and a lot of it's awful." He'd make the same remark about some overly plump female displaying more flesh than was demure. It was a gentle sort of wit, and in many ways Freddy was gentle.

When it came to fishing, though, Freddy was a driver. Hardly any day was too bad, hardly any water too rough. He taught me that if I wanted to be on top of the fish I had to be the first boat out in the morning; and more than one night he waited so long before he came in that I worried the tide would be too low for him to make it in.

"How about," he suggested, "you run *Nonny* and I'll run *Hazel Marie*, you pay your expenses and I'll pay mine, but we'll throw into the same box and share and share alike." It was fine with me. The hard days, the days when three or four fish were all the fleet caught, Freddy usually had them all, or most of them. With my two hands and a more able boat I could more than make up for it on the good days. We pretty well gave up night fishing, though we laid out a great many nights in order to get the daylight rise of fish. Freddy's comment was, "If you can't catch 'em when you can see 'em, you surely can't catch 'em when you can't see 'em, and can't-see to can't-see, daylight to dark, is long enough for even us fools to fish."

There was a great deal to learn, and no teacher except "cut and try." Artificial lures, excepting eel skins, Jap feathers and tin jigs, were all but non-existent. Striped bass were where you found them, or so we thought. (Frank had said, "Fish have got tails, they go where they want to," which is only partly true.) Though Freddy had trimmed Whit and me with rod and reel versus handline the year before, handlines were still the usual gear. Plugs, blown-up fresh-water plugs, were just beginning to seep into local usage, though we heard rumors they were being used at the Cape Cod Canal.

At Freddy's insistence I bought a second-hand rod and reel from Kid Baker, a Montague "Off Shore," a meat ax of a split bamboo rod, and a deep-spooled Penn #65, Long Beach reel. We both used "Cuttyhunk Style" linen line, usually forty-five-pound test. I had some years before adopted Polaroid (Freddy invariably referred to them as "Pulverized") sun glasses because I could see so much better into the water with them. It may seem peculiar that they be included with the tackle we used, but we wore them from sunrise to after sunset and would have felt naked without them.

One by one, plugs came into use. The first we had was a white swimming plug with a red head, made, as I remember, by Heddon. Then came the Martin "Mackerel," a very deep-swimming plug which worked much better after the original blue "mackerel" color had faded out. The first surface or "popping" plug we had was the Point Jude "22-A Blue Mullet." Next came the "Cap'n Bill" series in both swimmers and poppers, numbered one through eight. (As a matter of record, seven out of nine years running I brought into Rock Harbor the first striper of the year, each caught on a beat-up Cap'n Bill Number Seven, an almost white plug with pale blue streaks running diagonally down and fading out at the belly.) It was (and still is if you are lucky enough to have inherited one) a spring plug, I rather suspect because the alewives are running at that time of year. It is worth little later in the season. Creek Chub began showering us with plugs about that time, and while they were undoubtedly the best-made plugs we had, only the "thirty-oh" series of jointed plugs of varying colors worked for me. Eventually Bob Pond came out with the original Atom plug, the "Blue Herring-Scale," and then he finally evolved the plastic Atom, both swimmer and reverse. Then the market broke wide open and no one, including the tackle stores, could keep up with the flood of new plugs.

We not only had new gear, including braided nylon squidding line and flat spool reels, we learned how to use it. We soon learned not to come charging into a school of breaking fish — we put them down if we did. We learned that too long a trolled line gave a hooked fish a chance to head for the bottom to scrape the hooks off his mouth, but that the lure had to be far enough back from the boat (mostly we settled for from forty to fifty yards), or stripers wouldn't take it (unless the school was breaking wildly, in which case we could shorten up). We learned to circle a school in shallow water, or better still, to lay off with the sun behind the school (which made seeing difficult but tended to spook the fish less) and cast into it. We learned never to cast ahead of a fish, but to explode the plug on his tail. Gradually we learned the precept: the darker the day, the darker the plug.

We gradually discovered new fish grounds, most frequently by seeing fish break water, although a few secrets leaked out of Wellfleet and very occasionally a sportsfishermen came up with a new location. With perhaps the one exception of the so-called "New Ground," which really is not a specific location at all, we found every spot where striped bass are found consistently today. For these fish do not wander aimlessly; they locate in a very specific area because of food and/or the conditions caused by the tide running over the bottom. As long as there is sufficient food, stripers "stay put" all summer, and come back to the same areas year after year. We found that at certain locations the stripers fed on the ebb tide, that flood tide was feeding time in other areas.

Not that we learned this all the first year, but little by little we pieced it together. And we shared what we learned with the fleet, which was gradually building. "If you find something new and tell me," Freddy said, "and I find something new and tell you, then we'll both know something. But if I find a secret and you find a secret and we tell no one, then neither of us will know anything."

It was not all profitable. Our experience was limited, our tackle was rudimentary, and the fish didn't always co-operate. Our patience was limitless, but our credit wasn't. After three weeks of fishing and no fish I found my credit at the gas pump cut off. I couldn't really blame old Art Smith who owned the gas pump. The only time he ever saw me was when I was pumping gas into a tank which seemed always empty. But it was a shock; I very nearly went back to quahoging in Pleasant Bay.

Freddy said, when I told him, "Stick it out one more week. I'll lend you the money for gasoline." After an all-night discussion with my wife I agreed: one more week and then back to hanging onto the end of a quahog pole.

Don't you know the next day we loaded up with almost two hundred dollars worth of stripers? But others had been as hard hit as we by the shortage of fish and the expense of running. They had quit fishing and gone to waiting on the shore for us to find fish. We argued with them that if we all spread out we had a great deal better chance of someone's finding fish. Their attitude seemed to be, "Why should we waste time and money? You fellows know more about the business than we do, so go ahead and find the fish and we will come and help you catch them." It was upsetting to say the least.

We knew that two-hundred-dollar day that if we brought all those fish to the dock we would have a dozen or more boats following us the next day. We rebelled. Freddy put all the fish he had caught aboard *Nonny*, since she was the more able boat and I was known in Sesuit. I headed into that harbor. Old Howard met me at the shore and when I tossed out fish after big fish his eyes bugged out. He lent me a tarpaulin to cover the fish there on the beach, and I bribed him with one of the smaller stripers to keep his mouth shut for a day or two. Then I backed out and headed for Rock Harbor. Freddy was cute enough to know there would be some telltale signs, so we agreed to keep a couple of small fish apiece, not enough to arouse anyone's cupidity, but enough to explain the random scales which always escaped, and enough to give us an excuse to drive off toward Chatham to the fish buyers.

It worked — well, it worked one day, for it took that long for the word to filter down to Rock Harbor. We had one more day and then the whole fleet was out and everybody caught fish. From then on we had good days and we had bad days.

One particularly windy day we had skipped the morning tide, the wind was blowing so hard. On the high water that afternoon Freddy headed *Hazel Marie* out.

I shouted, "What's the matter? Are you nuts?"

"Come on, if I can go in this you can do fine in *Nonny*."

I said, "No you don't. I think too much of *Nonny* to put her through an afternoon like this."

It must have been blowing all of forty from the sou'west, but Freddy was going anyway — alone. I looked at his one arm. (No one who knew him well ever referred to it.) I thought of him all alone in that leaky boat with an ailing motor. I went with him. He sneaked up along the Brewster shore, making what little lee he could, though we were both soaking wet before we ever got far enough to catch any fish. But did we ever catch fish! Freddy had his hand full of boat, but all I did was haul lines, every one with fish on, first one and then the other, never paying any attention to where we were or how rough it was. I remember coming in as the tide fell and throwing fish out onto the dock until one of the dragger captains said, "Look at those two fools. They go out on a day when nobody else is foolish enough to go, in a boat that is good for nothing but a bonfire, and make more money than I can make on a good day, with a good boat, working all day." That was one of the good days.

I remember one day on the edge of the Shoal Ground when stripers were breaking all around us as far as we could see — and not the first fish could we catch. I finally caught one with my fly rod, and Freddy managed to foul-hook one. Though the weather was fair, that was one of the bad days.

Sometimes, looking back, I marvel how we trusted those little boats. After fishing all day, we went out again one night. Freddy was going to try the Brewster Flats, while I planned to find the edge of the Shoal Ground, three quarters of an hour out, with the fathometer, and work my way out and back. I went all alone, but Freddy, who had a license to carry paying passengers, took with him for pay a doctor he had picked up somewhere along the shore. The plan was to fish until we tired — tired, for goodness sakes? We had fished all day since daylight. Then we were to meet at Billingsgate Light to catch a few hours' sleep.

We went our separate ways, and I fished out along the Shoal Ground and back. It was clouding over so I finally stumbled to Billingsgate. No *Hazel Marie*, no Freddy. "Well," I thought, "maybe they went by The Ship." I ran the couple of miles back, but they weren't there, so I chucked over my anchor, left my anchor light burning, and turned in.

To show how tired I was: When I woke up the next morning the doctor was crowded into the spare two-foot bunk and Freddy, wrapped in rain gear, was half in, half out of *Nonny*'s cabin and I hadn't heard the first sound of their coming aboard.

# 23

~~~~~~~~~~~~~~~~

# The Ship

Now that I have brought The Ship into the story, I should explain. She is not an abandoned lightship, as is frequently claimed by people who write about Cape Cod. She was not wrecked there nor was she sunk by German torpedoes, as is occasionally claimed. She was, and is, the *James Longstreet*, official number 242-396, built by the Houston Shipbuilding Corp., Irish Bend Island, Houston, Texas. Completed in October 1942, she went ashore on the New Jersey coast October 27, 1943, at 40.27 N, 47 W, on a voyage to Southampton, New York. On November 23, 1943, she was refloated and towed to New York where she was dismantled. She was towed to where she is now the following spring and sunk "for gunnery target practice" (this specific information thanks to Charles W. Miller, Sr., Esmond, Rhode Island).

At first two men were kept aboard her. There had been installed a massive diesel pump and what looked to be a line of smudge pots all along her rail. On unannounced days a Coast Guard cutter would come from P'town and very politely come alongside each boat. It was, "Will you please maintain your present position," or, if a boat was too close, "Will you please move off to one thousand yards." The men aboard had meanwhile filled the smudge pots with fuel oil and lighted them. The cutter would take the pair off, and very, very high up a plane would drone over. The plane would drop two bombs, practice bombs of some sort with no explosives. They must have been very large because when they hit the spray would fly as high as the mastheads of the *Longstreet*, sitting there on the bottom in three fathoms. The cutter would put the men back aboard and head back for P'town. The men would put out the smudge pots and we would go back to fishing.

The cutter was always very polite, almost apologetic, about the whole thing — except on one day. Asa Lee and his son Dick were dragging quahogs right up under The Ship in *Helen* when the cutter came prowling around the bow. As soon as they were within hailing distance someone yelled on the bullhorn, "Get the hell out of there!" Asa, who could use some pretty fancy language himself on occasion, was so surprised at this rudeness that all he could stutter was, "Y-y-yes, s-s-sir." Needless to say, he got away from there.

Not everyone did, and yet no one was ever hit, to my knowledge. A character showed up during that summer in an old Coast Guard surf boat. He had built a sort of Quonset hut amidships for living quarters. I don't know that anyone ever got very friendly with the cuss, though he tied up for awhile in Rock Harbor. Harris and I both tried to teach him how to catch stripers, but like a lot of greenhorns he knew more than we did.

On the day he didn't run from The Ship, we were fishing Stony Bar, north and east from The Ship. The cutter came alongside and warned everyone. The smudgepots started to smoke. The plane came over, and then, to my horror, I saw the surf boat hove to, just clear of The Ship's stern. Never waiting to haul in my lines, I hooked up and headed for him, thinking he must be broken down. The plane made a dry run, then circled back quite low, forward and aft of The Ship. It dropped two little bombs, crunch, crunch — like that. The surf boat just lay there. I was getting closer now, my lines were in and I was busy faking down a rope to tow with. Again the plane circled, this time lower than before; this time it dropped only one little bomb, so close it splashed water into the cockpit of the surf boat. At that this character reached over, threw his boat in gear and moved off toward me perhaps a hundred yards.

I was puzzled as I came alongside, for his motor was running, idling. "Hey," I said, "you all right? You want a tow?"

"Oh, I'm all right," he drawled, "I just got my lines tangled and came over here to make a lee while I untangled them."

"But that plane is dropping bombs!"

"Oh, I don't think he will as long as I am here," said he.

I screamed at him, "What the hell do you think that plane just dropped? Eggs?"

"Oh, no," said he, "they were little bombs, but you saw how careful they were not to hit me."

I got away from there, and he eventually moved back to the fleet. Maybe the pilot would be careful not to hit him, but I had seen a good many times when the bombs didn't go precisely where they had been aimed. In fact, the next year, after the men had moved off The Ship and the planes went to bombing any old time with little nine-inch, cast-iron bombs with a charge about the size of a 10-gauge shotgun shell, they got mighty careless with them. We live three-quarters of a mile from shore, which would put us over three miles from The Ship, and twice, during the years, bombs have dropped in our front yard. The story seems to be that the bombs stick in their racks, and with the weather just right the planes make their turn before the bombing runs just over our house and the bombs which have stuck in the racks shake loose. I don't suppose they would do any real damage, but one would make an awful mess of Sunday dinner if it came through the roof.

In later years they got to firing five-inch rockets from jets, and that was a bird of a different feather. The TBF's (whether that's what they were or not, that's what we called them) were one thing; we could see them coming and get away from the target area, and they always made one dry run. The jets, however, fired rockets before we even knew they were anywhere around. On top of that, the little bombs the TBF's dropped hit once, made a flash and a puff of smoke, and that was that. The rockets, however, even when they hit The Ship (and they usually came pretty close) would go right through both sides of The Ship and ricochet as far as two miles — they were five feet long. In spite of the fact that the "Danger Area" on the charts of recent years had been set at one thousand yards, complaints to the Coast Guard seldom produced much satisfaction, even when we were many times one thousand yards away. "You are in a danger area," they would inform us (just as though we didn't know), "You'll have to move out." Thanks for nothing.

While The Ship was a nuisance at first — they plunked it right in the middle of the very best striper grounds we had — it proved a benefit in a great many ways. First, it made a lee in stormy weather: many a sunrise found twenty or thirty boats anchored snug up to it. It was reasonably safe, for the planes seldom bombed it before sun-up, and never in thick weather. It hadn't been there a month before we were using it to range on. "Put the foremast under the crooked tree at Campground," and we had one range for the Sandpatch striper ground, and so on. After so many years of depending on it, I sometimes wonder if anybody could find his way home without The Ship to guide on.

For years there was no light anywhere near it. We petitioned the Coast Guard, saying that it was a navigational hazard at night or in a fog. The answer we got was, "Small boats shouldn't be out at night or in a fog." Thanks again for nothing. Then all of a sudden there was a little green blinker flashing merrily a quarter of a mile to west-'ard. It seems that Zibe Crosby had some high Navy Brass with him one early morning before daybreak in *Marilyn*. Zibe ran his course out, swung up into the wind, and there was The Ship looming over him. "Where's the light on that thing?" says the Brass. "No light," says Zibe, "We're not supposed to be out at night or in the fog." It's wonderful what scaring the right people can do.

Sometimes the wrong people got scared, though. The way this particular trip got started is a little round-about, but bear with me. Harris had a license to carry passengers for hire — I had none. (I got mine the next year.) Harris also had free-loading friends. Sometimes when he had a paying party he put his free-loading friends aboard *Nonny*. We were packing fish at Thompson's Snow Inn one after-noon when Harris said to me, "Will you take this fellow out fishing tomorrow? Name's Farnum," or some such. Thinking he was one of Harris' friends, I said why not.

We arranged for Farnum to meet us the next morning at the dock at four a.m., sailing time. He was there on time and so was I, but Harris wasn't, and Harris was never late. We waited and the tide kept dropping until it looked as though we had all waited too long. At the last minute Harris wheeled into the parking lot with one of his free-loading friends. George had gotten drunk the night before and was sick on the way to the harbor, and that's why Harris was late. (He'd slept at George's house.) It also developed that there were two other characters waiting in the parking lot to go with Harris. "You take George and Farnum," Harris said, "and I'll take the other two."

I was considerably irritated — I get that way when things go wrong and I've been fishing twenty hours a day for so long I can't remember when I've had a full night's sleep. George handed me a bottle. Had I not been irritated I would have refused it, figuring I had enough trouble without the booze. As it was I put it to my head and found it was empty.

I chucked the bottle out into the creek and said, "If you have got to go, come on." Hardly waiting for them to get aboard I slipped the dock lines, fired up the Redwing and took off. As we went by the range light pole at the entrance to the harbor Farnum said to me, "That looks like an electric light pole."

I said shortly, "It is, or was."

The tide had dropped so far the sedge grass showed on both sides of what little channel there was. Farnum said, "That looks like grass."

I said even shorter, "It is."

Now, long before my time it had been the custom of the fishermen out of Rock Harbor to pump down a line of pine trees, trimmed at the bottom but with their needles still on at the top, as a guide to where the deepest water was. With the tide dropping vertically six inches every fifteen minutes it is easy to see how eight or ten inches more water might make a difference. As we went by the third or fourth tree, Farnum said, "My god! Aren't those pine trees?"

I felt *Nonny* scrape bottom and I was in no mood for idle explanations. I said, "The damn things will grow anywhere." Then, having cleared the last tree I hooked open the throttle and headed off north-by-west. It was cloudy and blowing fairly hard from the sou-'west. *Nonny* was a rocking chair in a trough, but she could throw a considerable spray. I said brusquely, "You better get below before you get wet."

He went below into *Nonny*'s little cabin — briefly. It never entered my head he would get seasick and I wouldn't have cared anyway. I was concentrating on holding a lively little boat on a compass course in the dark and the wet, and it bade fair to be very rough before the day was out. I ran my time out with not a soul saying a word. Twenty minutes, and I hauled up into the wind and cut my throttle. There, looming directly over us, was the bulk of The Ship. I cut a tight circle, stopped the ignition, and went up forward to drop the anchor.

Poor Farnum. If ever a man had cause to be frightened, it seems he had. It turned out he had never been to Rock Harbor in the daylight. He said, "I thought you were drunk with that bottle you threw overboard, then we rushed by utility poles, through tall grass, and even pine trees like somebody's pasture. Then you sent me below decks where I got seasick. I came on deck to find the boat rolling horribly, then I thought you were going to kill us all because you said, 'Good, there's The Ship,' and you almost ran into what I thought was a freighter under way."

The day was saved when at the crack of dawn we got into wild fishing. It was so rough I had my hands full of boat, but George was experienced and he bawled orders like a bucko second mate on a windjammer. "Haul that line! Gaff that fish! Get out of the way or make yourself useful!"

Said George afterwards, "I thought he was a friend of yours — I didn't know he was a paying guest." I didn't know he was a paying guest either until he handed me the ten dollars Harris had told him I charged. But Farnum was game: he came back again and fished for years with Harris. I guess one trip on *Nonny* was enough.

# 24

~~~~~~~~~~~~~~~~~~~~~~~~~~~~~~~~~~~~~~~~~~~~~~~~~~~~~~~~~~~~~~~~~~~~~~~

# Harris and I Make Hyannis

We fished through that summer, learning a great deal and earning a sort of living. Fall came and we decided to take both boats around the Cape, *Hazel Marie* into the Town Cove for some badly needed repairs, and *Nonny* to Pleasant Bay to go back to flounder dragging. (On this annual migration Harris agreed to pick up Gene Fulcher, in the boat which later became known as *Wild Duck*, and tow him from Chatham over the bar into Town Cove so Gene could work on the boat that winter.)

In the middle of the night we left in *Nonny* and got as far as Herring Cove, just south of Race Point. It was cold, so before we turned in to wait for daylight I lit a fire in the Shipmate with charcoal briquettes. It was a wonder we weren't both asphyxiated, for we closed *Nonny*'s sliding hatch tight and both turned in. We awoke about the same time, both of us groggy and with a raging headache, but the clear, cold morning air cured us, and we went the long, uneventful trip to Nauset. Chatham Inlet is rugged enough, but Nauset Inlet is usually worse. It changes with every storm; that trip it was not too bad. We had studied the shifting channel from Nauset Heights the day before we left Rock Harbor, and while an easterly swell was gradually building from a storm offshore, *Nonny* was such a little lady she brought us through with hardly a drop of water on deck.

We were ashore just long enough to gas up *Hazel Marie*, then took off for the Cape Cod Canal, to go around the Cape the other way. Harris' headache had come back (the guy never did eat properly, living while he was offshore on peanut butter and jelly sandwiches,

Hershey bars and Coca-Cola). With our very old chart I made the Canal entrance as best I could, while he tried to sleep off his headache. He took over at the entrance, and with no knowledge or thought that we should report to the Army Engineers we started through. The Engineers caught up with us and were pleasant enough; they wanted to know simply where we were from, where we were going and other relevant information. Then we proceeded on our way until we came to the railroad bridge.

It wasn't open and we innocents didn't know enough to blow a horn to get it open. So we circled there in frustration. There was a strong-running tide west (or south as they figure it there). Harris finally brought *Hazel Marie* up into the tide, and we backed under the bridge, letting the tide carry us gently. There was less than a full inch clearance. I couldn't put my hand on top of the running lights, which were atop the cabin overhead, without scraping the skin off on the ironwork above us. Once clear of the bridge we hooked up and made our way down Buzzard's Gulch ("Bay" on the chart).

Wood's Hole and the fast-running tide there was new to both of us, but except for an encounter with a tug bringing through what looked to be about a half-mile of dredging barges — which called for some fancy dodging — we had no trouble. The day was overcast but there was little sea, and we banged away, planning to spend the night in Stage Harbor or Wychmere and continue the next day. That's what we planned, but we didn't get there.

We were just in sight of Bishop and Clerk's Light, off Hyannis, when the motor came to a coughing halt. It was getting on toward dark. Said I, "What do you suppose is the matter?"

Said Harris casually, "Oh, I suppose we're out of gas." Just as I had done the previous spring, he too had laid by a five-gallon G.I. can for a spare. But he, too, had neglected to bring along a funnel or pouring spout. Putting gasoline into a one-inch pipe on *Nonny*'s stern was one thing, but *Hazel Marie*'s filler pipe, being also an inch in diameter, was up forward. There was no toe rail, no hand rail, nothing but a needle-sharp triangle of slippery deck. Furthermore, although we hadn't noticed it while we were running, there was a very decided swell, and *Hazel Marie*, once her motor was stopped, lay very uneasily in the trough. So there I was in the fast approaching dark, balanced against an unhappy swell, trying to get what I could of five gallons of gas down a skinny little pipe. Since I was a long way from the machinery, as soon as I poured in a little gas, Harris started the motor and jogged with the boat's head up into the sea. It was a slow, tiresome process, but finally the can was empty. I put the cap back on, flushed the deck (and my feet at the same time) with several buckets of salt water and worked my way aft.

I said, "Harris, you better make for Hyannis Harbor. I don't believe we've got enough gas to make Wychmere."

He said stubbornly, "We set out for Wychmere."

I said, "I'm aware of that, but I don't know how far it is and you don't know how far it is, and nobody's going to come looking for us if we don't get in. Damned if I want to spend the night drifting around Nantucket Sound because you were so stubborn."

He asked, "Have you ever been in Hyannis Harbor?"

I said, "My wife and I eloped to Hyannis."

With reason he asked, "What has that got to do with it?"

I said, "Nothing, but from the shore it looks as though the channel comes in straight enough. There's lots of boats use the harbor; seems as though the channel would be marked." (By now it was too dark to read the antique chart, and we had no flashlight.)

So we headed for Hyannis, and found that they were in the process of dredging and that there was a whole line of pontoons and dredging equipment to follow. Luckily, we got on the right side to start with and weren't hedged off from the dock. The harbor master was somewhat irritated with us for coming in at that time of night. (Goodness knows what *he* was doing there then.) Finally, he let us use a phone so I could call my wife to come after us. I don't know which was stronger, her relief at having us safely in for the night, or her irritation at having to bundle up the kids again and tool that old Model A all the way to Hyannis.

# 25

# We Run Nauset Inlet

After a reasonable night's rest my wife had us at Hyannis before daybreak, fueled and ready to go. The boat ride to Stage Harbor was not all that long after the day before, but I doubt we would have had gas enough to make it without refueling. The plan was — we had stopped on the way home to make sure — for Buddy Henderson, who was dragging quahogs off Stage Harbor at that time, to tow *Wild Duck* with Gene and his helper aboard to the Powder Hole at the south end of Monomoy Point, and to anchor her there at daybreak. *Wild Duck* was simply a stripped-down hull at that time, no motor of any kind, forty feet long and riding very, very high when we finally took her in tow — which was not immediately, for she wasn't at the Powder Hole. We waited and waited and finally set out for Stage Harbor. Buddy had brought her down as far as he was going, and there Gene had been waiting since shortly before daylight.

We hooked her on a long tow and started around Monomoy. Luckily for us we had little wind or sea as we made our way north past Chatham Inlet. Glancing back now and then to see whether our tow was riding easily, I realized a ten-foot swell had built up. The offshore storm which had made Nauset Inlet seem rough the day before — was it only yesterday morning we had run Nauset Inlet in *Nonny*? — had intensified and, while there was no wind chop to speak of, the swell was high enough so that there were times when *Wild Duck* was high above us, and times when all we could see of her was her wheel house.. About that time we also discovered that through our ignorance and the delay, we were now having to buck a fast south-running tide. We were covering bottom very, very slowly. I did a little calculation. "Freddy, do you realize we are going to hit Nauset Inlet with about a two-hour ebb, and the tide is going to be against this swell?"

"I also realize," said he, "we're damn near out of gas."

I said, "Now aren't you glad I remembered to bring along that funnel?" I was, because just before we got to Nauset Inlet Freddy hove to and I went up forward on that wet, narrow, triangular fore-deck to pour in our last five gallons of gasoline.

While we were hove to Freddy said, "Get Gene to shorten up the tow, 'way up, about thirty feet behind us."

I protested. "Not in rough water. Nobody shortens up a tow in rough water, you lengthen it out."

Freddy had thought ahead of me; he pointed out that there were two right angle turns in the channel and he couldn't possibly control *Wild Duck* if she was too far astern. I conceded his point but shuddered at the thought of that great ark so high over our stern. I talked Freddy into letting me rig a sort of bridle from the cleats on our counters. I let it drop back nearly twenty feet from our stern, then rigged on it a snatch block which I moused closed, and to which I secured the tow rope. Now whichever way Freddy turned, the strain would come from that side and we would have better turning power. I cleared every movable thing from the deck and secured or lashed down what I couldn't stow below decks or in the cabin. I pumped the bilge dry. Freddy asked if I wanted to put on a life jacket.

I said, "What the hell for? If we do sink we wouldn't stand a chance with that monstrosity running us down. Anyway, we're not going to sink so why the life jackets?"

I don't know about other people at a time like this, but I begin to sweat no matter how cold it is. My mouth gets dry. All my senses seem sharpened, I see better, hear better, smell better, and if I don't have to talk — because if I do I tend to stutter — I think more clearly.

*Hazel Marie* was not the handiest-rigged boat I was ever on: all the controls were in the little stoop-over cabin. In order to see forward clearly Harris had to stick his head out one of the two little forward windows like a turtle from a shell — and then he couldn't see aft. So we lay hove to, waiting for a slack spell in the breakers

— with the ebb tide and the easterly swell there were breakers clear across the Inlet. Freddy crouched in the cabin with the motor idling. "Tell me when." His voice was hoarse with strain.

It was not simple. It's one thing to wait a slack spell at the mouth of an inlet when the boat's running free and can jump from a standing start to full throttle in seconds. It was something else to have in tow a boat that weighed four or five times as much as we did, to judge the seas far enough back to get ourselves and our tow underway. I counted seas. Somewhere, I recalled, I'd read that the notion that a sequence of seven big seas is followed by a series of smaller ones is sheer superstition. Maybe so. Maybe so. We waited out a series of three. Another series of three — no, four, five, six, I could see behind the seventh one — it looked reasonably calm — I yelled to Freddy, "Pour it to her!"

The motor raced, the wheel dug in, and the tow rope came tight with a jolt that slewed us sideways for an instant. Up we rode on that breaking crest as it roared under and by us, leaving us with a barrel or more of water aboard. The downhill pull of that sea started *Wild Duck* flying behind us. All the way in to the first turn we rode in comparative calm, but I could see a big one building behind us as *Wild Duck* towered over us.

"Cut it, Freddy," I yelled. "Let this one go by." It went by, most of it. It was a good thing Freddy had slacked off because it would have caught us broadside just as it broke. As it was, our slowing down and the added push of the wave brought the helpless *Wild Duck* roaring down on us, right down on our stern.

"Go!" I shrieked at Freddy, and go he did, right on the back of the wave, at right angles to the course of that behemoth bearing down on us.

The *Wild Duck* on the end of her short tow fetched up against our straining bridle so that the snatch block was jammed clear against our starboard cleat — she had gone right ahead of us. That five-cylinder Gray never faltered, and by the time the next sea broke *Hazel Marie* was clear of the first bar. The next sea broke aboard *Wild Duck*, but we had her pulled clear before another one could come. The second right-angle turn was not so bad for the seas weren't half the size of the ones on the outer bar.

When we were through and headed up the channel into the Cove, Freddy said weakly, "Come take over, will you?" He was not a swearing man, Freddy, other than an occasional "hell" or "damn," but he came on deck and shook his fist at *Wild Duck*, riding serenely behind us. "Before I'd ever go through that again," he said, "I'd take the goddamn motor out of the goddamn boat and shove it down the sonofabitch's throat." That was all he ever said about that trip. If someone else mentioned it he would give a sickly smile and change the subject.

Of all the men I ever went fishing with, perhaps only five would stand up to a frightening experience like that trip: Freddy, of course; old Captain Dave Delano, who had fifty years' experience including trips undoubtedly far more dangerous; Captain Art Gorham (of whom more later), who had thirty years experience as a fireboat captain; my own son Pete, who is as silent and as fast-thinking under pressure as anyone I ever fished with; and one mate, Arnold Miner, who later went into the merchant marine. That's not a very long list after thirty-five years of fishing, but it is amazing to me how many men go all to pieces when they need most to be steady. Twice in my winter fishing in Florida I had to take over a boat or be drowned, once in Hillsboro Inlet and later in St. Lucie Inlet, because the skipper quit in sheer terror and let the boat go where it would. A number of times fishing northern waters I've had to threaten violence to control passengers or helpers, and then there's the type who simply freezes, seeing nothing, hearing nothing. I suppose it's something a man can't help, but it's awfully comforting to have a partner like Harris who settles down and does what has to be done. It was shortly after that trip that Harris put aboard *Hazel Marie* the bronze plaque which he later put on both *Kitty W.*'s. It said, "Oh, God, thy sea is so big and my boat is so small." And that's not a bad thought to have in mind when you're boating or fishing.

# 26

~~~~~~~~~~~~~~~~

# Lobstering

We put the mast and boom and hauling gear aboard *Nonny* that fall and went to flounder dragging until we finally got frozen in The River in Orleans. Then we went to work on *Hazel Marie*, putting in a new deadwood. She needed a new horn timber, too, but Harris would spare neither the time nor the expense of putting one in. We patched her as best we could with a rubber gasket made of an old inner tube, covered with sheet lead securely tacked with a double row of copper tacks. The poor old thing was so flexible, we found the next year, and her stern wagged vertically so much, that the flexing would break the best sheet lead clear across in three days.

Instead of putting the time into *Hazel Marie* we came up with the idea of going into the lobstering business. Knocked-down lobster pots, even in those years, were selling for around six dollars apiece, and since we needed at least a hundred pots this seemed like too much money.

After shopping around we bought five hundred square feet of unseasoned, unplaned white oak, an inch or more thick, in random widths and twelve feet long. We carried this to a mill in Chatham and had most of it ripped into quarter-inch laths, the balance into two-inch pieces for frames. It was beautiful stock, clear and knot-free and I agreed with the mill owner it was a shame to cut it into laths, but we carted the whole pile home and I went to building lobster pots.

Lobster pots, or traps, vary from one location to another, but in principle most of them work the same. There is a front section with an entrance on each side (in some areas it is customary to have only one). This section is usually about one third the total length and has a spindle set midway on which to secure bait. Between the front section and the "parlor" or back section there is a twine funnel, operating on the same principle as the center "nozzle" in an eel pot.

While our dimensions were not standard, this being the first time either Harris or I had dabbled in lobstering, the pots we built were about four feet long by two feet wide by a foot and a half high. (They were too big to be handy.) We built rectangular pots for two practical reasons: first, a rounded top meant steamed bows, which was complicated; and second, in the water we planned to fish, tide run was not a major factor (the theory being, as we understood it, that a fast tide run was less apt to roll over pots with a rounded top).

Dowelling the corner pieces presented a problem. After the devil's own time we managed to borrow a female auger that was probably left over from the days of the wooden wagon wheel. Applied to the end of an inch-square piece of oak, instead of boring out the center and leaving a hole, it bored away the outer edge and left the center, a round, projecting, dowel three quarters of an inch in diameter.

In order to get out the lobsters we might catch, we made a slatted door on top, hinged with strips of old tire casings and locked with extended battens which caught under the top of the main pot. The heads ("funnels" or "nozzles") I netted of a two-strand, soft-laid nylon heading twine, made especially for the purpose. The number of meshes and the ratio of tapering fitted the dimensions of the pot, of course. While the nylon was soft and smooth to the touch, by the time I'd pulled the knots tight enough my hands were as sore as hard work ever made them.

Since we would be fishing in water usually eight and no deeper than ten fathoms, and since the tide run was not fast enough to pull the buoys under, we spliced on the front top of each pot a twelve-fathom buoy line. We made cedar four-by-four buoys two-feet long, painted (the State, which licensed us, allowing us to pick our own colors) white on one end, orange on the other, with a narrow black stripe to set off both colors. Peter Bruce made us a branding iron, and into each pot and buoy we burned the initials "PJS."

When my cellar was cleared I went into construction, while Harris took it into his head to go off gallivanting to Florida and Louisiana with Bruce Hammatt (who, by his tell, had been a Louisiana cowboy before he came to fish on Cape Cod).  All that winter I worked building lobster pots (Harris came back later and brought his friends to help).  Then evenings I netted nylon heads until my hands were so sore I had to ease off for a while.

It wasn't as monotonous as you might think, for most of the fishermen were frozen in and had nothing to do.  Knowing that I would be in the warm cellar busily pounding galvanized nails into oak, they would show up one by one until the cellar was so full of laughing, joking, horse-playing fisherman there wasn't room for me to work.  I'd pound on the kitchen floor overhead and shout, "Coffee break!"  And in due time my wife would stomp back, "Coffee's on!"  We would troop upstairs, dragging sawdust, mud and snow into the house.  After a quick cup I'd head downstairs again, and one by one the fishermen would disperse, leaving me to get something done and my wife to clean up after them.  My wife used to say, "I don't mind the four or five pounds of coffee a week we're using (although with no money coming in it was an item) but I can't keep cookies or pie or cake in the house.  And besides, I do wish they'd clean their feet before they come clumping through the living room in their rubber boots."

Harris' coming home from Louisiana put a stop to most of the gamming.  He brought home five pounds of what he called "Louisiana coffee."  Cooking, it smelled like ether.  I phoned Ann Hammatt to ask how she brewed it.  "Oh," said she, "just like regular coffee."  We brewed it that way.  Strong?  It made coffee so strong the boys said it broke the cups, ate away the silver on the spoons, and dug furrows in their teeth.  Maybe yes, maybe no, but it effectively drove away the company which was welcome enough but totally distracting when it came to getting the lobster pots built.  I came to like the stuff, somewhat diluted.

That spring I took time out to go to the Coast Guard Headquarters in Boston to get a license to carry passengers for hire.  The test was somewhat different from that given today.

The August Person who gave out Master Mariner's tickets examined me.  "How many years have you been fishing?" he asked.

I counted on my fingers.  "Thirteen," I finally answered.

"Why did you never come for a license before?"

Very brashly I said, "I never needed it before, but with the price of fish where it is, it looks as though I'd have to start carrying tourists or quit fishing."

"Can you box the compass?"

"Yes, sir."

"Start at north-by-west and go backwards."

I gave him half a dozen points.

He reached over and put his signature on my license. "Try to stay out of trouble," he grumbled.

I said, "Yes, sir, thank you, sir."

I came home and slapped a quick coat of paint on *Nonny*. We came around the Cape together to Rock Harbor. No sweat, no trouble. Does it gradually come clear why I loved *Nonny* so? She was always ready to go, no troubles, no leaks; she needed nothing but a scrubbing and a couple of coats of paint.

We left the mast and boom in and added a heavy davit, our plan being to sea-scallop most of the day and haul lobster pots to finish out. We set the pots on Dennis Ledge, in areas where the rocks were so rough no one could drag. I'd built the pots solidly, with so much wood they wouldn't sink the first day, so we had to go in and steal half of the Dennis breakwater to add rocks to each pot. After they'd soaked up enough water we took the rocks out, but we still had to leave in eight red bricks. Although the pots were oversized for the water we were fishing, they did fish well. Everyone said we wouldn't get any lobsters the first few days, until the air bubbles had quit rising, and April was too early to start anyway. Everyone was wrong. Almost without exception the pots caught lobsters as soon as they were set — setting them all took several days for the most *Nonny* could carry was fourteen pots per trip. True enough, most of the lobsters were cripples, one-clawed, no claws, or with their shells cracked or damaged one way or another. I always thought they must have wintered there and been damaged by the sea-scallopers. But since no one else was bringing in local lobsters at that time we could sell all we caught right on the dock, including cripples.

For our first bait we scrounged trash fish from the sea-scallop draggers: skates, sea robins, sculpins — almost any fish they caught and would normally have thrown away. Later on we went to ale-wives we caught ourselves in the local herring runs and salted in barrels, and still later we bought menhaden from the fish traps.

During the winter, Harris, who had a ham radio license, suggested we put in two-way radio telephones. This was far out because electronics wasn't yet playing a big part in fishing, particularly not in the Bay. Bruce Hammatt in *Ann H.* and Freddy in *Hazel Marie* had put in radio phones the previous year: war surplus monstrosities (Russian tank radios, actually) they bought at Macy's or some such place. Bruce and Freddy spent more on having them converted than they cost in the first place. The sets drew an awful lot of power and were such murder on batteries that neither of them could be kept on for more than a few minutes at a time.

The radio idea sounded good, so in the middle of winter when there was absolutely no money coming in, Harris sent off for a couple of Islip ten-watters. We built home-made antennas by winding a cane pole with a specified length of wire. I know nothing whatsoever about radios, but this I know about those rugged little ten-watters: They were the Model T's of the radio world. They were crude, and they were eventually outlawed by the FCC, but nothing seemed to hurt them. *Nonny*'s was hung on the cabin bulkhead so I could reach it through the companionway. It got rained on, it got doused with salt water, it got banged with everything including people who went through the companionway — and it kept right on working. When I turned the switch on in the morning it sounded as though I had set off a bunch of firecrackers. It would snap and crackle until I thought it was going to blow up. Then it would quiet down when it had dried out and I was in business.

Fishing the way we did, with two boats more or less independent of each other, the radios made sense, except for one thing. One or the other of us would have enough of the chatter-chatter, yak-yak that went on, even in those days, and he'd shut off the set. Then, of course, he might as well have left the set at home for all the good it did.

When the stripers arrived in May we split up and went to using *Hazel Marie* for striper hunting and *Nonny* for lobstering. We struck the sea-scallop gear and simply left winch and davit. I rigged with a slatted car, big enough to hold all the lobsters I would be apt to catch, attached a flag buoy, and added twenty fathoms of buoy line and a good, light anchor. If Harris called me, as he frequently did, by the time I got where the fish were hitting I had my outriggers over and my lines ready. As I reached the spot I'd chuck the lobster car overside, and follow it with the flag and anchor. It would stay there until I was ready to go, and the lobsters wouldn't suffer from being out of water all the while I was fishing. It was a way of making bread-and-butter money for both of us and still covering the striper situation where a great deal more money might be made.

# 27

## Plug-Casting

That year we started after stripers with outriggers and handlines, but before the year was out almost all our fishing was done with "fish poles." ( A word about "fish poles," "fishing rods," and "sticks": The absolute greenhorn who never saw salt water before will usually say "fish pole." The neophyte, the novice, will say very properly, "fishing rod," "rod," and then "fish rod" in that order, as he progresses. The semi-pro, so to speak, will refer to his "stick." Into this category fall most tackle store operators, most sports writers, most beach buggy operators, and those moonlighters who can't quite stay away from fishing. It is only after a fish pole becomes almost an extension of a man's arm and hand that it again becomes a "fish pole.")

It began to look as though this year was a continuation of the year before, but no two years are quite the same. All the stripers in Cape Cod Bay went into shallow water, and we got so we literally knew individual fish in each school. We spent untold hours in shallow water, on the Brewster Flats, at Sunken Meadow, in the holes back of Billingsgate (the west side, that is) and at Ryder's Beach. We would be there when the tide began to drop, at low water, and on the first of the flood. It was difficult fishing, but the lessons we learned could never have been learned elsewhere. Here *Nonny* was at home. I don't doubt I scraped inches off her skinny little white-oak keel, for I was forever running aground on one or another sand bar, not accidentally, but deliberately to chase the elusive striped bass.

That was 1947, the year we learned to plug-cast for stripers. With all the fish in shallow water, in water where trolling was not only impossible but completely unproductive, casting for stripers became a way of making a living. The set-up was quite different than it had been before. The water was shallow, the bottom was clear, white sand, and we could — under most conditions — see every fish. As I said, we got to know individual fish in various schools, where they would be at what time of the tide, and how they would react.

There was one twenty-five-pounder, for instance, who had been hooked before. He wore a blue plug crossways, just back of his eyes. If we threw a blue plug at him he went elsewhere, I suppose because he had had enough of blue plugs. There was another fish of about the same size, the whole side of whose face was white scar tissue. One really big fish, so far as length went, lived in the hole on the south side of Billingsgate Island; apparently he was sick because, while he was over four feet long, he was as skinny as could be. Then, there was a small, very dark striper that I took to be a tautog the first time I saw him. (Tautog come up into shallow water to spawn in the early summer.) But the little fellow was a striper all right, for when he turned on his side to scrape off the sea lice I could see his stripes quite clearly.

Living with fish as intimately as that, we got to know when and where they would feed. We learned an amazing accuracy in casting, though we had no need to learn distance casting. We regularly wore out a line a week, just shooting it out through the guides and crank-ing it in.) Harris got so good, with his one arm, that at seventy feet and using a tin jig, he could make a drifting quart oil can jump three out of four trys.

He got the notion that if the fish wouldn't bite his lure, maybe he could harpoon them. He made what was in appearance a brass knitting needle, slightly more than a quarter-inch in diameter and about fourteen inches long. He sharpened the leading end to a point and then hacked notches in it to act as barbs. He drilled a hole in the other end and threaded through a strip of cloth to act as feathers do on an arrow, and also tied his line here. Time after time he wait-ed until a big striper got within range, and then — slam! Every time it looked as though he had harpooned his·fish. Every time the needle bounced or slid over the fish. What blew the whole thing was that on one of his casts the striper he aimed at actually turned about and bit the needle. Harris was so mad he cut his line and threw the brass thing at the next fish that came along. He was none the happier for our kidding suggestions that he solder hooks on the rig and maybe invent a new lure.

We learned to cast behind a fish rather than in front of him. We learned a surface plug, or popper, works better if cast across the wind and twitched in the trough rather than downwind or upwind. A hundred other lessons we learned, some of them without our realizing we had taught ourselves something new.

All that early summer, while we were chasing stripers, I was tending lobster pots for eating money. It was just as well, for we came on a long, dry spell, when it looked as though all the stripers had left the Bay. One by one the other boats quit until only Harris and I remained. The fishing was so poor, in fact, that Sarge Sargent, who was then running the *Sou'wester* and who later became and now is the governor of Massachusetts, actually gave me a twenty-five-pound striper to eat. I filleted it and saved the gurry for lobster bait, backbone and all. Harris went with me that next day to tend lobster pots. When we got to the striper tail he said, "Don't use that for bait. I want it." So he saved backbone and tail.

I had at that time a five-hundred-pound halibut box for a fish box. Into this I usually put the lobsters, covering them with wet burlap bags to keep them damp and cool. We used it that day, but on the way in, after soaking the lobsters well, Harris arranged the fish tail and box cover so one end of the tail showed quite clearly.

We were met by the usual reception committee. "Oh," said Bruce Hammatt, "I see you've got a striper." At his disbelief of Harris' negative, Freddy pulled off the cover to show the clean backbone. At the gas pump it worked again. "No, we didn't catch a striper, we caught you, too, Mac." (Thus the fish called a "utoomac.") Three or four times that afternoon that fish tail caught the unwary.

It worked better than that, though, the next day. Coincidence took hold and the big stripers showed up offshore while we were tending lobster pots. We caught a dozen forty-pounders. Harris wanted to take them into Sesuit.

"I don't think we need to, Freddy," I said, "We've still got that striper tail from yesterday." We put first in the big box the dozen stripers, then wet burlap bags, then the lobsters, then more burlap bags, and last of all the backbone with the tail sticking out of the box as it had the day before.

The reception committee met us again. This time they weren't going to bite on the same bait. Nobody asked us if we had caught any fish. Everyone eyed that fish tail and shied off. All but Jackie Crosman. Jackie came bouncing down onto the deck without so much as a by-your-leave. He flipped the fish tail with his hand and sat down on top of the box. "Huh!" he said, "Who do you think you're going to catch twice on the same fish tail?" And he sitting on top of almost five hundred pounds of stripers! We told him the next day when we came in with another, bigger load, but I don't think he ever quite forgave us.

# 28

~~~~~~~~~~~~~~~~~~~~~~~~~~~~~~~~~~~~~~~~~~~~~~

# Charterboat Lessons

Gradually this year I began to learn the many, many lessons of charterboating. Getting business, customers, wasn't the problem. They came to me. Word got spread around that more striped bass were being unloaded at the dock in Rock Harbor than anywhere along the coast, and people came to see. Some nights twenty or thirty boats each unloaded from one hundred to five hundred pounds of big fish in disorderly, romantic heaps.

The tide situation had always been a nuisance, but I found that it worked to the charterboatman's advantage. Since the harbor is land-locked all the time except for two and a half hours each side of high tide, and since the tide is roughly an hour later each day, our sailing times had to vary with the tide. When we were commercial fishing we left at two, or three, or four o'clock in the morning, without much thought about the time except to be on the grounds at "just-can-see." We came in on the next high water, or the next-but-one, chiefly because we had fish to unload, or we needed supplies. Hours and daylight had no particular significance except as they bore on catching fish.

In the charterboat business things were different. People not used to getting up in the middle of the night objected; also the good, old-fashioned habit of being on time had been lost. More than one party, getting to the dock a half hour or more late were surprised and up-set to find the tide down and *Nonny* gone.

The tide, however, worked to the advantage of the charterboat-man whose first consideration was catching fish. There was no com-ing back into the harbor because someone was tired, or because the

weather turned foul. Until the tide came in, we couldn't, so we fished, and many unlikely days brought fish to the dock when, if the
customers had had their "druthers," they'd "druther" have gone
home. The second benefit was that all the boats came in at the
same time. An evening when there had been a big day would see a
whole line of boats following each other like beads on a string, across
the mile of flats, into the harbor, and to the dock to await their turn
to unload. People coming to the shore to watch the sunset were also
treated to the sight of boat after boat unloading at the dock. And
every one of those people, innocently coming to the shore, became
a potential customer. In later years when I sailed from Wellfleet or
from Barnstable, it seemed strange to me that the crowds customary
at Rock Harbor were never at the dock to meet me when I had a load
of fish.

In spite of the gradual change in our way of fishing, we did little
to change our gear. We put no fancy chairs aboard; we bought no expensive tackle. The customers sat on the fish box while they waited
for the fish to bite, and hauled fish in when they did bite on handlines. We rather frowned on customers who brought their own tackle
aboard.

There were exceptions, of course. There was Mr. T. who fished
with me and *Nonny* until he finally bought a boat of his own and
hired a year-around skipper. In spite of the fact that he was probably a hard-nosed business executive, when he was with us he was
gentlefolk. He never presumed to try to tell me where to go or how
to fish. The deal was that if the fishing was hot he would get out of
the way and sit in a little canvas deck chair while I went to hauling
handlines. When the fishing was slow I'd take in one or two handlines and he'd put over his own tackle. He had an ancient, split-
bamboo boat rod with a permanent set which made a half loop of
it, and I think what was probably Mr. Vom Hoff's first salt-water
reel — at least it was very old. Mr. T. had a bad heart and carried
nitro pills. There were days when I came near to having a heart at-
tack myself, for Mr. T. with a big fish on his ancient rig would suddenly stop cranking and fumble at his vest. It fell on me to get out
the little vial, drop a pill into the palm of my hand, and slide it into
his mouth. Then we'd go back to fishing. He paid ten dollars a day

and seldom took more than one fish, no matter how many we caught.

Then there was Barney, a great bear of a man, and his crew. The original deal was three men, forty dollars, and they take all the fish. Barney got cute and worked in four men, but when he tried five *Nonny* was just too small, and that was the end of that. He later bought his own boat, but admitted he never did as well as he did fishing on *Nonny*. I excused a lot in Barney because he was one of the very, very few men I ever fished who, having a newcomer in the party and hanging the first fish himself, would hand over his rod to his guest and say, "Here, you crank in the first fish, I'll get mine later."

# 29

## My Wife Goes Partner

The summer drew to a close and it got to be time again for my pilgrimage around the Cape. It looked like a big scallop year in Pleasant Bay, and since Harris' one hand made it impossible to do well opening scallops we came to the end of our partnership. It was his doing rather than mine, really, for while he'd put up with flounder dragging and lobstering, and assorted attempts to make a dollar, his heart was entirely in striper fishing. If it wasn't striper time he might be talked into doing some other kind of fishing but only because he was bored and had nothing else in particular to do.

This trip my wife, pet-named "Reddy" in our courting days because of her long, chestnut-colored hair, went with me. It was the only trip she ever made around the Cape with me, not that we had a rough trip — for the most part it was a lovely day — it was simply that she never seemed to care much for boating, having other things she'd rather do. From time to time I have said, "We called my wife from such a harbor and she came to get us." Many times through all my years of boating the telephone would ring at home and I'd be calling from some unexpected port for her to come and get me. In later years when we had a radio receiver in the kitchen, never once did I call over the air and say, "Reddy, meet me at such a harbor at such a time," but she was always there, patiently waiting when I came in. She shared all the trials, all the sinkings, all the motor troubles, all the midnight boat drills. She knew when I came home down in the mouth what had gone wrong before I ever told her. Or if, as occasionally happened, I had an unusually good day, I could never hide it. I'd come home and pretend to moan and groan though I was twitching with my good luck, and she'd say quietly, "Was the day all that good?"

She could have gone with me a great many more times than she did. Though she could get seasick in the cabin with *Nonny* tied to the dock, rough weather never bothered her when she was on deck. For the most part, she only went along for company when I had no one else. That particular trip around the Cape, as I say, was a lovely day to be on the water, although Race Point was pretty sloppy. Before we got there, with a following wind, she felt a little squeamish, so she went up forward of the sprayshield. When we got to the Race I suggested she come back since it was going to be rough. She would have none of it. Remembering the hole close inshore I sneaked in as close to the beach as I dared and, except for two or three masthead-high seas, we "skun" through with no trouble.

She did go scalloping with me that winter in Pleasant Bay. The mast, boom, and winch worked beautifully. When we left The River in the morning for the half-hour run to Big Pleasant Bay, she'd fire up the Shipmate stove with charcoal briquettes and sit cozy-warm until it was time to go to work. Then on the way home she had a comfortable place to ride. It is cold, scalloping in the winter, and she wore so many clothes I figured if she fell overboard there would be so much air trapped she could never sink. She never came close to falling overboard so I never found out. She wore her underwear, a suit of my longjohns, her dungarees, a pair of my dungarees, then her hip boots, and one of my woolen shirts over her sweater, then a jacket, and over all a set of regulation foul weather gear. It was lucky she had to walk around very little for with all her clothing she moved like a mechanical doll rather than the spry little person she really is. She did have a little trouble going to the head, though.

We got scallops that year. Yes, we did! The town let us take five bags apiece. (She had a commercial license, as did many of the fishermen's wives.) That meant over thirteen bushels of scallops to open after we were through dragging. Some nights I didn't clean up until after midnight. (Later in the season when the scallops came a little harder, I'd have to carry over a bag or two a day so that by

Sunday, when the law wouldn't allow us to go, I had a whole day's work ahead cleaning up the carry-over.) We should have made a lot of money, but as always happens when there is an abundance of fish the price was down.

# 30

~~~~~~~~~~~~~~~~~~~~~~~~~~~~

# Night Trip

Another spring came and another trip around the Cape from Pleasant Bay to Rock Harbor. *Nonny* and I had been ready for three weeks for the trip, but every day the wind blew easterly. The seas raged on Chatham Bar — not even the hardiest and hungriest of the trawlers put out. Stripers were already in the Bay for Sim Smith in *Lucky Lady* had caught the first one. (This was one of the two years out of nine when *Nonny* didn't bring the first striper into Rock Harbor.) At last, about noon one day, the wind moderated. Late in the afternoon it looked as though the sea would die down at sunset, when the tide turned to run with it. On an impulse I drove over to Bob Whiting's house. "Want to make a trip around the Cape to-night?" I asked.

He hesitated only a moment. "I've got to go carpentering tomor-row," he said. "What time will we get in?"

I figured the tide. "Well, we can't get in much before ten o'clock because of the tide," I said. "How about going as far as Province-town with me? Your wife and mine can pick you up — oh, say some time around midnight."

We left it that way and my wife drove me to the boathouse at the head of Meetinghouse Pond where *Nonny* lay. Bob stopped long enough to buy a couple of steaks and a bunch of bananas — that's rations for a night sea trip for you!

It was just dark when we left Meetinghouse Pond with all the length of Pleasant Bay to run, Likey's Point and Namequoit, the Narrows and Dogfish Bar, then Scatteree and the flat to south'ard in Chatham, the names of which I did not know. A full moon was ris-

ing, it was flat calm, and we never touched bottom all the way to
the Inlet. There it was a different story. The moon went behind the
clouds and only by scrooching down could we be sure there were
breakers ahead. I hit what I hoped was the hole out, and Bob, flat
on his stomach forward of the sprayshield, coached me when there
seemed to be breaking seas. We headed due east and never once did
we take any appreciable amount of water aboard. Once clear of the
Inlet I let her go to nor'ard and turned the wheel over to Bob. I
went below to light the Shipmate, broil steaks and fry bananas.
When I came on deck I asked Bob if we had gone by Nauset yet.

"I don't think so," he said, "I'm pretty sure that is Nauset Light
up ahead."

It couldn't be, and yet it was, and then it suddenly came to me
that with the full moon, we were bucking a tide figured on the calen-
dar as a twelve-footer. The inshore tide must run over four knots on
the way from Nauset to Chatham, and with *Nonny*'s top speed only
slightly over eight, it meant we were doing no more than four over
the ground.

"Well," I said, "I guess the girls will have a long wait. I figured
six hours from Meetinghouse to P'town." It took nearer eight.

We pulled into the dock at P'town in the wee hours of the morning and the town police — not our wives — were waiting for us.

"You out of Chatham Inlet?" one asked.

I said we were.

"How many horsepower in that boat?"

I said, "Forty-five at twenty-three hundred revolutions."

The cop laughed, "You better tell your wife, she thinks you've got
four."

I thought that over. "She must mean four cylinders. But my wife
— where is she?"

"Oh, she went home an hour ago."

They took us to the police station where they let us call to tell our
wives we were safe. Bob was going to sleep overnight with me in
*Nonny* and we were going to try sea-scalloping on the way home.
Millie was to call Bob's boss to let him know Bob wouldn't be carpentering the next day. We planned to put in to Sesuit Harbor about
noon. My wife was to meet us there.

This time it worked out as planned.  Bob wouldn't turn out in the morning when I headed for Dennis Ledge but kept on snoring in the cabin.  I got even with him — the first sea I took when we got out from under Land's End bounced *Nonny* just hard enough to bring a can of beans off the rack down onto Bob's head.  For years he laughingly warned my charter customers, "If Phil tells you to come on deck, you better do it, because if you don't he's liable to hit you on the head with a can of pork and beans."  We got enough sea scallops for supper on the way home.

# 31

~~~~~~~~~~~~~~~~~~~~~~~~~~~~~~~~~~~~~~~

# Publicity and Parties

Sea-scalloping couldn't hold my interest long that year because the stripers were in the Bay when I got there. That year, without Harris' support, I began to build a charter business. I learned about publicity and I learned about sports writers.

With the sole exception of Henry Moore of the *Boston Herald*, I found that sports writers never bothered to check a fish story and would print almost any lie a fisherman wanted to feed them. Barney came up from Connecticut one day early in the year. The trip was scheduled for five a.m., but I didn't like the looks or smell of the weather. I said, "Barney, we'll fish until the six-twenty Coast Guard weather comes over the air. If they say 'small craft warnings' we'll stay, but if it's storm warnings we're coming back in."

We went out and the fish went crazy. We got seventeen fairly good stripers in an hour, not big fish, but good, solid twenty-pounders. At six-twenty the Coast Guard said, "Storm warnings, forty to fifty no'theast and rain squalls." We headed back in at the last possible moment. Bobby Gardner, who had been fishing alone in the same school, came in when we did.

Bobby naturally didn't have as many fish as we did, but he did have one forty-five-pounder, which Barney bought. Barney paid me the price of a full trip and took off for wherever he came from. What happened that afternoon didn't make ripples here until later, but it seems that one of Barney's party had a brother who ran a boat livery at Niantic in Connecticut. They got home early in the day and went to a police photographer who took a picture of them and the fish. Then they went to the local paper and fed the reporter a story that came out in big headlines, "Record Catch of Stripers at Niantic. Eighteen big stripers weighing up to forty-five pounds."

Laughing about it later, Barney said, "They ain't caught a fish as big as that in Niantic in one hundred years, but Nick's brother's boats were rented out a week in advance, and they had to call out the state police to handle the lines of traffic."

We fishermen found, however, that false publicity was worse than none. Some whopper would appear in the Boston papers and we would be flooded with calls and customers. The trouble was, we couldn't produce. We did all we could to spike the lies.

One picture was printed over and over again in the western Massachusetts papers. I caught two twenty-five-pounders one day, and since it was a case of "too many to eat and not enough to sell," I iced them down and kept them, hoping to catch more the next day. The reporter who took the picture the next day had me hold up one fish and Alan Corbett, a local carpenter who happened to be at the harbor but who hadn't been fishing all summer, hold up the other. The picture came out the first time captioned, "Captain Fred Harris and Captain Phil Schwind holding two big stripers this reporter caught yesterday." I don't know which of us was supposed to be Harris for we both had two hands. Not once but many times that picture appeared, under different headings, seldom mentioning my name. I got a spate of letters asking, "Isn't that *you* holding up the fish on the right?"

I found that sports magazine writers, by and large, knew very little about fishing. One writer, who later became a steady customer and a good friend and to whom I owe a great deal for his encouragement when I began writing about fishing, booked *Nonny* for a four-hour trip, over the high tide.

I never liked the four-hour trip, except for family parties when there were small children and any kind of fish, mackerel, harbor bluefish, tautog — anything that would bite — would do. It was a foggy, foggy day, and the only stripers were way out on the "Flag Ground," a good three quarters of an hour run against the tide for *Nonny*. That meant an hour and a half running in the fog out of a four-hour trip — if I could find the flag buoy which marked the ground where the fish were supposed to be. But my friend insisted, so we rubbed out of the harbor as soon as we could on the coming tide and I ran three quarters of an hour with my eyes glued to my compass. Wonder of wonders, I hit the flag dead on. As my friend was letting his line out I said, "Wait a minute. Your partner's line looks all right, but that line of yours looks mighty frayed. Is it new?"

"Oh, yes," he said, "New forty-five-pound linen."

We went round and round the flag with nothing biting. Gradually I became aware of sea gulls yammering off to nor'ard. I got my two anglers to reel in and I shut off *Nonny*'s motor to listen. Sure enough, the gulls were putting up an awful fuss. I hated to leave the flag, since with it in sight I knew where I was, and I also knew what my course home was. But if I could catch my anglers just one fish apiece . . . I headed north, and they let their lines run. It was fish on the surface, all right, big fish. Both lines went tight at the same time. The doctor's line held, but my friend's line, the one I had questioned, went pow! No line, no lure, no fish!

I said, "That's new forty-five-pound linen!"

"Well," he said, "it was new last year." Wouldn't you think a man who made his living writing about how to catch fish would know enough not to take a chance on an old line?

The doctor's fish weighed over forty-five pounds and I managed to get them each one more fish, my friend using my rig, before we had to head for home.

I began to learn about charter parties, too. Many times since I began taking out parties for hire, friends have said, "I'll bet you can tell some pretty wild stories about people who went fishing with you."

I can't really. I found that most people who wanted to go fishing were pretty nice. There were a few — but for the most part that type of trip is happiest forgotten. Once in a while, though, a party came along that no one could forget.

A friend in town, to whom I owed many favors, came to me one afternoon with a request. Could I take fishing two friends of his, a dentist and his wife?

I said, "Look, I'm awfully sorry, but there's no way I can fit him in. I'm double-booked the next two weeks, an eight-hour trip and a four-hour trip every single day."

"Please! He's an awfully nice guy. He's been fishing for ten years and never caught a striper. Just him and his wife."

I said, "Look! I've got an eight-hour trip booked for eight o'clock in the morning and a four-hour trip booked for tomorrow afternoon from half past four until half past eight. If your friend wants to go at four in the morning and be back at eight, the trip will be a little short on time and it will mean over sixteen hours straight for me, but, I'll take him."

"Beautiful," my friend said, "He'll be here early, and don't worry about him, you'll love the guy."

Four o'clock a.m. sailing time means three-thirty for the skipper, to get the boat and tackle ready. I was ready to go on time. My friend's friend, the lovely guy, wasn't there. He and his pretty wife didn't show up until almost five. I was not in a pleasant mood. I hardly waited for them to get aboard before *Nonny* was taking us out of the harbor, again on that long run to the Flag Ground. The dentist had not only shorted himself on his time by being late, but he had missed the best fishing, the daylight rise, which so often produced all the fish caught before evening.

There was little talk on the way offshore. When we got there I explained about the tackle, dropped over an eelskin rig, ran off the right length of line, explained the star drag. "Now, look," I said, "there are big fish here. They'll hit like an express train (if we're not too late). Don't try to stop one if he hits, don't put your thumbs on the reel whatever you do, don't yank to set the hook. Hold your rod tip up to make the fish fight the rod and when you can gain, start winding in line. Do you understand? Whatever you do, don't try to set the hook, the fish will do it for you."

He said very snuffily, "I've been fishing for ten years."

I thought, "Yeah, and without a fish."

I rigged another eelskin for his wife and dropped it over the stern. She seemed to understand. Almost before we had squared away a fish hit. Yes, he hit and my customer yanked his rod tip so hard he brought it clear over his shoulder and almost hit me with it. The fish was torn loose.

I wound the line in, straightened out the eelskin and dropped it over again. It couldn't happen three times in a row — but it did. (I hadn't expected to get three hits on the entire trip.) I took the rod away from him and put it in the holder after I had run the line out again. "Now," I said, "don't touch that rod until I tell you." And I stood over him to see he didn't.

He was very indignant, all the more so because his wife said very gently, "Maybe the captain is right, dear. Why don't you try it his way?" He did, whether he wanted to or not, because I stood in his way. Sooner than I expected he got his fish. Before I let him touch the rod the fish had run off a good fifty yards of line, but the point was, he hadn't been set so hard the hook pulled loose.

Every skipper who ever used eelskin rigs consistently knows that there are times when only one rig in the boat will catch fish. I had found that one rig, so, to even things up, when I put over the gear the next time I made sure the lady got the hot eelskin. (Neither of them ever realized the difference.) Sure enough, on the next pass she got a hit and handled it very well — for a minute or two. Don't you know that clown reached over and snatched the rod out of his wife's hands! "Here," he said, "I'll take that. That's too big a fish for you."

I could have belted him one, but his wife flashed an apologetic negative at me, so I let him keep the rod until he had landed his second fish. The next time I made sure she got the same rig, and this time when she hooked a fish I just happened to be standing in the way so he couldn't grab the rod. He was furious I was in his way, but by this time I had had enough. I told him to shut up and sit down, and something in my voice convinced him it might be just as well if he did.

Once her fish was in the boat I headed for Rock Harbor. I had over-stayed my time as it was, bound as I was that the lady was going to get a fish. Said the dentist, "Where are you going?"

"Rock Harbor. Your time's out."

"Oh," said he, "I'm not going to Rock Harbor yet. I'm going to stay a while longer."

"Then," said I, "you better get your Jesus shoes out and start walking on the water because the rest of us are bound in."

"If you think," he said, "if you think I am going to pay you for a full trip when you deliberately made me lose three fish, and we have only been out three hours, you're mistaken."

I chewed on that for a while. "Well," I finally said, "all right. I expect when people come in to have their teeth fixed they tell you what they are going to pay, but I suppose fishing is a little different. So, I'll tell you what you do, you pay me what you think the trip is worth. Whatever you pay me — it'll be nice to know just how cheaply you'll sell yourself."

He paid the whole price but then had the nerve to ask me to clean the fish. "No," I said, "I usually do, but I'm almost a half-hour late, my boys on the dock are frothing at the mouth, the tide is dropping — and look, Doctor, don't ever come back. People like you I can do without."

And over the next twenty years of charter fishing that was the rare send-off — very, very rare, because most people were very nice. There were the people who never caught a single fish, but who said on the way in, "Captain, this trip has been the highlight of our whole summer's vacation. We know how hard you tried, and if we're back on the Cape next year we want to go with you again." There were husbands who came secretly to me and tried to bribe me so their wives could get a bigger fish then they, and wives ditto. "Here's an extra five dollars, Captain, see that my husband (or wife) gets the biggest fish of the day." Did you know there are people that nice in this world? There are. Lots of them.

The kids — I should have paid the kids instead of their paying me. I wonder how many kids have steered my boat across the Bay. So we wandered zigzag, first too far east, then too far west! More young tongues were chewed and more energy was expended, but almost without exception, whether their parents thanked me or not, the youngsters came and solemnly shook hands with me, and thanked me for letting them steer. As far as fishing was concerned, if you want to see some real excitement you let a little tacker, eight or nine years old, tie into a forty-pound striper. Man! I mean that's real fun. And if once in a while a fish got away? Isn't that what fishing's all about? I loved every minute of that kind of fishing.

Speaking of kids, perhaps my most memorable trip with kids was with little Murphy. The trip was some years after *Nonny*, when we were fishing in *Whitecap*, but it stands out as an all-time great trip. We had been fishing six boys on four-hour trips, a whole series of trips with the littlest boys from a boys' camp. Murphy was the very littlest. He was a black Irishman, with jet black hair, the longest black eyelashes and eyes so dark blue as to be almost violet. There were school stripers aplenty on Brewster Flats, three- to five-pound, boy-size fish. All five of the other boys that trip had caught their fish, all but Murphy. Time was running out. I had maybe fifteen minutes — which I usually allowed in case something went wrong on the way in.

It came on to rain, a light "cow-stormy" drizzle, so the other boys crowded into the deckhouse. Not Murphy — he sat there with goose-pimples on his skinny arms, from his T-shirt to his wrists, working his fish pole, concentrating on getting his fish. My mate caught fire — he wanted a fish for Murphy almost as much as I did. I heard him chanting to the fish, "Come on, fish. One more fish for Murphy. Come on, fish. Bite, damn you."

One of the bigger boys — the oldest was no more than eight — came back with his jacket and settled it over Murphy's shoulders. Another came and put his cherished baseball cap over Murphy's seal-wet, black mop of hair.

I spoke to the mate, "I'm sorry, Bill, but we've got to . . ." and the fish hit. Murphy's rod hooped over and he started to crank frantically. Bill handed his rod to one of the older boys to get the line in out of the way. That crew literally held their breath while Murphy manfully wound his fish to the boat.

Once the fish was over the rail and in the boat I hooked the throttle to the firewall, heading for the harbor, for we had really over-stayed our time. Bill unhooked the fish to let Murphy hold it, and the other boys broke loose with cheers. They screamed the camp cheer — it was long and involved — for Murphy. Then again for Murphy. Then they cheered Bill. Then they cheered *Whitecap*. Just as we got to the harbor mouth they looked shyly up at the flying bridge and cheered the captain. By the time we had docked they had all but forgotten their own fish and were hoarse from cheering, and little Murphy just stood there hugging his fish. The other boys' fish were all cleaned and scaled, but not Murphy's — no knife was going to touch that fish yet a while. His T-shirt was a mess of fish slime and soaking wet, and I expect the drops of water on the ends of those long, black lashes were rain drops — yes, that's what they must have been.

# 32

$\infty\infty\infty\infty\infty\infty\infty\infty$

# First Tuna

The seasons wore on and somehow the years blended into each other. In 1949 the little bluefish came back after an absence of twenty years, and we had to learn a whole new technique of fishing. They were little fellows, a pound to a pound and a quarter, a lot of fun to catch and good eating, but commercially hardly worth the bother of catching.

About that time the school tuna showed up south of the Shoal Ground. They were bigger than the bluefish, twenty-five to forty-five pounds, again fun to catch — though none of us knew anything about tuna fishing — and again not worth the bother to catch commercially, bringing only three or four cents a pound with their heads off. Some of the fleet went to tuna fishing in a big way, neglecting good bass fishing, and only settling on bluefishing when there was nothing else to catch.

As far as I was concerned, I had fished too long for market, for edible and hopefully high-priced fish, to be much interested in tuna, which more often than not wound up in the dump. But I did get talked into a couple of tuna trips in *Nonny*.

The first grew out of a phone call when the caller asked if I would take him "tunny fishing." I couldn't talk him out of it. He wasn't the least bit interested in striped bass — he'd caught three or four of them. My explanation that I knew nothing about tuna fishing, that there were skippers in the harbor who were making tuna fishing a way of living, had no effect on him. He wanted me to take him tunny fishing and that was all there was to it. So we went tunny fishing with striped bass gear.

I cheated a little on the way out (I still dislike an empty fishbox almost as much as I do trouble); I stopped long enough to catch a couple of big stripers, my crew of two objecting strenuously. We went on across to the north side of the Shoal Ground where tuna were reported in plenty, on a lovely afternoon I hated to waste at such nonsense. The water was flat calm and the temperature almost too hot. We came on school after school after school of little tuna, placidly and swiftly minding their own business.

Now, mind you, I had never caught one of these critters on rod and reel, but I had listened to many discussions of the best way to catch them. We put over various lures, tin and feathers and the like. We trolled short lines, then long lines, we trolled both fast and slow at different times. I found I had a pair of anglers who would rather not catch tuna than catch anything else, and for a long time we "not caught tuna." In every school there has to be one idiot, and such an idiot tuna got himself hooked on a trolled striper tin jig.

It upset him and he tore off a good three hundred yards of line, which was about all I was carrying on that reel. My angler sat down to fight him. He was skillful enough, but he and the fish were a long ways apart, and I had no idea how to fight that sort of fish with the boat. I threw out of gear the way I would with a striper, turning only enough to keep the fish square off the stern. That was all right so long as the fish was a long way out, but when he got closer I found myself kicking the boat around in a circle almost continuously. I think we turned nine complete circles before the fish got where I could boat him. He weighed just under forty-five pounds.

In the meantime, as I said, it was a hot day. A hot day while trolling along at a pretty good speed is one thing. A hot day lying idle while an angler fights an irritated fish is something else again. My angler got redder and redder in the face until I began to worry about sunstroke. Finally, at the angler's own request his friend bailed up a bucket of salt water and poured it — swish — over the angler's head. And again, and again.

With the fish in the boat, beating the bottom out of my fishbox, I gathered the gear together. "Okay! We found out how to do it. Come on now, quick, let's catch another."

My angler's friend looked at me with disbelief written all over his

face. "If you think I'm going through what he's just gone through
. . . Oh, no you don't. We're going home."

I said, "Look fellows, we can't get back into Rock Harbor, allowing we've got an hour's run to get there, for at least two hours more.
Let's try for another one. No? Well, let's go back and try a little
striper fishing."

They'd had enough, so we jogged back to Rock Harbor and lay at
anchor for two hours while they drank beer and congratulated themselves and me on our successful trip. P.S. They didn't want any fish
but left them all with me.

# 33

## More Tuna and Whales

My second tuna trip was with a very nice, apparently stodgy couple from Boston, and was memorable, not so much for tuna, but because of Willy the Whale. The first day they were with me both husband and wife proved to be excellent fishermen. On the way in they asked if I was booked the next day. When they found I was not they asked if I would take them tuna fishing.

On the strength of the previous trip we went tuna fishing the next day, again with striper tackle. The tuna had moved to Race Point so we churned the two-and-a-half hours north and found the P'town fleet of charterboats busily fighting small tuna. When he saw we were having no luck, Cap'n Jerry Costa, charterboat *Inca*, out of P'town, swung alongside and tossed me a couple of blue and white, half-ounce bluefish feathers. "Fish 'em fast and short," he yelled. We were in business. I really don't remember how many we caught, three or four, but it was Willy the Whale who made the day.

I had been watching Willy for some time as we fought tuna. He was a little whale, thirty or thirty-five feet long, quite famous along the outer Cape shore. For a while he had made regular daily appearances near the Nauset Light shore, but for some reason, food probably, he had moved down P'town way. The bait that day, whether herring or sperling or whatever, was bunched up in schools so tightly packed they almost seemed to the casual observer to be a solid object several feet across and floating just below the surface. Willy would blow steam through his blow hole, take a deep breath and sound. When he came up it would be with jaws gaping under a school of baitfish. He'd gulp and swallow a whole washtub full of bait and then settle until he found another school.

My lady angler saw Willy's spout. "Oh," she said, "I think I just saw a whale's spout."

I said she had, and that it was Willy.

"Can we get close enough to get a good look?"

I said we could. I trolled over, watching Willy as we went. Timing it just right I lay hove to with the next school of bait beyond Willy just off our stern. (Our lines were in.) We got a good look at Willy, all right — when he came up with his jaws spread wide I could have stood on *Nonny*'s stern and pushed a full-grown collie dog into Willy's mouth.

My lady angler screamed, "Let's get away from here!"

I kicked *Nonny* ahead because really we were just the least bit close, but I don't believe we bothered Willy at all. He closed his great jaws gently on that whole school of bait, lowered his head, and settled right under our stern. As he slid under us I realized there was a great semi-circular chunk out of his back, cut out by a ship's propeller. Dug into his hide was a collection of striper plugs that would have stocked any charterboat. There were blue plugs and green, amber plugs and yellow. I don't know how to account for them unless various foolish fishermen, seeing Willy in the surf, had decided to catch themselves a whale and had cast over Willy's back and so snagged him.

Never could I understand the mania which seems to overcome so many otherwise sane people when they see some great and wonderful beast like Willy. They must immediately kill it, kill it, kill it. (Our blackfish driving was different. There we were killing for a commercial product, though the killing has left a bad taste in my mouth to this day.) Usually the object of their kill lust is perfectly harmless if left alone. I have found many of the beasts almost friendly. I eased *Nonny* alongside not only Willy, but blackfish swimming free, great sea turtles, porpoises, and one memorable day a great thresher shark, the upper lobe of whose tail was almost as long as *Nonny*'s cockpit. The saddest of all are the great ocean sunfish. The fishbook says those found in these waters are probably sick, and certainly they're not good for anything, nor do they do any harm. Usually a fisherman will first notice one as the creature sluggishly waves his great dorsal fin, perhaps five or six feet long, like a great, black ironing board on end. He'll pay little attention to a boat coming quietly alongside. What is it that makes people want to kill a pathetic and slightly comical being like that?

The orca or killer whale is supposedly an exception among the generally harmless sea-dwellers, and yet he is not. His name or reputation is enough to scare people away, but I remember one exciting day just off the Eastham shore when a whole school of orcas, with their very formal black and white markings, played and chased mackerel under *Nonny*. They were almost as long as *Nonny*, but infinitely more graceful and much faster. Excited, I called the fleet to tell them, for I had never seen orcas so close. The air was promptly jammed with calls, "Get away from there. They'll upset your boat and eat you!" I turned the radio off and sat and enjoyed their play. They didn't upset *Nonny* and they didn't eat me. They broke up the school of mackerel and went off to find other company.

# 34

## P'town Striper Trip

So much a part of our routine had the trip become, so trusted was *Nonny*, that trips around the Cape got to be commonplace. Sometimes I had company, sometimes not. Once we ran into stripers near Peaked Hill Bars and caught so many we put back into P'town. In fact, some of my fishing even stretched out to a four-hour run to the Peaked Hill country, and to that part of the Truro outer beaches known to surf casters as "The Meadows."

Jimmy Andrews and I had run out of fish in Cape Cod Bay. We worked the Pamet River one morning at dawn and picked up three or four school fish. Jimmy said wistfully, "I caught a forty-nine-pounder last spring at The Meadows. How about we finish the day down there?"

It was all right with me. "You take her around, Jimmy," I suggested. "You slept all the way to Pamet this morning. Wake me if you see anything interesting." I turned in and went to sleep, lulled by the steady drone of *Nonny*'s Redwing. I slept until Jimmy kicked my feet.

"I think you ought to take a look at this," he said. "See what you make of it."

All the seagulls in the world were having a convention. I never saw so many gulls. We couldn't push *Nonny* any faster, so for nearly half an hour we shivered and shook with excitement. We laid out spare plugs, we checked and re-checked our gear. As we got nearer we could see great splashes under the gulls. It was literally miles of stripers gone mad, feeding on blueback herring. We got to the fish, threw out of gear, and let drive with our plugs. Two fish on. We boated the fish and kicked ahead to keep up with the school. From then on it was a madhouse — whoever got his fish into the boat first kicked the boat ahead, and let the slow one fight fish and boat at the same time.

Suddenly Jimmy stopped casting and started to change plugs. I yelled, "What the hell are you changing plugs for?"

Jimmy explained, "We're both using orange plugs." (They were Captain Bill's number three poppers.) "And the stripers are feeding on blueback herring. I thought I could catch more fish with a blue plug."

I asked, "How can you catch more fish than one every time your plug hits water? And don't cast so far, there's fish right close to the boat."

By this time Jimmy had tied on a blue plug and let it sail. A sea-gull picked it right out of the air and started off with it. Jimmy's line came tight and the gull dropped the plug. Another caught it on the wing. Three different gulls had the plug before it could get wet. Jimmy changed back to an orange plug, which the gulls were smart enough to let alone. In the meantime I had boated two fish.

We caught fish that way until it got so dark we lost the school. We had somewhere around seven hundred pounds. The fishbox was overflowing and there were stripers everywhere on deck, even in the cabin. I headed back around The Race. "Jim, we've got to go back into P'town to ice these fish down, and we've got to be back out here at daybreak."

The trip around Race Point in the dark was long — we had been underway since four that morning — but it was calm and eventually we came to the dock. Not a soul was stirring. (It must have been near eleven o'clock.) The only ice we could find was under the ice breaker, but we scooped all that up and it was enough to partially ice down the fish. We set the dollar alarm clock early, knowing the draggers would take off before daylight and we could discharge our fish then.

I woke sometime during the night. We lay bow to the dock on the east side, and the wind had come in strong easterly. The waves, hitting the stern, were being blown clear through the companionway and were soaking us both. I kicked Jimmy's feet to wake him.

"Come on, we'll be pounded to pieces here.  Let's get around to the lee side of the dock."

Jimmy was a little slow getting the lines in, so that by the time we had made the west side of the dock several of the draggers were under way, and they, too, were moving to the west side.  I could visualize tender little twenty-five-foot *Nonny* tied between those rough old eighty-footers, and I was having none of that.  I said, "T'hell with it.  Blowing like this, we can't go outside tomorrow — or today, or whatever day it is.  Let's run across the harbor and make a lee under Corn Hill in Truro.  We can get into Rock Harbor by nine o'clock."

It was dark and it was rough, but *Nonny*, the little lady she was, jogged and flirted her way across that black, black P'town harbor.  I was running on Highland Light and Jimmy stood beside me, shivering in the wet and the dark.  Gradually the Light drew down so I knew we were getting pretty close to the Truro shore.  I said, "Jimmy, go down and turn the fathometer on, and while you're there get me some dry matches; mine are soaked."

Jimmy is well over six feet tall, and just about the time he stuck his head down the companionway it was — "kling-up!"  We'd run into something.  Jimmy fetched up with his head clear up into the eyes of the boat.  I heard a muffled, "Damn you, you did that on purpose."

I chopped the throttle and threw the motor out of gear.  "Jimmy," I said, "I think we just ran into a fish trap."  We had.  Not only had we bumped into it, somehow missing all the various guys and stays in the dark, but we had literally run into the trap, right through the netting, so only *Nonny*'s stern was clear of the twine.  I went up forward and untangled us, and I'll bet that trap's owner was mad the next morning, for we left a great hole in the trap through which every fish must have escaped.  But it was his own fault.  By law the trap was supposed to have a light on it, and nary a light was there.

By this time I had had enough of the Truro shore, and the way home was pretty much lee, anyway.  I said, "Jimmy, turn in, I'm heading for Rock Harbor."  And that's how we finished the trip.  It blew for three days after and by the time we could get out again that school of fish had left.

# 35

## Foggy Trip

One last trip around the Cape in *Nonny* was quite eventful. Johnny Shakliks had begun fishing out of Rock Harbor in a little double-ender that summer. When he heard I was going around the Cape he asked to go with me. We left before daylight; the sun never came up until we were just short of Wood End. With the sun came a thick fog. I hesitated. Much as I wanted to run around the Cape, I didn't want to do it in a fog. We jogged on with a fair tide to Race Point, figuring that if it was still foggy by the time we got there we would put back into P'town, call my wife to come and get us, and finish the trip the next day. By the time we got to Race Point the fog had burned off and except for a heavy swell from the southeast it looked like a lovely fall day.

"Johnny," I said, "hold her on the last point of land to southeast you can see. I'll straighten the gear." (I had put aboard mast, boom, and all the scallop gear the night before.) "Then I'll fire up the stove and make us some hot coffee."

I was still below when Johnny said, "What do I steer for now?"

I came on deck and we were again in thick fog. I said, "Oh, damn! How long have we been in this stuff?"

"We went by a lighthouse 'way up on the bluffs," he said, "just a little bit ago."

That would have been Highland Light. The trouble was, if we followed fairly close to shore our course would continually change. Unless we went farther offshore than I wanted to go we wouldn't be able to steer a straight course. So we ran for a half hour generally southeast, then let her come sou'west until we could see dimly through the fog the white lace of the surf as it ran back down the beach. Then off southeast to give us sea room, then sou'west looking for the surf.

We had zig-zagged a number of times when suddenly we ran out of the fog just as though someone had pulled aside a curtain. We were right abreast of Nauset Light; but, with clear visibility, we realized there was a pretty fair swell built up, nearly fourteen feet from trough to crest.

"Johnny," I said, "I dunno. Chatham's the original fog factory, though it looks clear enough ahead. If I can find a break in the surf at Nauset I think I'll head in there." Nauset Inlet was one solid wall of surf, not only on the outside bar but clear up into the Inlet. We lay to, jogging long enough to tell there wasn't going to be any slack spell to let us through. We picked up again and headed for Chatham.

Before we ever got to Chatham Inlet we ran into the thickest, blackest fog I ever saw. I hesitated for several minutes. Just out of curiosity I picked up a fish pole and cast a plug out into the fog. It was so thick I couldn't even see the splash when the plug hit the water. I cranked the plug back.

"Well," I said, "we've got to go somewhere. I haven't seen the Inlet since last spring, and for all I know it's changed. I'm going to make one pass. There is, or was, a nun buoy just on the edge of the outer bar. If we can find that I'm going in. If we can't, I'm going to run off and throw over the hook and wait, either until somebody comes along who knows the way in, or until this fog lifts."

We came on the seas breaking on the outside of the bar. There is an uncertain feeling in a fog. Things lose proportion; perspective is all out of whack. At times you feel you're rushing around and around in a circle though the compass holds steady. At times you feel as though you're climbing a long, long hill, and at other times you feel as though you're plunging down into an abyss. One thing was certain; we had more sea pounding in than I was happy with.

"The sand bottom on the edge of the bar, Johnny," I said, "I'm going to be busy watching it — I can see it here. Do your watch off the port side, and if you see a wave that looks as though it's going to break, sing out, and sing out quick."

He asked, "How will I know if it's going to break?"

I said, "It'll be all hollow on the leading face, and there'll be feathers all along the top edge." I crept along, riding the backs of the seas which were breaking on that shallow bar. It seemed as though we must have gone miles beyond the Inlet when Johnny nervously cleared his throat.

He drawled, "I don't like the looks of this one."

I took a quick look. My God! I didn't either! I spun the wheel to turn us offshore, straight into the sea, and chopped the throttle. The sea was higher over us than the fourteen-foot mast, and it was all hollow along the face. Just as it got to us it began to curl over. No boat ever responded as quickly as *Nonny*, and her quickness saved our lives. Pointed straight at that mountain she climbed gallantly. Her nose pointed right up in the air, and we had just way enough on so she climbed and climbed until at last the wave broke side of us, all around us. We shipped maybe three or four barrels of water, even so. What would have happened if *Nonny* hadn't turned so quickly? We'd have been drowned right there, that's what.

I jumped the throttle ahead as we ran down the back of that wave, then slowed again as the next wave lifted us. We climbed that one, up, up, and over, and were clear of it just before it broke. The third one was easy, *Nonny* was so quick to respond. I could see no fourth one and swung south again, and there — bless it! — was the nun buoy. I could have kissed it if I'd had time. I whirled *Nonny* around and headed due west, racing through the Inlet before the next wave could catch us. The remnants of a wave very soon caught up with us, but it was only broken water which whirled us along at a dizzy speed, rail high and choked with sand, but nothing to hurt us.

There was a second bar ahead. The fog was lifting slightly and I could see waves breaking, but the slot seemed right before us so I let *Nonny* run.

Just when we were in the middle of the smaller breaking seas, dancing on top of them, Johnny said, "What's that?"

I flashed a look, then my attention whipped back to the seas around us. I asked, "What did it look like, Johnny?"

He said, "I don't know. It could have been a barge, or a sailing vessel. I thought I could see a flag or something. Maybe it was a sail. But something is there in the breakers."

We had run out of fog; inside the Inlet it was as clear as we could wish, and had been all day. I spun *Nonny* about and headed offshore to try to find what Johnny had seen. Almost immediately we were back in the fog again, and there, right ahead of us loomed this great thing Johnny had seen. We tried to get closer, but it lay right in the breakers. I nosed *Nonny* into the whitewater until she buried her nose clear back to her sprayshield. She had hard work shaking that one off. Still we couldn't figure what was there in the breaking seas.

Johnny said, "Now it looks as though it might be a sail boat bottom up."

We finally turned back. Johnny was nearer right than he knew. It was a boat, bottom up, though not a sailboat. It was the forty-foot Nova Scotia line trawler, the one that drowned Archie Nickerson and Roy Larkin. We didn't learn that though, until we got home that afternoon.

We had a little time to spare before my wife was to meet us at the River Road Landing, so we got a mess of scallops for Johnny and a full commercial limit for me in Pleasant Bay. When I got home the phone was ringing. It was the Nauset Coast Guard Station.

Whoever was on the other end of the line said, "Phil? Is that you? You didn't get drowned?"

I asked if I sounded drowned, and what did he mean. (I'll say one thing for the Coast Guard, they were very diplomatic. Never, after looking for me unsuccessfully, did they call my wife to upset her further. When I had finally gotten home and they did call, they always made sure it was I who was talking.)

He said, "We heard there was a small boat overturned on Chatham Bar and we figured it had to be you, since you were the only small boat out that we knew of."

# Part Four

WHITECAP

# 36

≋≋≋≋≋≋≋≋≋≋≋≋≋≋≋≋≋≋≋≋≋≋≋≋≋≋≋≋≋≋≋≋≋≋≋≋≋≋≋

# Wellfleet to Rock Harbor — the Hard Way

It was excursions of this sort that finally brought me to look for another boat. *Nonny* and I had come through too many tight places where a larger boat would have been not only more comfortable but in all probability somewhat safer. Furthermore, *Nonny* was nearing her fortieth birthday, and just how long could I expect a boat to take the pounding I had given *Nonny*? Few small boats in these waters fish more than a hundred-day season, but *Nonny* and I had gone over two hundred days several years, and once or twice over two hundred and twenty. (As a matter of record, when I sold *Nonny* she went to New London, Connecticut, after unhappily thrashing around in Rock Harbor for a couple of years, and from there she went to Block Island, where she may still be running for all I know.)

There was another reason for getting a bigger, faster boat. In spite of the fact that there was a law against seining for striped bass in Massachusetts, seining was still going on, and the bottom had dropped out of the market, which meant that the only way I could stay in the striper business was to go for charter, where I had my day's pay in pocket before I ever left the harbor. *Nonny* was not big enough for parties of five and six people, which were the trend in those days. Besides, school tuna fishing was becoming more and more popular. A lot of the boys had gone around the Cape to fish from Wychmere and Chatham and had done very well. *Nonny* was neither big enough nor fast enough for that kind of fishing.

I heard *Whitecap* was for sale in Wellfleet. She had come into the Bay back when Whit and I had first fished *Nonny* together, and she had taken my eye even then. I went to Wellfleet to talk with Arnold

Hanson, who, with his brother-in-law, had bought *Whitecap* from the War Shipping Administration on a sealed bid for ten dollars. She was a Robert Rich boat, built in Maine and snatched by the Coast Guard for patrol work in those waters before she was ever finished. She was cedar-planked, with white-oak ribs, and a keel that was fourteen inches deep at the shaft log. Thirty-five feet on her waterline, she was nine feet six in beam and drew thirty inches standing. She was rigged with a big Hathaway winch driven off the propeller shaft, a short mast and boom, and a stern "gallows" rig for scalloping. She had for power an old six-cylinder Gray marine motor, and, said Arnold, "There's another, a spare motor just like this one, in the garage in North Eastham." He spoke truer than I knew; there was another motor "just like this one" — which was not good.

We took *Whitecap* out into the Bay on a smokey sou'wester that would have been an "I'd be smarter to stay at home" day in *Nonny*. I drove her. I hooked her wide open and headed into the sea, I laid her in the trough and let her wallow. She was wet, she was always wet, but how she took those choppy seas! She held up into the wind well, too, when she was idled down to trolling speed. (I didn't find out until later that she was a dog at half throttle in a following sea. She was so deep forward that she'd stick that long nose of hers down and rootle, broaching to one side or the other, and all I could do was drop her down to nothing and let her wallow, or kick her wide open to lift her bow. That was a small matter — no boat is perfect — and I much preferred a boat that would hold up into the wind while trolling than one that ran true before the wind, since I had no inlets to run and when I was trolling most of the time was spent headed up into the wind anyway.)

I fell in love with her. It was a strange thing with *Whitecap*; she always had the reputation for being a lady. When I took her from Wellfleet, the local boys, who were never very fond of the Rock Harbor fleet, bemoaned the fact that I was taking away the nicest boat that had ever come into Wellfleet. During the years I went back there from time to time, *Whitecap* was always made welcome, even if I wasn't. Before I made a deal with Arnold, I made sure of two things. One was that I had a buyer for *Nonny*, and the other was that the only reason Arnold was selling *Whitecap* was that he and his brother-in-law had split up their partnership and Arnold wanted a bigger, heavier boat with which to drag quahogs. I bought her in late September, just before the scallop season opened — and there was a trip!

It was unseasonably warm with little or no wind. High water was about five o'clock. I waited until my son Peter had come home from high school; then my wife took us to Wellfleet. I made sure I had gas enough and took along a new piece of three-quarter-inch rope. I had bought *Whitecap* bare: except for the anchor and one fire extinguisher there wasn't a piece of gear aboard. I found out before the trip was out that not even the running lights worked. Pete and I left in our shirt sleeves for Rock Harbor. The last thing I said to my wife was, "If we don't push it should take us an hour and a half, but don't worry if we're a little longer than that."

We cleared the harbor and swung slightly off course to clear the rock at Lieutenant's Island and Wood's Beach Rock. Everything was working smoothly. Ahead of us we could see the quahog draggers had finished their day's work and were heading one by one for Rock Harbor. It was getting along in the afternoon but surely we'd be in Rock Harbor before dark. We weren't.

We had gotten just about abreast of the Ship and only a little off the edge of the flats when the motor just stopped. I did the routine checking. Fuel? Plenty. I tried the spark — there was the trouble; the spring on the ignition points in the distributor had broken. I suppose the motor had been used so little recently that the spring had rusted, and the little use I had given it in trying the boat out had not been enough to break it. But it was broken now, and there we were, a mile or so offshore and only a couple of miles from Rock Harbor.

Pete had thrown over the anchor at my suggestion; I didn't want the tide to carry us farther offshore. "Well, Pete," I said, "I guess we're here until somebody comes to get us."

We inventoried our stock in the fast-thickening darkness: No tools of any kind except the knife I carried on my hip and the wire-cutting pliers most sportfishermen carry. A hardwood pole for a harpoon, miles of eight-pound, tarred handline. Under the stern deck a bale of about forty new burlap bags. A canvas deck chair, and in the cabin a whiskey bottle half full of kerosene or something. No life jackets, no coats, and only half a package of cigarettes in my shirt pocket. No water or food. Neither of us was thirsty but Pete could have eaten a sandwich.

Pete said, "I'm cold." So we cut out the seams of half a dozen burlap bags and made a sort of blanket for him. It very soon became apparent that no one was going to come looking for us from Rock Harbor, for by the time we were settled in for the long wait the tide had dropped. The wind pricked on from the north, but not strong enough to make us too uncomfortable. Then, as it got darker, we could see car headlights blinking and blinking at us from Rock Harbor.

I said, "Pete, there's your mother blinking headlights at us from Rock Harbor, so she must be able to see us."

It turned out that she couldn't. Someone had told her that the range lights were out and she was afraid we couldn't find the harbor. It got really dark and Pete's stomach was a little squeamish; after all, he hadn't had a bite to eat since his school lunch. We stretched him out in the air in the canvas deck chair and bundled him up in layers of burlap bags. I tried to doze off in the cabin, but I wasn't all that tired. I came back up on deck. Realizing that at the rate I was smoking I'd smoke up all my cigarettes before midnight, I broke each one in half, so I could smoke more often if not as much. I got to thinking about that whiskey bottle in the cabin . . . "you don't suppose . . . naw, for all Arnold was a drinking man . . . Well, why would he have kerosene?" I didn't guess he'd been around that long. Using kerosene to dry out ignition wires was an old-timer's trick. I fumbled my way down into the cabin and brought the bottle up on deck. I sniffed it. I tasted it. By golly, it was whiskey. I spoke softly to Pete, thinking a drop or two would help fight off the cold, but he had finally dropped off to sleep. I decided to have a small drink of whiskey on the hour and half a cigarette on the half hour.

In the meantime my wife had gotten tired of blinking headlights for a husband and son who obviously weren't going to come home that night, so she'd driven off to find help. Her first thought was Johnny Shakliks. Why she didn't think of Freddy, who was far more experienced and would have been far more resourceful, neither of us

will ever know.  She called Johnny's home and finally tracked him
and his wife Mary down in Orleans.  Johnny started looking for me.
He tried Boat Meadow and First Encounter Beach, and then Kings-
bury Beach.  Then, for some reason he could never explain, he skipped Thumpertown Beach, which is where we were.  I had in the
meantime, when the tide had stopped running, pulled the anchor to
let the wind carry us closer to the beach, until there was a bare three
feet of water under our keel.  I suppose we could at any time have
jumped overboard and waded ashore, but the thought of leaving that
lovely new boat all alone just never entered our heads.  Johnny went
all the rest of the way, Camp Ground, Cooks Brook and Sunken
Meadow, then he went to Wellfleet thinking we might have turned
back.  When he had made the rounds he called my wife and said there
was no sign of us and maybe she'd better call the Coast Guard.

She called them, and after a long delay, somewhere around two
a.m., the DUKW went rumbling down the road past our house.  Pete
had awakened by this time, and he and I saw the lights of the "Duck"
swing the corner of First Encounter Beach, and we saw her take to
water.  It was a clear night, though there was no moon.  We watched
the "Duck" as she set a course for the Rock Harbor lighted buoy,
which is a good mile offshore from the harbor.  From the buoy she
changed course and went right to the little green blinker which lies
west of the Ship, and then, when she had come out from behind the
Ship, she headed straight for Billingsgate Island.  She rounded the
Billingsgate Light, and for a few minutes her spotlight played on the
Island, then she reversed course and headed back to the green blinker.  About that time a stray plane came over to do a little practice
bombing on the Ship, and the Coast Guard inexplicably doused
their lights.  The next time we picked them up they had turned the
corner at the Rock Harbor buoy light and were headed for First
Encounter, where they landed and wheeled out of sight.

It was nice to know they were looking for us, and it helped to pass
the time, but it seemed a silly sort of procedure.  When they finally
did hook onto us in the daylight, I asked why they had run that
course.

"We were running the channel markers," they said.

I was tired and exploded.  "Channel markers!  For God's sake, there isn't any channel where you went. The Rock Harbor blinker marks the entrance to the harbor, though it's a mile away. The green blinker marks the Ship and the shoal it's on. You ran right over Stony Bar, and the Billingsgate Light marks the Island. Another time you fellows go looking for a lost fisherman in the night, a fisherman who is taking a boat from one harbor to another on high tide, you draw a straight line on the chart from one harbor to the other, and he'll be somewhere along that line."

Well, they didn't find us during the night, and about sunrise the wind pricked on strong from the nor'west. I said, "Pete, I guess if we're going to get home today, we'll have to do it ourselves." We rigged the harpoon pole for a mast forward, and cut up more bags for a three-cornered kind of jib. Then we cut up more bags and sewed them together with fishline for a mains'l on the stub mast amidships. They worked pretty well, except that we couldn't get enough way on to steer, so we sort of washed along, closer and closer to Rock Harbor, going sideways all the while.

About the time we got rigged, here came the "Duck" again, this time out of Rock Harbor — and headed straight for the Rock Harbor bell buoy. Then they apparently saw our queer rig and squared away for us. The seas by now were four or five feet high and it was just the least bit sloppy. The "Duck" wheeled around and started backing up to us, against the wind. The boot in the stern threw a great armload of nylon rope right under her stern. Luckily the man driving the thing had sense enough to kick her forward so the rope didn't get caught in her propeller. I coiled down our new three-quarter-inch manila and yelled at the boot to catch. I nearly knocked him off his feet with it, but he managed to hang on. "Is it strong enough?" he yelled.

I called back that if it wasn't I didn't want to be aboard. Then, instead of running straight before the wind to Rock Harbor, they dragged us in the trough of the sea all the way out to the bell buoy, and then swung about and quartered into Rock Harbor.

I said to Pete, "They were bound to find us at that bell buoy, and since they didn't, by golly, they're going to take us there before they take us home." Well, they tried, and I suppose I sound ungrateful, which I'm not; they couldn't have towed us into Rock Harbor in the middle of the night anyway — though if they'd found us I bet they would have tried. No bones were broken and no harm was done, although both Pete and I were pretty hungry and cold before we got in. What a way to start off with a new boat, if I had believed in omens.

# 37

## Lily, Ruthie, and Flo

If the trip home from Wellfleet was a portent — and it was — it didn't worry me much. For the first time I had a boat big enough to compete with the big fellows on equal terms. I had a cable winch and could pull a full-size, fifty-four-inch drag instead of a little three-footer; furthermore, the gallows rig in scalloping was a big advantage, for instead of taking a loaded drag over the starboard side and necessarily lying in the trough, I could haul straight up into the wind while the drag came over the stern.

This was the year Bob Whiting and I developed a scallop drag which should have revolutionized the industry. For us it did, but for the rest of the fleet we were just a couple of lucky nuts. The year before, in Pleasant Bay, we had worked on little twenty-four-inch "planing" drags. To the traditional scallop drag which was nothing but an iron hoop followed by a bag, chain links on the bottom and twine on top, we had added a tilted board, a foot wide, and set at an angle clear across the bows. After much experimentation (we visited Peter Bruce almost every night on the way home) we arrived at a formula for the angle: the rise should be one third of the run. Contrary to appearances, the rush of water over the planing board did not force the drag deeper into the bottom, but created a sort of vacuum which lifted the scallops off the bottom. (Another local copied the plan but missed the idea entirely; sadly, many of his drags are digging deep into the bottom to this day.) Our drags, fished fast and with a very touchy scope, caught only light shack or trash. The old-fashioned "snowplow" drags and the imitations of our drags not only took longer to fill but caught mostly rocks, stones, mud, shells and relatively few scallops. With bigger boats and power winches, Bob and I went to the maximum fifty-four-inch drags, but instead of building them of inch-and-a-half iron, as was customary, we had Peter build them of half-inch iron with the planing boards. We had to tow them fast, five knots or more. True enough, if we hit a hang-up, a rock or whatever, the drag was apt to come in folded up like an accordion, but being only half-inch iron, we could beat on it with a maul and be back in business in minutes. The drags fished so much cleaner we did far less culling and caught a great many more scallops per tow.

It was the first time in years there had been a commercial crop of scallops in Eastham waters in Cape Cod Bay. *Whitecap* and I, and whoever I could get to go with me as a hand, went scalloping every day. That was also the year there was a bonanza crop of scallops on the Orleans/Chatham line in Pleasant Bay. This was outboard fishing, very shallow water where even *Sunshine* would have been cumbersome. Early in the morning my wife and I would set out from the Narrows in a big old skiff I had acquired, equipped with a five-horse outboard, a two-foot scallop drag, and two commercial licenses. Before eight o'clock we would be back in the Narrows with our limit of four bags each. Then, hurrying to Rock Harbor, I would pick up whoever was going with me at the time; Whit Scott went with me a few times, though he didn't much take to scalloping; Jackie Crosman, who later brought his own "Novie" boat around from Chatham, and Johnny Shakliks, who went until he took off for Florida about Thanksgiving.

Getting so many scallops opened was a problem. No one could drag all day and then open twenty-eight bushels at night. We were rescued by three ladies named Lily, Ruthie and Flo, and once they learned the business no one was ever better at it unless it was Lily, Ruthie and Bridgetta, who took Flo's place the next year. I was stuck the first day of the season for openers until Warren Baker called me to tell me of the girls. I showed up at Flo's house with the back of my Model A, a "tail-box" coupe, loaded high with scallops.

"I hear you girls want to open scallops."

They looked at me doubtfully. "Only if there's enough to keep us busy so we can make it pay."

Said I, "Oh, I'll keep you busy, all right. How's this for a starter?"

They agreed on seventeen cents a pound, which was a cent a pound higher than the going price. I unloaded the scallops. In Flo's garage they set up an old storm door on horses. We dumped all the scallops the door would hold, while the girls put on boots, gloves and aprons (rubber). Let me say, Lily was Ruthie's mother and several times a grandmother, while Flo had a couple of kids of her own.

I watched them dubiously as they started. The table was certainly inadequate, and inexperienced openers can waste an awful lot of scallops. Lily and Flo had obviously been there before, but Ruthie was not only unskilled, she was using the wrong sort of knife. A bay scallop knife is a highly developed tool with a short, wide, limber blade and a rounded tip. Ruthie's knife was carving the scallops, as the saying goes, "one third for the shell pile, one third for the cat, and one third for me." I remonstrated.

Ruthie snarled, "If you don't like my knife go buy me a better one." I did. Not only that, but I ground the knife thinner so it was more flexible and would follow the shell more closely, and I built up the handle so it wouldn't cramp her hand so quickly.

She tried a scallop or two in the way I showed her and then fired the knife into the shell barrel. "I can't use it and I won't," she yelled and tramped home across the street, boots, apron and all.

That was a nice start. The other girls looked embarrassed but kept on whittling. "Well," I asked, "what now? You girls can't open all of these by yourselves. Can you get anyone else to help?"

They shook their heads. So we took away a third of the scallops to a family in North Eastham I had heard of. That tribe opened only one lot for me because the next night when I brought more they were having fried scallops — mine — for supper, which I didn't object to overmuch, until I saw in their freezer a good gallon of scallops, also mine. That made me change my mind, pay them for the scallops they had opened, and carry off the fresh ones to open myself. With scallops bringing close to a dollar a pound and a gallon weighing nine pounds, I couldn't afford that.

About the third day Ruthie came back, somewhat chastened, and in due course became a first-rate opener, fast and clean. I got used to her snarling every night and her calling me Simon Legree. I could bring her right up on her tiptoes by searching in her shell barrel as though for wasted scallops. So we enjoyed each other all winter, as long as the season lasted, and all the next season. The girls were embarrassingly honest; they insisted on paying for every scallop they ate, even though I assured them it was common and accepted practice for openers to have a meal of scallops on the captain occasionally.

With the problem of opening the scallops out of the way we settled down to steady dragging. And then I started to have trouble with that damned motor. Nine times that winter Bob Whiting, who had bought *Peepot*, a little boat not much bigger than *Sunshine* but with considerably deeper draft and higher sides — nine times Bob had to tow me in. I went to the garage in North Eastham and picked up the other motor, which presumably had been newly overhauled. Maybe it had been, but it was no better than the first motor. We discovered that the blocks of both motors, being salt-water cooled, were completely clogged with rust. Both motors eventually cracked their blocks and sprayed water all over the cabin. That wasn't too much bother as long as the bilge pump took care of it, but finally the cracks got so big they sprayed water all over the distributor and plugs and something had to be done.

I tried drilling and tapping a series of holes all around the crack, then covering it with a heavy gasket and a sheet of copper. I got a couple of days out of that rig; then it, too, gave up. I got Peter Bruce to come and braze the crack shut, right there in the boat. That cooked it, figuratively as well as literally. It loosened so much rust the motor refused to run at all. Luckily for my peace of mind the Bay froze over about that time so I couldn't go scalloping anyway.

With the charter season coming up in four or five months I went shopping for a new motor — not a second-hand one this time, but a brand new one. I finally settled on a one-hundred horsepower, so-called "industrial," flat-head Ford V-eight. Of all the buys I ever made, except perhaps *Nonny*, it was the very best. Eleven hundred and fifty-eight dollars, specially painted, special hangers, ready to install, with a two-to-one Paragon clutch and reduction gear. Ten years I ran that motor; thirty-seven thousand gallons of gasoline went through it. At the end of that time it still had the original pistons and I had lost a total of a day and a half because of breakdowns. Oh,

I took care of it; a new carburetor every year, new points and plugs three or four times a season, a change of oil filter every time I changed the oil, and the oil the very best I could buy. I had it re-built three times, but each time the mechanic would say, "I don't know why you're wasting your money, there's nothing wrong with it the way it is." It was wonderful to go out every day and never have to worry.

# 38

Admeasured in P'town

When I bought *Whitecap*, while she was a pretty thing to look at, she had the fault of many southern boats; too much house and not enough work room (*Nonny* actually had more work space); and a fault which is peculiar to a good many northern boats: the house was without headroom, so low it was nothing more than a cuddy for the storage of gear. The motor was in the cabin and the standing room was decked so low it was impossible to put in scuppers. Finally, the deck had been built of two layers of one-by-six-inch matched hard pine with a layer of tarpaper between. Both above and below the paper the decking was rotten. Wood has to dry out sometime or it will surely rot.

Before installing the new motor I put in a new bed so the motor was some forty-four inches aft of where it had been. I put in new deck timbers, crowned to carry off the water (though they could have stood more crowning), and a new deck of square-edged, fir flooring about two inches above the water line. This could have been another two inches higher but I wanted to keep our weight as low as possible. I cut down the cabin and moved the deckhouse forward so the motor was all clear of the cabin.

The interior re-building was about finished when the Customs Department caught up with me and I got a notice that *Whitecap* had to be newly admeasured, either at my own expense in Rock Harbor, or at the government's expense in Provincetown (P'town being a port of entry). Without checking the tide I made a date in Provincetown.

The date came, and I realized that to make P'town, be admeasured, and get back to Rock Harbor on the same high tide I was going to have to fly. I had made trial runs and it seemed the new motor was going to give me a lot of speed. I talked Captain Art Gorham into going with me.

Captain Art, a retired fireboat captain with some thirty years of experience, was as salty a character as Old Dave Delano. Rough weather in a small boat was his dish of tea. But it wasn't rough, it was foggy, and the tide for some inexplicable reason was late. We waited and waited. Finally, Art went up town and bought a small bottle of rum. "We ought to be able to get out on this," said he.

We did. With the first signs of a flooding tide in the harbor, I backed *Whitecap* off the whole length, clear to the gas pumps, then I hooked it to her and we hit shallow water at the entrance wide open. Wonderful! She lifted with the thrust of the prop in that shallow water and literally planed across the flats.

Now I had another problem. I had a new boat and motor, and I also had a new compass. By the chart, to clear Billingsgate Island on my way to P'town the course was north-by-west, but how far out was the compass? I had had no chance to find out. In *Nonny* north-by-west for twenty minutes would bring us to the Ship. We never saw the Ship, though both of us craned our necks once we left the shallow water of the flats. In twenty-five minutes I looked over the side and said, "Art, I believe we're on the Shoal Ground."

He scoffed, "No way! You think this clunker will fly?"

I said, "Art, there's eelgrass patches under us in about five feet of water, and you won't find that anywhere except on the Shoal Ground." I let *Whitecap* run another ten minutes on the same course, and then hauled due north. I wasn't sure what my course should be, but I wanted to give us plenty of sea room.

Art said casually, "Cap, the cabin roof's on fire. Where's your bucket?"

To get rid of the nuisance of a water-cooled exhaust running clear the length of *Whitecap* I had run twin exhausts up the sides of the deckhouse and out through the overhead. The miniature water-jackets I had put on the exhaust lines from manifold to deck, and the asbestos covers from deck to overhead simply had the effect of carrying all the heat to the overhead. I slacked off and we bailed buckets of water at the joining of overhead and exhaust lines, and then we were on our way again.

It is about nineteen land miles from Rock Harbor to the dock in P'town Harbor, and I figured it would take us nearly two hours. Mind you, we were all this time in thick fog and had seen nothing of the shore, and only that short glimpse of some part of the Shoal Ground as we passed. "Art," I said, I think I'm going to haul her more to east'ard. We'd look pretty silly if we missed P'town altogether."

"You're crazy," he said, and threw the empty rum bottle overboard. "We're nowhere near P'town."

"Be that as it may," I insisted, "I'd much rather run aground somewhere along the Truro shore than miss P'town entirely and wind up in Boston or someplace." I hauled her around no'theast, never slacking the throttle. "Art," I said, "We're in deep water. I think we've gone by Wood End."

He started to object, then hesitated. He pointed through the fog. "That there," he said, "is Race Point Light."

So much faster was *Whitecap* than *Nonny* that we really had come close to over-running P'town. We doubled back, following the vague shoreline, and were some twenty-five minutes getting back into the harbor. The Customs men had just about decided to leave when we came steaming to the dock.

"Where did you come from?" they asked.

"Rock Harbor."

"In this fog?"

I said, "Look, fellows, is this going to take long? I'd like to make it back to Rock Harbor on this tide, if I can."

They were nice guys. They measured *Whitecap* fore and aft, up and down, and sideways. Art, in the meantime, went up town and bought another bottle, a very small bottle of rum. The Customs men finished just as Art got back. "How long do you figure it will take you to get back to Rock Harbor?" one asked.

"Hour and fifty minutes."

"Have you got that much time?"

"Got almost two hours. C'mon, Art, let's go." The Customs men shook their heads unbelievingly.

An hour and fifty minutes later, having seen no land since leaving the P'town dock, not even land under us on the Shoal Ground, and having adjusted our southerly course by guess, I said, "Art, we ought to be pretty close to somewhere."

He had been peering over the bow. He yelped, and it was one of the few times I ever heard him yelp. "Haul hard back! We're up in somebody's front lawn at Brewster."

We just nearly were. We must have almost split the Rock Harbor bell buoy, though neither one of us saw it. I backed around, headed east-north-east, and in minutes there was Rock Harbor ahead of us.

Wild as the trip was, my point is that I was acquiring the hard way a kind of extra sense. Shallow water looks one way, deep water another. Without any instruments, I began to know when I had gone far enough in one direction, or should go in another. It was not altogether a thinking thing, but more a subconscious warning that something I was not even aware of was right — or wrong.

I put on a flying bridge and remote controls, and a fish box in the stern, and I was ready for the charter season.

# 39

## Shallow-Water Stripers

For years Harris and I and the fleet generally had watched stripers in shallow water on the Brewster Flats. While *Whitecap* was not as handy in shoal water as *Nonny*, that shoal-water fishing I knew, and *Whitecap* carried me there. I came ashore one day, frustrated and tired.

"Are there any stripers around?" asked Freddy MacFarlane in the Goose Hummock Shop, the local tackle shop.

"Tens of thousands," I said, "on the Brewster Flats. It's like a goldfish bowl; you can look at them but you can't catch them."

I hadn't meant the statement for the press, it was a mere statement of fact, but I was quoted the next day in the *Boston Herald* in Henry Moore's Rod and Gun column.

Bob Pond, who made the Atom plug and later successors, said, "If the fish are there I can catch them."

We made a deal. "If you can catch one fish, I'll give you the trip for free because I will have learned something. If I can show you ten thousand fish, by your own count, and you can't catch one, then you owe me sixty dollars worth of plugs."

He came the next day and gave me more than sixty dollars worth of plugs, win, lose, or draw. It was a trip neither he nor I will ever forget. The day was perfect for sighting fish; flat calm, the tide starting to drop at noon when the sun was right overhead. He and a buddy, Art Posgay, and Bill Fitzpatrick of the Massachusetts Department of Natural Resources (who was along because I had seen nine-inch stripers, something new for these waters) coasted out of the harbor. We sped to the Brewster Flats, where I slowed down. Bob and his partner started to cast off the stern while I was still under way.

"You're wasting your strength, fellows," I said, "I can see every inch of the bottom and there are no fish here." Then I nudged Bill. "See that patch of rough water over there, a quarter of a mile south? That's stripers."

"No," whispered Bill, "that's a wind slick."

"You think I don't know stripers when I see them? That's a school of fish."

We crept down on the rough water. It was a quarter-mile-long school of big stripers, thirty- to forty-pounders, finning, as they were wont to do in the shallow water of Brewster Flats at that time of year. I said casually to Bob and his partner, "You want to see a few stripers? Put down your rods and come up forward."

They came, they looked, they scrambled back frantically for their rods and we got closer and closer. I shut off and coasted close to the school. Bob and his friend cast and cast, surface plugs and swimmers, big plugs and small, red plugs and blue. The fish were not feeding and simply turned out of the way of the plugs.

"Here," I said, "I can get fish to follow a plug — which you obviously can't do. Let me show you." I jogged easily ahead until we came to a new school of big fish, fish that hadn't been alerted by Bob's frantic casting. The fish were all easing lazily nor'west with the tide, their dorsal fins and the tips of their tails showing above the surface. I popped a surface plug just astern of the last fish's tail and exploded it. I made all the commotion in the water I could with that one plug. Every fish in the school turned to follow it. I cranked and popped, cranked and popped all the way to the boat with the whole school following curiously. Not one fish tried to bite my lure. When my plug reached the boat and I had to lift it out of the water the fish turned away, not scared, just not hungry and not particularly interested.

"Come," I said, "west of here are slightly smaller fish. Sometimes they bite better. And west of them are still smaller fish, schoolies; sometimes they will bite when the big ones won't."

Bob said, "You sound like a fish market; big one here, medium-size ones next to them, and little ones at the end of the counter." But that's the way it was: So constantly we lived with the fish, we knew their habits well. Finally, after the turn of the tide, when the wind sprang up and ruffled the surface of the water, Bob's partner managed, with my coaching, to catch one lone fish, a twenty-five-pounder. Neither he nor Bob ever quite got over that day, though they fished with me for years afterwards.

Every day was different — there is no monotony for people who really love fishing. I will concede there were days when I felt as though I were running a ferryboat. I went endlessly in and out, in and out of the harbor, taking aboard a new party, carrying them back to take aboard another. I looked back on the old, carefree days with *Nonny* when we came or went on a whim. That was the way to fish.

# 40

‱‱‱‱‱‱‱‱‱‱‱‱‱

# Too Many Tuna

I enjoyed most people who came aboard. Those who didn't measure up, the complainers and the drunks (and there were very few of them), were asked not to come back. Even though we were out for only a day on the water, I was very much aware that I was responsible for the lives of everyone in the boat, and I didn't care to take that responsibility for people who couldn't behave.

We had memorable trips, trips that no one aboard would ever forget. One was a tuna trip — this was before the *Silver Mink* (Captain Manny Phillips, out of P'town) came tuna seining in the Bay and scooped up all the little tuna, or scared them offshore into deeper water.

The gentleman who hired *Whitecap* that day was a regular customer, a good fisherman, though somewhat inclined to over-react, a feisty little man — my kind of people. He called to arrange the trip. "I want to go," he said, "as early as we can get out of the harbor, and stay as late as we can. I'll gladly pay for the overtime, but my son is home from college and has never seen real fishing."

We went as early as we could rub out of the harbor, my regular customer, his son, and two friends. I had invested in new light tackle for tuna fishing, 6/0 reels, rods custom-tied in Florida for amberjacks, and eighty-pound dacron line. I had four swiveling fighting chairs made by Peter Bruce of sheet steel well padded with foam rubber. We churned our way north to Race Point early in the morning.

Arnold Miner was mating for me that year, as good a mate as ever fished out of Rock Harbor. Alert, clean, handsome and blond, he was all business. "Come on, Little Mother," he'd say to any woman angler over thirty fighting a fish, "you can beat any fish silly enough to bite a hook." The men anglers liked him, too, he was so sturdily masculine. But his training was all on stripers; tuna he had never caught. He set out the baits at my direction and we ran the suds, the edge of the breaking seas of the Race, looking for fish. We found them! We found four at once. All four lines screamed off the reels — and for some reason one of those new eighty-pound-test lines popped. It broke clean off. No matter for the minute. We still had three fish on, which is enough for any skipper. (We never had a chance the rest of the fourteen-hour day to rig a bait on that fourth line.)

I had learned about playing tuna by this time, as usual the hard way, so I favored one angler, only watching to see I didn't foul him with the other two. That first screaming run, that unbelievable stripping off of as much as three hundred yards of line from a reel that gets so hot the grease melts in the bearings, that's my thrill from tuna fishing. Papa grabbed a rod and had his fish beat in minutes. Turning the boat over to Arnold, I came down off the flying bridge to gaff the fish. Jimmy Andrews, who had mated for both Charlie Mayo in *Chantey III* out of P'town and Joe Eldridge in *Striper* out of the Canal Basin when both skippers were concentrating on tuna, had taught me how to get the big fish: Always gaff up under the chin or through the gill plate so blood won't fly all over everything.

I hand-lined the fifteen-foot wire leader, jabbed my short-handled gaff under the tuna's chin and heaved him over the rail, a good hundred and twenty-five pounds after he was gutted. By this time one of the guests had his fish close to the boat. I turned the first fish loose to beat himself to death in the cockpit and gaffed the second one. (No fish we caught that day weighed less than one hundred and twenty-five pounds after it had been gutted and bled.)

Thinking Arnold had seen enough, and knowing how skilled he was in gaffing stripers (he never knocked off but one bass in the two years he mated for me), I climbed back on the bridge to let him handle his first tuna. Papa's big, just-home-from-college son had on the third fish. He was irritated (and saying so) that Papa had his fish in first. He finally brought the swivel to the rod tip and Arnold literally rolled up his sleeves to do the gaffing — but not in the chin as I had done it! He got him in the belly, like a striper! The tuna resented it. In a great flurry of bloody water he took off, with the gaff and almost with Arnold trying to hang on. Arnold let go just in time to stay in the boat. The line screamed off the reel again, and Arnold, quick as always, reached up with both gloved hands to stop it. Before I could yell, "No!" he grabbed the line and wrapped it around both hands. The line stopped running out, but the tuna didn't. That eighty-pound line snapped like thread. Arnold turned with tears running down his cheeks. "What did I do wrong?" he said.

In the meantime, Papa had kicked over his feather lure, and almost before we knew we had lost a fish we had on another. And so it went all day. Arnold did get a chance to bend on a new lure on the line he had broken, but the fourth rod sat in the holder, unused all day until we started home that night. It got rougher as the day wore on, about as rough as *Whitecap* could live in, far rougher than *Nonny* could have fished in. Nobody but I seemed to notice. We had at least one fish on at all times that day.

After the first three fish were aboard I found time to come down off the bridge to suggest we turn the rest of the fish loose. They were worth only three cents a pound in P'town, dressed and with their heads off. Certainly three fish, each weighing over a hundred pounds, were all any party could use. We could bring the rest to the boat, cut the leader, and let them go.

"Oh, no," said Papa, "I want them all." So all day long Arnold gutted the fish when he had a chance, threw them in the fish box for their dying struggles, then slipped a noose over their tails and towed them behind us to wash out their blood. The bottom of the fish box, meant for relatively quiet stripers, was knocked loose. There was blood and fish guts all over the cockpit. Nobody seemed to mind. When we had boated our ninth fish ( it had gotten so rough I had my hands full handling the boat) I headed for home, a good two hours away.

Some clown threw over one of the baits, and even though I was turning top speed we hooked another tuna. I was irritated because I was used to parties doing as they were told. I got that fish headed south, then I cranked up the motor and headed for home, letting the angler hang onto the rod as best he could. I ran that fish all the way from Race Point to Wood End, with the angler hanging on for dear life and *Whitecap* digging through the rough water for home. Finally, I slacked off on the throttle long enough to let Arnold lead a very tired, very beat-up tuna to his gaff. I expect the angler was tired, too.

As I said, I had begged Papa to turn loose every fish after the third one, and he had said, no, he wanted them all. Halfway home in the dark, he climbed the ladder to the flying bridge. "Phil," he said, "we can use one of those big fish; you can have the others."

"Oh, no, you don't!" was my tired, testy reply. "You wanted 'em — you got 'em. If you think I'm going to drag those fish back to P'town tonight after fourteen hours offshore, for three cents a pound, you've got another think coming. They're your fish; you wanted them all; you get rid of them. Tell Arnold to start throwing them overboard if you want, but once they reach the dock, you take them off."

We got to the dock and the television people were there — word had gotten out. It was an historic trip: ten tuna, the smallest dressing out over one hundred and twenty-five pounds. Papa, after we had racked up the fish and all had our pictures taken, backed his little coupe around to the rack. I said, "Wait a minute. Let Arnold go aboard one of the quahog draggers to get some burlap bags to pad your car."

"Oh," said Papa, "that's all right. It's a rented car."

But it wasn't easy. We got eight into the trunk, but the other two just wouldn't go. So there we were, left with two large tuna.

One of the dock-watchers, a lady, came shyly to me. "Do I understand you are giving those fish away?"

I was tired, wet, cold, bloody, hungry and grumpy. Arnold and I had to clean the boat to make ready for a trip the next morning, less than eight hours away. "Lady," I said, "if you want one of those fish, you're welcome to it."

"Well." She hesitated. "I'm staying in one of Captain Elmer's cottages. Do you think he'd like a tuna fish?"

I said, "Lady, he'd love it."

"But how can I get it home?"

I said, "For all of me you can sling it over your shoulder. If you don't take it I'll take it offshore tomorrow and dump it overboard. Now if you don't mind, I've been offshore for fourteen hours, it's after ten o'clock, the boat is a stinking mess, and I've got a trip out of here at six tomorrow morning."

She backed her car around, we shoved the thing in the trunk, and that was the last I saw of that fish. (Arnold lugged the last one home, cut it into steaks, froze it, and doled it out to the local cops with whom he was in some trouble for hot-rodding.)

But it wasn't the last I heard of the fish the lady had carried off. Captain Elmer's son, Simmy, one of my very good friends, ran a charterboat out of Rock Harbor. Simmy fancied himself a tuna fisherman, but he hadn't been able to catch a tuna in two weeks (he wasn't out on our big day). He came to me several days later.

"Did you give a female a tuna fish the other night?"

I said I might have.

"You sonofabitch," he said, "I had to bury the goddamn thing two days later."

It was a shame, because bluefin tuna, properly gutted, bled, and cared for (as ours were) make delicious eating, although if it's not bled there's not a self-respecting cat on Cape Cod that will touch day-old tuna.

That was one of the good trips. A few days later Papa and more guests went with me on a four-hour trip for harbor bluefish, little fellows a pound or so in weight, caught on light tackle. After the seventh or eighth fish he climbed part way up the ladder. "Cap," said he, "if you want to turn the rest of the fish loose, it's all right with us."

"Why," I said, "nobody ever turns bluefish loose; there will be a hundred people at the dock who'll love them." I thought a little. "Oh, ho!" I said, "The tuna — what ever happened to them?"

He grinned sheepishly. "I had to hire the boy next door to bury them."

That's one way to cure a fish hog.

# 41

# No-Tuna Trip

On the strength of that famous trip I had another tuna trip. That's the way the business is built. This one wasn't so happy, though it came out well enough in the end.

Friends of Papa's wanted to duplicate his trip, but when they showed up at the dock I said, "Why don't you go home? This is no day for a tuna trip. The wind has been pricking on sou'west since sunrise. If we were lucky enough to get a fish on I couldn't hold the boat still for you to play it."

The folks who had booked the trip, who fished with me many times afterwards, were one of the nicest husband-and-wife teams I ever took along. They were agreeable; they knew I knew whereof I spoke. After all, if a charterboatman loses a trip because of the weather he can never make it up. It's one of a hundred trips of the season, one day's pay out of his year. But their guest hadn't learned.

"I heard about Cape Cod fishermen," he said, "how they are chicken."

That did it! I said, "If that's the way you feel, you asked for it. I think it's stupid to go, but I can take it, the boat can take it — let's see if you can take it."

We went, and it was stupid. (I never did such a thing again, preferring to be considered chicken than to submit people who trusted me to such a beating. There were many days when it took more courage to stay ashore or to turn back than it took to go.) The southwest wind was doing a good forty when we left the harbor. We ran before the wind, more or less, until we crossed the Shoal Ground, then Arnold set out the baits and I let her go downwind. Somewhere off the Pamet shore we hung one tuna. He peeled off a couple of hundred yards before I could bring the boat up into the wind. Then the line went slack and he was gone.

I should have turned back then, but instead I kept on going downwind, thinking if I could get in the lee of Race Point maybe I could make a day after all. It was warm although the wind was whistling. Once I had rounded the Race, sneaking in through that hole again, and hugged in under the land, I had second thoughts. The tide was still on its way out; the wind by now was blowing so hard it was blowing all four lines to one side of the boat.

"Arnold," I said, "pick 'em up. We're going back."

"Chicken!" the guest snorted.

Chicken or no, when the tide started to run against the wind we would be in for no picnic. As a matter of fact we were in for no picnic as it was. A trip which ordinarily took me no more than two hours took us more than four. *Whitecap* was always a rough weather boat, but that day she buried her bow clear back to the sprayshield time after time, even throttled down as she was. One of the big seascallopers, heading for a lee, said afterwards, "Cap, you went by me, and most times all I could see was a welter of water and your outriggers and radio antenna."

Eventually I made a lee at Billingsgate Island and we went to fishing for little bluefish to pass the time. Friend guest climbed part way up the flying bridge ladder. "Captain," he said, "I have an apology to make. I have never been so frightened in my life. I didn't know a small boat could live in such water."

But it wasn't worth it. Never again but once (and we got a bum weather report that day) did I let anyone — and I had some pretty angry, disappointed parties — talk me into going when I knew the weather was wrong.

# 42

〰〰〰〰〰〰〰〰〰〰〰〰〰〰〰

# Hurricane Carol

Chartering in *Whitecap* was quite a different thing from chartering in *Nonny*. My own son, Peter, started the first year with me; before the year was out I had so much business I had to put on Jimmy Andrews as an alternate mate. An eight-hour trip over low tide and a four-hour trip over high water was the regular schedule, but we were catching a lot of stripers and even though I had gone to sixty dollars for an eight-hour trip, an unheard of price in those days, I was turning away more business than I was taking. Over the high-course tides, with high water coming at noon and midnight, we began to take two eight-hour trips a day. With *Whitecap* at Wellfleet, where I could come and go any time, after the second trip on a twelve-hour day I was ready for three or four double eight-hour days. I'd pick up mate and party in Rock Harbor in the station wagon at three in the morning, drive to Wellfleet, and leave the dock at four. By noon I was back in Rock Harbor with the party, where their car was. I'd take aboard the alternate mate and a second party, and fish until eight that night, when we'd make Wellfleet. Then I'd pack them, their gear and fish into the station wagon and take them back to their car in Rock Harbor over the road. It was a grueling schedule, but the money was good and the two boys made it possible. When we left Wellfleet at four in the morning, Pete (or Jimmy, whoever was with me) would take the wheel once we were clear of the harbor while I curled up in a corner of the flying bridge to take a nap. We fished a lot at Ryder's Beach that year, and it was an hour's run, from either harbor. When we neared the ground the mate would wake me and we would fish until it was time to go home. Then the

mate would take over and I'd get another hour's nap in spite of the
overhead exhaust roaring in my ear.  For almost three months that
motor never cooled off.

The motor paid for itself the first year, for that was 1954, the
year of Hurricane Carol.  We got a bum weather report, "Rain and
small craft warnings, thirty to forty mile no'theast wind late in the
afternoon."  The trip was scheduled out of Rock Harbor at three
a.m. (there really are people who like to start the day's fishing at
that time) and I had come on a terrific school of stripers the afternoon before.  Most of the fleet had come in just before midnight
and weren't planning a trip until late in the day.  The crowd I had
were sunrise fishermen and had been at the harbor an hour or more
before I got there.

Harris was the only one stirring while we got ready.  "You going
this morning?" he asked.

"Sure," I said, "Why not?"

He sniffed the weather.  "It doesn't smell good, and the twelve-
twenty weather from the Coast Guard said, 'rain and no'theast winds
. . .' "

I said, "Hell, I'm not so sweet I'll melt with a little rain, and if it
comes heavy no'theast, what of it?  I'm going to fish Ryder's, and
that's a lee shore.  Anyway, if the storm is too bad I can get in by
eleven, and surely it won't blow up a storm before then."

He shook his head, and I took my party aboard.  The course from
Rock Harbor to Ryder's Beach is dogleg, and it was my habit when
running at night to swing wide.  Not that I was afraid of running on
Billingsgate Island, but what was the use of worrying when there was
plenty of time?  The party was mostly old friends, and I steered
casually from down below, swapping lies and checking only occasionally on the little tell-tale compass I carried below for rainy days.  The
wind, right out of the sou'-south-east, was right on our tail, and while
it wasn't *Whitecap*'s best quarter, the seas were hardly high enough
to be bothersome.

I ran my time out and went topside.  Pete put down the outriggers
and got the rods ready.  The party had one last beer and settled in
their chairs to do some serious fishing.  It was a lowery morning and
oppressive.  The wind seemed to have increased considerably, and

while it was close to sunrise there was hardly any light. I realized I had let myself run a little far offshore so I headed due east before slowing down. It was light enough to see the rod tips when I slowed down. I told Pete to let the lines run. He hadn't finished setting out the fourth line when we had our first fish on. It was a little fellow, eight pounds, and shouldn't have caused any trouble, but in the half light, the lines got fouled. Trouble was going to be our companion that day. It seemed like forever before the lines were unsnarled and the fish boated. Eventually we squared away, still headed east. I became aware that the wind had hauled southerly and was blowing so hard it was picking the tops off the waves. I swung and held right into the wind until Pete got the lines out again, then instead of heading toward shore I kept working south, back over the ground we had just run.

It was uneasy weather. I felt a little difficulty breathing. The east had finally brightened to a dirty, brassy yellow. The water was a dead grey tipped with dirty white caps. I held on a little south and east until I was sure where I was, then I thumped on the cabin overhead for Pete. The party was strangely silent, as though they, too, felt the oppression. I said, "Pete, pick 'em up. I don't like this weather. We'll go back to the Eastham shore and fish for harbor blues or something until the tide comes in."

Pete told the party and they helped with unexpected alacrity. Usually they would have griped mildly, but this time they seemed more than willing to get away from there. Once the lines were in I hooked up and headed south and came downstairs to explain. There were no arguments. "You know best, Cap," and "Whatever you say, Cap."

The wind continued to freshen, though it was still slightly east of south. I calculated the tide in my head; it must be pretty near dead low water. I let the boat fall off a little to the west to give myself ample water to cross the Shoal Ground. Then the fog and the rain set in simultaneously. All in a minute it was raining so hard the seas were flattened, and the rain and fog together reduced visibility until I could hardly see our bow. I paid off slightly more to the west and pushed on the throttle to be sure I was wide open. We came into shallow water, and it seemed too shallow so I had to reduce speed.

Again I let us fall off to west'ard until I was running due sou'west. The water should deepen soon.

Pete, who had taken off his glasses and was peering around the starboard, dry side of the cabin said in a strange voice, "Pop, there's a high, dry bar right ahead of us."

Speed was cut down even more while I looked. I climbed onto the flying bridge, rain or no, for better visibility. He was right, though we were in relatively deep water. I studied the bottom as we worked sou'west. Pete stuck his head above the edge of the cabin overhead. "You know what that bar is, Pete?" I asked. "It's the high bar just east of the 'Outside Hole.' There ought to be three feet of water over it on this tide."

As I worked my way sou'west I recognized one stretch of bottom after another. After all, I had been fishing this country for almost twenty years and if I couldn't tell where I was by reading the bottom I was never going to learn. The tide was a good three feet lower than any tide I had ever seen here. I had to keep swinging wider and wider to west'ard to keep water enough under me. The rain had let up slightly, but the fog and wind were increasing. My neck and wrists were wet from rain and spray, but my armpits were dripping cold sweat from sheer nervousness.

The seas right in front of us seemed suddenly mountainous. We had reached the south edge of the Shoal Ground. I cut the throttle until we were just holding our own against the wind. The flood tide had started to run. We were in about four feet of water, and I could see the eelgrass all pointing south. I lay there, jogging, studying the seas, the tide, and the wind. The waves were running a good eight feet high, maybe higher, and the waves on the channel side of the Shoal Ground are like no other waves in the Bay; they chop right straight up and down; often there is no more distance between crests than the height of the waves.

At a time like this there is a loneliness — not fear (a man who could be afraid has no business being here) — the decision is the captain's alone. Against him are wind, rain, fog, and cold salt water as high as the flying bridge, sólid water with the power to reduce him and his boat to waste fragments in seconds. But he feels not that these forces are against him, only that they are trying him, to see whether he is fit. With me, and on my side were a sturdy wooden hull, a motor I could feel throbbing, awaiting my command, though the wind carried away all sound except its own. I weighed twenty years' experience against an impersonal force, a constantly shifting danger. I turned back. I might have made it across the channel into the comparatively shallow water on the edge of the flats off Rock Harbor, but I would surely have taken every window out of the deck house doing it. If there was *any* truth in the weather report, the wind was going to back around to the east.

I turned back, scurrying before the wind. I planned to lay to under the lee of Beach Hill until the wind moderated or shifted. If it did neither — well, we could jog in that lee all night if we had to.

We worked our way back in what seemed like minutes to the high bar we had passed on our way south; then, knowing the water was deeper inshore, I headed east again, letting the wind carry me slightly north. The rocks under Beach Hill began to trouble me. I knew there was a gaggle of them. Ship Rock I didn't worry about — I was sure I could see that — but what about all those little rocks close in-shore? I held up closer to a due east course. The waves seemed a little less wild here, though the wind whistled louder and louder. Finally, I could see bottom, not more than three feet beneath the keel. I thumped on the deck and bawled for Pete.

"Pete, get the anchor ready, bring all forty fathoms of rope out through the hawse hole so you will be able to get it over in a bundle. And be sure you make that end fast."

Pete was never one to ask questions. He crawled forward, undid the tie ropes on the little seventeen-pound Danforth anchor, and then hauled all forty fathoms of half-inch nylon out, coiling it be-tween his knees to keep the wind from snatching it away. I saw him tie it to the bow-post, again and again. He must have shouted, though by this time the wind was howling so I could hear nothing else. He half turned on his knees and waved his hand. I slowed until we were barely holding our own and made a throwing motion. The anchor went over silently, then the rope, coil after coil. I realized we were going straight backwards, though the motor was in forward gear. I opened the throttle slightly. Pete waved to push me back, so I let us fall back again. The rope came tight, two hundred and forty feet in a ruler-straight line to where that little anchor lay in no more than three feet of water. I watched Pete down; then, leaving the boat still in gear to take some of the strain off the rope, I climbed down myself and wrung the water out of my collar and neck band as best I could.

My boys, the party, were apparently as glad to see me as if I had been off on a trip somewhere. They pressed beer on me but I told them, "I've got to have what little brains I have without I fuddle them with beer. Thanks. Now look, fellers, we're back of Jeremy's Point. I can run you ashore into less than three feet of water. You'll get wet, but you are wet anyway, so that won't matter. Less than a hundred yards due east is land. You can wade ashore, then turn to your left and walk until you come to a road. There are houses there, and no doubt somebody will carry you to town. Or I can call the Coast Guard and maybe they'll send the DUKW to take you off. What say?"

They hemmed and hawed. Finally, someone said, "What are you going to do, Cap?"

I said every dollar I had was in *Whitecap* and I wasn't about to leave her as long as she was afloat.

Somebody else said, "You wouldn't stay here if you didn't think the boat would make it. I'm going to stay right here."

Somebody else spoke up. "What about me? You forget my foot is in a cast."

Good night! I had forgotten that. One of the party had broken his foot, which was still in a cast. This was the first day his doctor had let him out of the house. I said, "I guess that settles it." I idly pulled the electric bilge pump switch.

Pete saw me. "It's busted, Pop, I tried it a little bit ago." So he set up a hand pump in the cabin and the party formed a bucket line, passing bilge water which was mostly rain from hand to hand to throw it into the air, where the wind picked it up and carried it away. It was good to give them something to do to keep their minds off their situation.

Back on the flying bridge again I turned on the radio telephone. I had only put out one call when Dick Clark came back to me. He screamed into his handset, "Where have you been? We've been trying to get you for two hours. Don't you know we're going to have a hurricane?"

As calmly as I could, I said, "Cappy, we ain't going to have a hurricane, we got one. The wind is moaning so loud I can hardly hear you. Now, listen, I'm anchored right up behind Jeremy's Point. I don't dare to try to make it across the channel. We're all right so long as the wind holds where it is, and if we had to we could walk ashore. I'm going to try to make it into Pamet River about noon — there won't be enough water before then. Will you get word to my wife to meet us there? Do you read that?"

Dick came back, "Phil, you'll never make it. The wind is blowing eighty with gusts a lot harder. Can't you come through the Slew?" (The Slew is the narrow gut between Jeremy's and Billingsgate Island. It's a place to stay away from when the wind is blowing forty, let alone twice that hard. It pays to know your own waters.)

I tucked my head down below the flying bridge coaming. I said, "Listen, Dick, I can hardly hear you because of the way the wind is moaning, that screaming sound you get only in a hurricane. I'm going to try Pamet River about noon. Repeat, I'm going to try Pamet River about noon. Please tell my wife. Repeat. I'm going to try to make Pamet River about noon. Please tell my wife. Do you read?"

Once more Dick came back. "Okay, you stubborn bastard. I'll tell your wife. The lines are all down, power, phone, everything, but I'll drive and tell her. Good luck. I hope you make it."

Before I could shut off the radio, Charlie Mayo, *Chantey III* out of P'town, came on the air. "*Whitecap*, if you're all right where you are, stay there. I'm down off Corn Hill and I can't handle the boat with twin screws. Do you read?"

It was amazing how comforting it was to talk to somebody. I said, "Yeah, I read you, Charlie. Much obliged. But that wind is gradually hauling west and I'm going to be blown right onto the beach if I don't move pretty soon. My anchor rope right now is parallel to the beach; in fact, I'm going to pick up now before it's too late. See you in Pamet, Charlie." I shut off the radio and put away the handset before he could discourage me.

The fog had lifted slightly, though the rain still poured as it does only in the tropics or in a hurricane. All this while I had been guid-

ing the boat with one hand on the wheel, because that faithful
motor was still turning over a good twelve-hundred revolutions to
take the strain off the anchor warp. The tide, once it started in,
came very quickly and we now had so much water under us I could
no longer see the bottom — which meant the waves were considerably higher.

I thumped on the cabin overhead for Pete and when he showed
his head I motioned toward the anchor. As he worked his way
around the weather side of the wheel house I leaned over and yelled
in his ear. "It's going to be rough, Pete. I'm not even sure we can
get that anchor back. Take your time and stuff that rope down the
hawse hole as you gain on it, otherwise it will blow overboard. I'll
keep enough way on so you shouldn't have any trouble bringing it
aboard. When you've got it all in and the last of it's straight up and
down, take four or five turns around the bow-post, then slide back
a little so if it breaks it won't hit you. I'll put on full power, but you
may have to cut. You got your knife? He nodded and patted his
hip. "We'll try it with power first, but that Danforth's probably ten
feet down in the sand by now. Go!"

He went, and I put on enough power to slacken the rope. It was
amazing, the tachometer showed seventeen hundred, which was tuna
speed, and still the rope was tight. I pushed to two thousand and
Pete waved one hand. Gradually, he got the rope back and stuffed
it down that vertical inch-and-a-half pipe, until, after endless jockey-
ing, I saw him take three quick turns around the bow-post.

I cut the wheel hard over to try to go around the anchor as I opened the motor. I eased it up, twenty-five hundred, twenty-eight hundred, three thousand, thirty-three hundred — that was all the power
I had. We lay there, straight up into the wind in spite of my rudder's
being cut hard over, the bow pulling slightly down with the strain.
For minutes we lay like that. I could feel the boat shaking, the vibrations of the motor racing, though I could hear nothing but the
wind. Gradually, oh, so gradually, we swung around until our stern
was pointing nearly toward shore. Then, all of a sudden, Pete waved
wildly and we surged ahead. I was sure we'd broken the anchor rope,
but no, there was the anchor scaling alongside. I slacked off, lying
in the trough until Pete had secured the anchor on deck and worked
his way back to the cockpit, grinning triumphantly.

We lay now in the trough of the sea, but fortunately headed off-shore. *Whitecap* wouldn't have turned downwind without plenty of sea room, for I poured on the gas and she simply scaled on her side, right in the trough. Little by little, as the wind exerted pressure on her cabin and deckhouse, which were somewhat higher than her cockpit and stern, she came around. I found myself headed down-wind toward Pamet River.

The trip to Pamet was dream-like. I saw nothing I recognized. We might as well have been in foreign waters for all I knew where we were. I kept the speed as slow as possible, a bare thousand revolu-tions, to give the tide all the time I could, and still keep steerage way. I didn't want to have to try to come back up into the wind. (A friend who has a cottage on that shore said he saw us go by and we simply scudded. "You must have been doing all of twenty knots," he said.)

I had barely time to go below and insist that everyone put on life jackets backwards, that is, tied behind so the flotation of the collar would be where it belongs, under their chins. We put two extras on the engine box for Pete and me. I didn't want to be hampered by anything as bulky as a life jacket.

I explained what I was trying to do. "Listen, fellers, there's two jetties about a hundred feet apart, at right angles to the beach. Usual-ly, when you go in, you go down north of the north jetty, swing east, then come back to south'ard, just outside that jetty. There's a bar which starts at the end of the south jetty and runs northwest. I've got to jump that bar because I can never come up into the wind. I'll scrape the south jetty just as close as I dare, and hope we hit the bar on the top of a sea instead of in the trough. If I catch a sea wrong and we broach, we've got an onshore wind and a flood tide. Stay with the boat as long as you can, even if it sinks, but don't get bang-ed on the rocks of the jetty if you can help it."

I never did see the rocks at Ryder's Beach and Fisher's Beach; all of a sudden there was the south jetty a bare hundred feet ahead of me. I cut a little toward shore and watched my stern. Just as I got abreast the jetty a big sea came surging on us. I cut the wheel to starboard and jumped the throttle. For a second or two the sea car-ried us, but it was travelling too fast. Before we had cleared the bar it ran ahead and left us stranded high and dry on bare sand. The next sea picked us up almost before we saw it coming and surged us ahead again with the motor racing. I was never sure whether we hit two or three times, but those seas were crashing in and actually curling in between the two jetties. So the sea that finally carried us over the bar carried us right into the inlet — the sea and thirty-three hundred revolutions against a hard cut-over rudder. It was a near thing. I could have reached out and touched the north jetty with a surf rod.

# 43

≋≋≋≋≋≋≋≋≋≋≋≋

# Let-Down

There always has to be a let-down, I suppose, after a trip like that. Once we were safely into the harbor the hill at Fisher's Beach cut down the wind so I could handle *Whitecap* reasonably well. Charlie, in *Chantey III*, had made the harbor before I did, but he had drawn sand up into both water pumps and didn't want to run his motors for fear of ruining them. He had anchored well out in the harbor. I ran around him and drove *Whitecap*'s bow hard up into the sedge grass. (The tide was coming, I remembered.) Pete immediately jumped over and dug the Danforth into the grass. Right on his heels six very wet and very relieved fishermen hit the beach, including the one with a cast on his foot.

Dick had carried my message to my wife, and in spite of winds exceeding eighty miles per hour she had coaxed our boxy little four-cylinder Jeepster all the way to Pamet, and was awaiting us. I wouldn't leave the boat long enough to give her directions, but sent Pete.

"Tell your mother to take these men back to Rock Harbor, where their car is. Then have her go to the hardware store and buy me forty fathoms of new, three-quarter-inch manila. In our barn is a spare twenty-five-pound Cape Ann anchor. I want that. She better bring back a couple of blankets, a gallon of hot coffee in the thermos jug, and a pint of whiskey, because I think we're going to have to stay here all night. I'm afraid of the hurricane backlash."

Pete scrambled ashore to deliver my message. I watched the party (they had insisted on paying me for the trip though I would rather they had not) squeeze themselves and their gear, and the eight-pound striper (which they later had mounted and named Carol), into the little Jeep station wagon. My wife waved bravely and set out for Rock Harbor, almost twenty miles away.

Charlie, in the meantime, was having an awful time trying to get out another anchor. He put his mate and a spare anchor in a little round-bottomed dinghy. The boy would try to row up into the wind while Charlie payed out rope. The wind would catch the oars and lift them right out of the rowlocks. Time and again they tried while we watched. I said to Pete, "Come on, the wind's not so stiff here and we can run his anchor out for him."

We drifted alongside, took his anchor, and churned up into the wind until he waved we were far enough. We chucked over his anchor. I had been studying the harbor and decided that if the wind came nor'west, which I expected in the backlash, we would be better off over against the sou'west bank of sedge grass. We went that way, and Pete dug our anchor again into the grass.

In the meantime, my wife's troubles were continuing. One of the party was sick — she thought from reaction — and had to be let out of the Jeep briefly on the way back to Rock Harbor. (More likely the beer he had drunk during the day had caught up with him.) When she had bought the rope and whiskey, and driven back home to get anchor, coffee and blankets, she found a great pine tree near our front door had been blown down since she left the house. Our barn was swaying so she was not at all happy about going in to get the spare anchor. Then she had to drive back the twenty miles to Pamet, only to find that we had gone across the channel and were on the west, rather than the east, side of the harbor. So she had to back up and find her way along back roads to the point nearest us on the other side of the harbor. (All this sixty or so miles of driving was in the worst of the hurricane — the windshield was so sand-blasted it had to be replaced.)

While she was gone the wind moderated and I watched for the calm spell which would mark the eye of the hurricane. It never came. The wind gradually backed around to nor'west and moderated further. When my wife got back with anchor and rope I set them out so no matter which way the wind swung I wouldn't be blown ashore. Then I quit. Pete and I snugged everything down as well as we could, jumped over the side into waist-deep water, and had my wife drive us home.

There was never any backlash at Pamet from that hurricane. The wind died during the night, and Pete and I brought the boat home to Rock Harbor the next day. Just how exhausted we were we didn't realize until we came on a school of stripers chasing menhaden on top of water on the north edge of the Shoal Ground.

I said, "Pete, I believe that's stripers. Jump down and get a rod."

He said, "Pop, do I have to? You jump down and I'll take the boat."

I said, "T'hell with it." And for perhaps the only time in my life I went by breaking stripers without trying to catch them.

# 44

# Loose-Ends

Hurricane Carol ruined the fishing for that year. Just previous to it the fishing had been fantastic; there were fish everywhere. I had one party, a gentleman from Pennsylvania and his family, that set what I believe is a record for Cape Cod Bay. Trolling we caught five different kinds of fish on one trip. We started out by fishing Stony Bar for harbor bluefish. We put over fifty in the fishbox, fishing light tackle, and with them we caught a dozen or more Jersey bonitos (which are very rare in Cape Cod Bay most years). The party was bored with such easy fishing. "Cap," said one, "how about catching some mackerel?"

We moved off to the south edge of the Shoal Ground and started to catch mackerel, again on very light gear. There seemed to be no end to the mackerel so I kept trolling west. Howard Walker, who was dragging sea scallops in the eleven-fathom water north of the Shoal Ground in a boat called *Squid*, called me on the radio. "Phil, if you're interested in tuna, they're feeding all around my boat."

I relayed the information to the party because I could see Howard not so very far away.

"No," said Father, "let's go catch a striper."

"I want to go," said Mother (she's a little scrap of a woman), "I've never caught a tuna."

"Well," I said, "it won't take long to try, and I honestly don't know where we can catch a striper until after the tide turns."

We went tuna fishing, and in less than an hour we had a cute little forty-pounder aboard.

"Now can we go striper fishing?" Father asked.

I headed for the Barnstable shore where a few, a very few, stripers usually showed up on the first part of the flood tide. The party laid out their lunch on the engine box. Pete asked me about the tuna lures.

"Leave them out," I said, "We've got almost an hour's run. I'll cruise along at twenty-eight hundred rpms. We might hook another." We did; a little fellow not quite thirty pounds, the second smallest tuna *Whitecap* ever brought in.

Father was irritated. He snatched that fish into the boat almost before the fish knew it was hooked. "I want to go striper fishing." he said. So we picked up and ran wide open for Barnstable, and nary a striper was to be found. I had long ago learned it was silly to leave a school of fish that was biting for another that might bite. But if Father would rather not catch stripers than catch tuna — he was paying for the trip. Time was running short and I had another, a four-hour trip coming up. I headed for Rock Harbor.

Just east of Sesuit there used to be a little hole on the edge of the flats; it was a casting spot for stripers. Almost never could we catch them there trolling because the water was too shallow. As we churned our way east I could see birds working over the hole. I thumped for Pete. "Get a couple of eelskins rigged on bass rods."

By the time we reached the hole he was ready and I slowed down. He hadn't any more than run out both rigs than both came tight with quite respectable, twenty-pound stripers. I hadn't time for more, with people waiting on the dock, so I never turned back. (I came to the same hole with my four-hour people and the stripers had left, so I doubt another run through the hole on the first trip would have produced any more fish.)

That was the kind of fishing we had before the hurricane. Two days after Carol, looking for tuna, I went so far offshore that I put Highland Light below the horizon, and not the first fish did we see. Even that far offshore the water looked like a bilious yellow soup, so badly had the hurricane stirred up the bottom. The fish never came back that year.

* * * *

The next ten years sort of melt into each other.  There were poor
trips and there were memorable trips.  I gave up winter fishing most
years and went to Florida to try my hand, first at commercial king
mackerel fishing (which the fish buyers strangled) and then at chartering for sailfish (which was a lot of fun but not nearly as demanding
as striper fishing).  On the Cape in the summers we brought an awful
lot of stripers to the dock.  Tuna fishing in the Bay (except for the
giants, five hundred or more pounds, which I never messed around
with) was pretty well knocked on the head by the *Silver Mink*'s
seining.  Sixty, seventy, eighty thousand pounds Manny Phillips
would scoop up in one day.  I used to scream at the sportsfishermen
on the radio who would call, "Manny, come this way.  Manny, there's
tons of tuna fish here."  All I did was make myself unpopular with
Captain Phillips; he got the tuna fish anyway, and then went out of
business.  We all went back to striper fishing where we belonged.

* * * *

There was a college striper tournament one year, which Floyd
VanDuzer, Barnstable Harbor Master and boatyard owner, set up,
but it was set too early in the year — there were very few stripers
around. (The Stuart, Florida, sailfish tournament — for which I ran
the committee and press boat for three years — was much better
planned:  it was held right at the peak of the season). Harvard, Yale,
Princeton, Western Ontario, and the University of Massachusetts
entered teams. Massachusetts drew *Whitecap* — or I drew them, I
forget which. All of the rest of the teams had coaches, blazers and
a great deal of "rah-rah."  My boys were paying their own way, and
I was going to win the tournament for them or bust a gut trying.
The committee kept the boys up all night with lectures on how to
catch fish; by four a.m., when they came aboard, they were sound
asleep.
    Freddy Harris in *Kitty W.*, Jimmy Hardy in *Sea Duck*, Johnny
Shakliks in *Quahog V.*, and Lee Buck in *Betty B.* were my competi-
tion.  Four skippers harder to beat in these waters you couldn't

find. The first day was a nothing day. We all went to the conventional places, fished the conventional lures, and we were, every one of us, skunked.

That afternoon I talked to Herbie Lovell, lobsterman on *Mayflower*, out of Barnstable. "Herbie," I begged, "there must be some stripers, somewheres, up here in Barnstable harbor."

Herbie is one of the world's nicest people — the guy seems to live to help others. "There are," he said. "You go across that bar over there, and then you turn to west'ard . . ."

"Herbie," I objected, "there's no water over there."

"Not much," he admitted, "but you go . . .," and so he laid out my course.

We all left the harbor at four a.m. We rounded the lighthouse in Barnstable Harbor, and then I turned back.

"What's wrong with you?" called Jimmy Hardy on the radio. (Jimmy is ever sharp on the watch for tricks, but also ever sharp to help if a boat is in trouble.)

"Boys forgot their lunch," I lied.

We went back around the corner, out of sight, and worked back along the bar Herbie had indicated. We squirmed up a narrow, winding channel. We set out our lures in not more than six feet of water — with the tide dropping. My boys were all sound asleep in the warming morning sun. One of the rods began to twitch.

"Hey," I bellowed, "you got a fish on number three rod."

The youngster looked at it. "Naw," he protested, "that's just the spoon wiggling the rod tip."

I demanded, "Crank it in."

"It's only just the spoon . . ." but he cranked it in anyway, and we had our first striper, sixteen-and-a-half inches from the fork of his tail to the tip of his nose.

We set out again, the tide still dropping. We made two more passes in that scary-thin water, and caught one more striper just slightly bigger than the first. "C'mon," I said, "we're getting out of here if we have enough water." We dragged bottom, skirting that deadly bar, and went offshore. No more fish for anybody that day.

The next morning Jimmy said to me, "Where'd you get those fish yesterday?"

"I'm not going to tell you."

"Doesn't matter," said Jimmy, "I'm faster than you are. I'm going to follow you."

"Won't do you any good," I said, "I'm not going back. So far we've caught the first fish, the most fish, the biggest fish, the smallest fish — all the fish. If nobody catches any fish today we've got the tournament sewed up." I didn't go back. We fished all that morning in a thick fog and nobody caught another striper. I had been elected timekeeper. It was getting on toward noon, when the tournament was to end, and I watched the time. The night before, Herbie had told me of another spot, a flood-tide spot. When the tide turned I worked my way toward it. The time got tighter and tighter. Even though our total catch weighed less than five pounds, in another minute we would have the tournament won. Both hands on my watch went right straight up. I called on the radio, "Time's up. Do you read me?" One by one the other boats answered me. The tournament was over. One of my boys shrieked, "I've got a fish on!" So he did — a good fifteen-pounder, too late for the tournament by seconds.

\* \* \* \*

We had been trying for years to get the boats in the fleet to fly a flag when they had boated their first striper. My wife sewed up innumerable pennants of striped green and white ticking. The flags were a big help, really; not only were they a brag flag when we came into the harbor, but that little triangle could be seen as far across the Bay as binoculars could reach. Although the flags never really caught on, I decided if I was going to brag when I caught a fish, I was going to brag when I didn't. I picked up a beautiful yellow dacron flag in Florida, with a very realistic black and white skunk on it. "Skaneateles" we named the skunk (for no good reason) and he was the finest bit of advertising I ever bought.

"Ho," people on the dock would say, "If that skipper dares to advertise he didn't catch a fish today, chances are he usually does catch some — and they'd book *Whitecap because* we had caught no fish that day.

I had mates who hated that flag. They'd knock themselves out to catch at least one fish so they wouldn't have to run up Skaneateles on the way in. And that was good business, too.

One day I had a teen-age girl and her mother fishing with me. We caught no fish so on the way in we ran up Skaneateles. Several days later, through the mail, I got a package from Chatham, New Jersey, where they lived. It contained, without any question, the highest-smelling sachet there ever was. The note with it said, "Maybe if you put this with Skaneateles he won't smell so bad. Signed, Cara." As to whether the skunk flag smelled any differently, I can't say, but for the rest of the summer I didn't need the oil of pine when people were seasick — that sachet out-smelled everything.

Cara took another trip with me which was memorable. (She would say "memorable" was an understatement.) She and her father, mother, and brother had been with us all day. It was not a particularly good fish day and we had hung out, hoping to pick up something. A cold front moved in, and with it a thunderstorm. Now, thunderstorms are relatively rare in Cape Cod Bay. The old-timers say that when they dug the Cape Cod Canal they changed the air cur- rents so half the storms go out to sea around P'town, and the other half cut across the land by way of Yarmouth and Harwich. Whether this is so or not, thunderstorms in our waters are rare. When we do get one it usually comes in against the wind from the east and hangs here and hangs here until we wish it would go away.

Such a storm we had this day, oh, how it rained. There were seventeen boats all fishing the same area, all hanging to it for the last minutes of fishing, all taking off for home when the storm hit. Since we were all on the same course and visibility was extremely limited, I felt I should ride the flying bridge. We were within sight of the harbor. Cara had put on a poncho to crouch with me on the flying bridge. Steve Stevenson in *Shirley L.* and Al Taber in *Explorer* were on either side of us. A bolt of lightning struck somewhere very near — I don't know where — and it knocked both my hands off the brass steering wheel as though somebody had kicked my wrists.

"Oh," said Cara, "look at the flame between the spokes of the steering wheel!"

Look indeed! It was some moments before I dared gingerly touch the thing again. That was close enough.

* * * *

The fishing was changing (either that or I was getting too old). No more did the fleet call each other on the radio when fish broke loose on top of water. Cut-off lines, once a rarity, were becoming commonplace. Parties wanted more comfort — good fishing was no longer enough. I tore *Whitecap* all to pieces one winter, raised the bow fifteen inches and put ten inches more sheer in each side. I put on a new deckhouse, a new flying bridge, and a bigger motor to get there faster. It was no good. Fishing had been fun. The fact that we were making a living had been incidental. Now fishing was only a way to make a living — and a poor living at that, the season was so short.

One fall I had *Whitecap* hauled out and trailered to our front yard. In time I sold her and took up the job of shellfish constable for the town. I had gone full circle.

Now I've bought that new little nineteen-footer. Once in a while I can sneak away to go casting for stripers. I work the flats, where there are almost as many ghosts as there are fish. And that's fun, too. (Harris used to say it was all right to talk to the fish if they didn't talk back to you. If they did, you should stay ashore; you had been offshore too long.) I find I still have the knack of easing a fish over the rail. It has been a good life.

# SUNSHINE

Launching *Sunshine* in Bee's River.
All photos, unless otherwise credited, are by Helen Schwind.

(*Above*). The author with daughter
Paula, Irish setter Skate O'Shaugh-
nessey, and flounders for dinner.
(*Left*). Longraking from *Sunshine*
in Pleasant Bay.

# STRING BEAN

(*Above*). The author and son Peter aboard *String Bean* berthed in Bee's River.
(*Below*). With Paula and Model T gathering thatch at West Shore.

Blackfish driven ashore by the *String Bean*.

# NONNY

*Nonny* rigged for commercial fishing for striped bass and lobsters.

(*Above*). *Nonny* all prettied up for chartering, ready to be launched.
(*Below*). Son Peter became an expert with a rod when he was still very young.

(*Above*). *Nonny*'s first Rock Harbor charter berth, homemade of course
with driftwood.
(*Below*). Cleaning fish on *Nonny*'s stern in Rock Harbor. The flags on the
outrigger indicate we had a big day.

(*Above*). The author and
Fred Harris with lobster tr
built in the winter of 1946
(*Left*). The traps paid off.

(*Above*). Rock Harbor in the early 1950's. *Nonny* is the second boat from the harbor mouth.
(*Below*). With son Peter and a carload of stripers for the market.

(*Above*). Paula, home from college, scalloping with Peter in Pleasant Bay. Peter built the boat himself.
(*Left*). The author lobster fishing in *Nonny* off Dennis Ledge.

# WHITECAP

*Whitecap* after her first rebuilding.

(*Left and below*). We tried spray rails on *Whitecap* but they made her nose-heavy.

(*Right*). The final *Whitecap* at the dock.

*(Above).* *Whitecap* after her last rebuilding.
*(Below).* The author rebuilding *Whitecap* for the last time.

*(Opposite page, top).* The skipper spins one off.
*(Bottom).* Bob Taylor reaches for a big one. Photos by Bob Pond.

They're breaking water over there. Photo by Bob Pond.

(*Opposite page*).  This striper bottomed the scales.

A typical day in Rock Harbor.  Captain Freddy Harris is second from the left.

The author homeward bound in *Whitecap*.

The author.

The author giving a lecture on clam digging at the Cape Cod National Seashore.

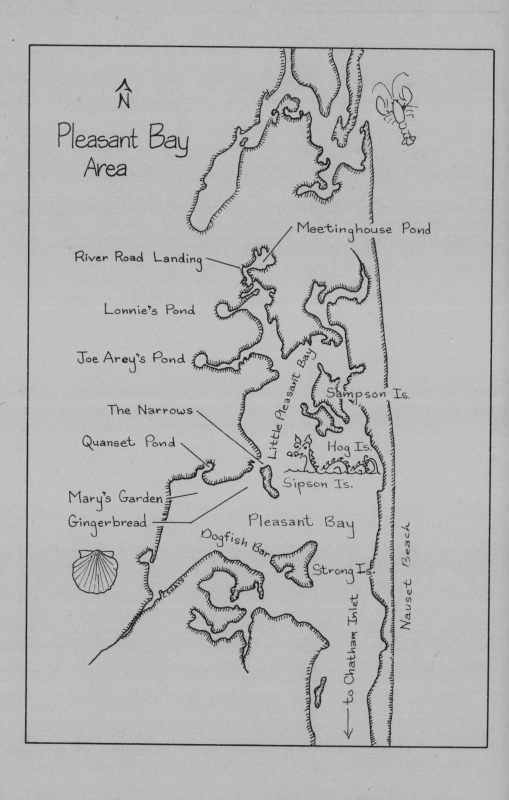

Pleasant Bay
Area

Meetinghouse Pond

River Road Landing

Lonnie's Pond

Joe Arey's Pond

Little Pleasant Bay

Sampson Is.

The Narrows

Hog Is.

Quanset Pond

Sipson Is.

Mary's Garden

Gingerbread

Pleasant Bay

Dogfish Bar

Strong Is.

Nauset Beach

to Chatham Inlet